CW00956576

TO GAYNOR JANE OUR QUEEN OF HEARTS.

WITH LOT'S OF LOVE
AND A FEW WISHES

LOVE BRIAN & WENDY XXX

THE ENCYCLOPEDIA OF MAGIC

THE ENCYCLOPEDIA OF MAGIC

Edwin A. Dawes
and
Arthur Setterington

GALLERY BOOKS
An Imprint of W. H. Smith Publishers Inc.
112 Madison Avenue
New York City 10016

CONTENTS

This book was devised and produced by Multimedia Books Ltd

Senior editor: Richard Rosenfeld
Editor: Patricia Hitchcock
Production: Karen Bromley
Design: Behram Kapadia
Illustrations: Angela Sutherland
Picture Research: David Sutherland

First published in the United States of America 1989 by Gallery Books, an imprint of W.H. Smith Publishers Inc., 112 Madison Avenue, New York, NY 10016

ISBN 0 8317 2780 2

Typeset by Text Filmsetters Ltd.
Origination by Peninsular Repro Services Limited
Printed in Italy by Imago Publishing Limited

"If you do things by halves, preferably do it in triplicate" must be the guiding principle for Mark Wilson and his Company, here displaying three severed ladies.

Note: This book tells you how to perform a great variety of tricks. The symbols and are used to denote descriptions and explanations respectively.

Paul Daniels, Britain's top magician, produces a white rabbit, the traditional symbol of the magician's art, from a top hat. This is the climax of a hilarious routine in which he tries to produce a toy rabbit from a hat placed on top of a very suspect-looking table. After many setbacks, including apparent exposure of the trick's method, the toy rabbit drives off stage in a miniature car. Seconds later, a real live rabbit pops out of the hat!

FOREWORD

I became interested in magic over forty years ago, when I went into my local library and borrowed a biography of the famous French magician Robert-Houdin. It was a wonderful story that immediately hooked me to the fascinating world of magic and gave me an insatiable appetite to read and learn more about magic and magicians. There were a few, to be honest very few, such books in the library and even fewer about the secrets of magic, let alone any explaining how to present or perform tricks. Nevertheless, I was determined to discover how they were done.

My start in magic was certainly not unique, for most amateurs become absorbed in the art as a result of reading a conjuring book or being given a box of tricks. Perhaps today that interest might also be sparked off by television magicians, such as the American David Copperfield vanishing a jet airliner whilst it is surrounded by members of the audience, or Paul Daniels carrying out a modern version of the cup and balls.

I regret that when I first became interested in magic there was no such book as this available. Had there been, I might have made progress much faster and more efficiently and saved my long-suffering audience of relatives and friends much boredom and embarrassment! For not only does this book trace the history of magic and the reasons why, in this very advanced technological world, tricks with playing cards or pieces of rope still intrigue people, but it also helps the beginner to attain a better understanding of the principles that make it possible to amaze as well as to amuse.

The following pages describe the lives of colorful performers such as Houdini – who so admired my first hero that he took his name, Houdin, and added to it an "i" to make what was, and perhaps still is, the most famous name in magic – and great magicians like Maskelyne and Devant who were, in their time, household names as Doug Henning and Paul Daniels are today. I found it fascinating to read again about such men who were "larger than life" and who presented "twice a night" miracles which drew thousands to the theaters in which they played.

What distinguishes this particular book is that not only does it so well portray the incredible men who were, and in some cases still are, great magicians but it also describes how some of the earlier magical secrets have been adapted to produce the marvels we see now on television or in cabaret. In addition, it helps us to understand how the master magicians create seemingly impossible new miracles, whether it be a girl floating on a fountain of water or the latest way of divining a chosen playing card. Students of conjuring need to understand the history of magic if they are to obtain the best possible satisfaction and enjoyment from this fascinating art.

Newcomers to magic will gain an enormous amount from reading this book. It is invaluable not only in the method of teaching but in the explanation of how one should approach each individual trick. And yet, as the authors so rightly point out, it is not how a trick is carried out which is important, but how it is presented. The secret of the trick is not in itself entertaining; it is the way it is performed that commands the audience's interest.

If you follow the expert advice and become an enthusiastic magician, then perhaps one day we'll meet at The Magic Castle or The Magic Circle or at one of the many centers around the world where magicians absorbed in the art of magic, be it as hobbyists, collectors or performers, meet to discuss their secrets.

May you get as much satisfaction and enjoyment from Magic as I have.

John Salisse 1986
Hon Vice-president of The Magic Circle
Former Secretary of The Magic Circle
Hon Life Member of The Magic Circle, London
Hon Life Member of The Magic Castle, Los Angeles

Above: Robin (Henri Joseph Donckele, 1811-74) was such a graceful performer that thousands of Parisians flocked to his shows. He presented both magic and scientific marvels at the Théâtre Robin, Boulevard du Temple, Paris, during the period 1862-9.

INTRODUCTION

Above: Mark Wilson and his Company present live on stage the colorful and exciting Cannon illusion.

Since the art of magic has been practised from the days of the Pharoahs, modern performers have a marvellous and spectacular tradition on which to draw. But while each new era has seen inspired inventions and developing technology add fresh possibilities to the magician's repertoire, many tricks are still based on ancient principles. Consequently, lasers, electromagnets and other modern apparatus now complement these older techniques, enabling contemporary magicians to produce dazzling effects.

While it has often been claimed that some of the greatest performers carried their secret methods to the grave, and their tricks remain unexplained, this was rarely the case. Most techniques are understood by fellow magicians; what distinguishes the great professional from the amateur is *skill and showmanship*.

Many of the basic principles are explained here, with clear instructions to enable the beginner to build an entertaining program. Advice on presentation and patter, the "tricks of the trade" that are vital to a polished performance, is also given.

Some tricks, of course, are still being presented and their secrets must remain with the performers. Detailed descriptions of these grand effects will nonetheless help the reader to see what can be achieved and will inspire him or her to ever more ambitious attempts.

When Houdini made an elephant vanish or David Devant made a painting come to life, audiences really did gasp in wonder. Such effects are beyond the scope of most magicians, requiring tremendous expertise and split-second timing as well as elaborate and expensive equipment. Only those willing to devote all their time and resources to a career in magic can hope to master such sophisticated illusions. Yet the amateur or novice can still achieve startling effects, whether producing ribbons from a hat or making a lady in a basket vanish. Always remember, though, that there is no substitute for individual flair – or for years of practice – and that grasping the basics of the performer's art is the first step toward understanding the exciting world of professional magic.

The Editors

Below: "Doctor" Walford Bodie (Samuel Murphy Bodie, 1869 – 1939) was a great Scottish showman-magician, ventriloquist, hypnotist, exponent of "bloodless surgery" and electrical wizard. His activities led to frequent lawsuits and this colorful lithograph, with Bodie in the role of "The British Edison", illustrates some of his electrical feats. He also antagonized the medical profession by using the letters M.D. after his name, although he claimed they stood for Merry Devil!

1

MAGIC PAST

Above: Top American magician Harry Blackstone Junior, famous son of a famous father, continuing the tradition of the big-time magic illusion show in the USA. His outgoing personality enables him to establish an immediate rapport with his audience and, of his smaller magic, the Floating Light Bulb is a masterpiece which never fails to amaze.

A scintillating display of magic, whether witnessed from the comfort of the theater or seen on television, rarely makes the spectator think about the history of magic. Contemporary stars – such as Doug Henning, David Copperfield and Blackstone Jr – are nonetheless the modern exponents of an ancient profession, the precise origins of which are shrouded in the mists of time.

The English magician Paul Daniels opens his full evening show with a trick that employs a beaker and a ball. The audience's attention is focused simultaneously on the performer and his apparatus. The ball appears and disappears in a most bewildering manner beneath the inverted beaker until the surprise climax arrives with the ball being transformed into a lemon. This is a humorous, modern presentation of the oldest sleight-of-hand trick in the world – the Cups and Balls. In its original form, which is still widely practised by conjurers, three goblets or cups are involved and balls appear and disappear beneath each of them. The twentieth-century single cup version is known to magicians as the "Chop Cup" because it was devised and first performed by an American magician, Al Wheatley, who worked under the name of Chop Chop.

Above: Matthew Hopkins, the self-styled Witch Finder General, as seen in this print by James Caulfield (1792), which was based on the frontispiece to Hopkins' *The Discovery of Witches*, published in 1647. The manual describes the techniques used when examining those suspected of witchcraft. Sleight-of-hand performers were often accused of being in league with the Devil.

Left: The dragon occurs with remarkable frequency in alchemy and can be interpeted as symbolizing life, power and creative energy, immortality and regeneration, and divine wisdom.

Right: One of the earliest illustrations of a performance of the Cups and Balls trick. This woodcut by an unknown artist for the block book *Wirtung der Planten* in 1470 was derived from the original *Children of the Planets* drawing by Joseph of Ulm.

Left: The Juggler by Hieronymus Bosch (c.1460-1516). This Flemish masterpiece depicts a conjurer performing the Cups and Balls to a group of suitably astounded onlookers, one of whom (*foreground left*) is blissfully unaware that her purse is being picked. Note too the wicker basket hanging from the conjurer's belt which contains an owl! (The original painting is in the Municipal Museum at Saint Germain-en -Laye, France.)

The Oldest Trick in the World

The first authenticated account of this ancient deception was written by the Roman philosopher Seneca, in the first century AD. The Cups and Balls was certainly already ancient by that time. Small wonder, then, that this trick became the conjurer's symbol and can be traced in word and picture up to the nineteenth century, when it was replaced by a new motif, a rabbit being produced from a hat. Although no longer a primary symbol, the classic Cups and Balls remains an essential item in the repertoire of many modern conjurers.

The earliest known illustration of the Cups and Balls is a colored drawing from 1404, *The Children of the Planets, Luna* by Joseph of Ulm. It shows the performer, a familiar figure in the town of Ulm, seated behind a circular table with a goblet in each hand. There are three balls on the table. This drawing was the forerunner of a series of fifteenth-century engravings that included Cups and Balls performers.

The most famous representation of a conjurer is *The Juggler* by the renowned Flemish painter, Hieronymus Bosch (c1460-1516). The performer stands behind a table on which the apparatus for the Cups and Balls has been placed. A touch of sly humor is introduced: a woman, astounded by the wonders being exhibited, is blissfully unaware that her purse is being stolen, although another young spectator points out the theft to his companion.

An explanation of how to perform the Cups and Balls was first published in Elizabethan times, in Reginald Scot's *The Discoverie of Witchcraft* (1584). Scot, a Justice of the Peace, was distressed by the cruelty involved in the then-prevalent witchcraft trials. Although not a complete sceptic, he disputed some of the current views of witchcraft. Scot believed that it would help to reduce fear of witches if he could explain how the wonders shown by sleight-of-hand performers were achieved purely by natural means and not by any diabolic assistance. At that time, tricks and showmanship were the preserve of wandering performers, who often were members of troupes comprising acrobats, musicians, jugglers and storytellers. Scot had no personal knowledge of conjuring, so he took lessons from a French performer, John Cautares, who lived in London. He was then able to devote a section of his book to sleight-of-hand tricks. His is the first book in the English language to explain these secrets and clearly Scot's conscience was pricked by his action, for he appreciated that exposure of the secrets would damage the reputation of "such poore men as live thereby".

The successful performance of the Cups and Balls depends upon skill and showmanship. Conjurers who watch an adroit fellow practitioner at work, while well aware of how the trick is done, should be unable to detect the precise crucial actions. An accomplished presentation of this magical classic will always evoke their admiration.

Another version of the Cups and Balls used to be common at race-courses where it was used by tricksters to dupe gullible punters. Known as the Thimble Rig, this version employs three inverted thimbles and a pea. While onlookers hesitate, having been invited to identify the thimble under which the pea is located, one of the tricksters (pretending to be a passer-by) takes easy money from the operator by repeatedly indicating the correct thimble. Yet when the "mark" tries his hand at this apparently simple way of making money, unaccountably the pea is *not* where he thought it was. Skilled manipulation ensures that the performer is in complete control – the pea can turn up under whichever thimble he desires.

Below: Parisian-style street magic in the early nineteenth century, as shown in this engraving by Brocas of *The Juggler of the Château d'Eau.* The site, close to the fountain near Porte St Martin and Porte St Denis, was regularly used by this conjurer, who is performing the Cups and Balls trick to an admiring audience.

Ancient Mysteries

The first recorded example of a genuine conjuring performance can be found in the Westcar Papyrus, now in the possession of the Berlin State Museum. It recounts how an Egyptian magician called Dedi was commanded to appear before King Cheops, builder of the Great Pyramid at Giza, in about 2600 BC. Dedi cut off and restored the heads of a goose, a duck and an ox but declined to do likewise to a prisoner whom King Cheops had thoughtfully provided for the occasion. Thus the decapitation illusion, which is still performed today in various guises such as the guillotine, has a long and venerable history. It became a feature of the English Miracle Plays of the fourteenth to sixteenth centuries and was explained by Reginald Scot in *The Discoverie of Witchcraft*. An illustration reveals how a trick called The Decollation of John Baptist was achieved and how the apparently severed head was displayed on a platter for all to see.

In the records of the mysteries enacted in the temples of ancient Greece and Egypt are references to apparent miracles that held worshipers in awe. These seemingly supernatural occurrences, however, can be explained. Many of them relied on scientific principles that were generally unknown to the public. Accounts exist of shrine doors that opened in response to the lighting of a fire on an altar, of urns that poured forth wine, vocal statues that responded to supplications, trumpet sounds that accompanied the opening of temple doors and even visions of the gods themselves.

Our understanding of how some of these remarkable effects were achieved is largely due to the writings of Hero of Alexandria around AD 62, and to the activities of archaeologists in later centuries. The opening of shrine doors, for example, was accomplished by the means shown in the detailed illustration below. The altar was, in fact, an airtight metal box connected to a spherical vessel containing water, which was sited in the cellars of the temple, unseen by the worshipers. The fire kindled on the altar caused the trapped air to expand and force water out of the vessel into a large bucket, suspended by ropes from a pulley. These ropes were wound round two spindles, which

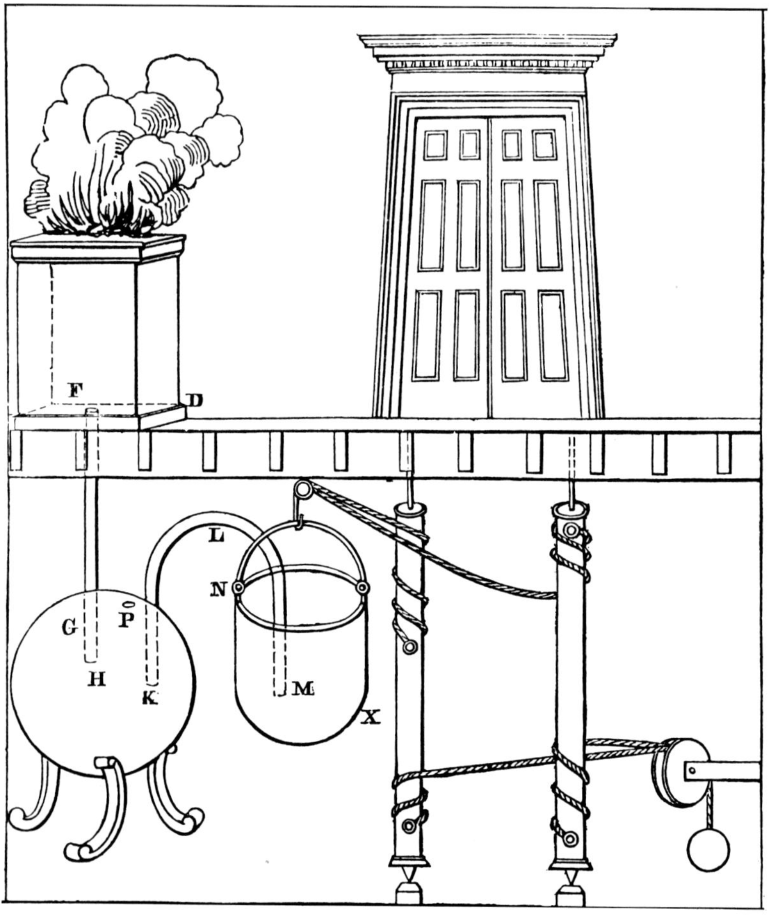

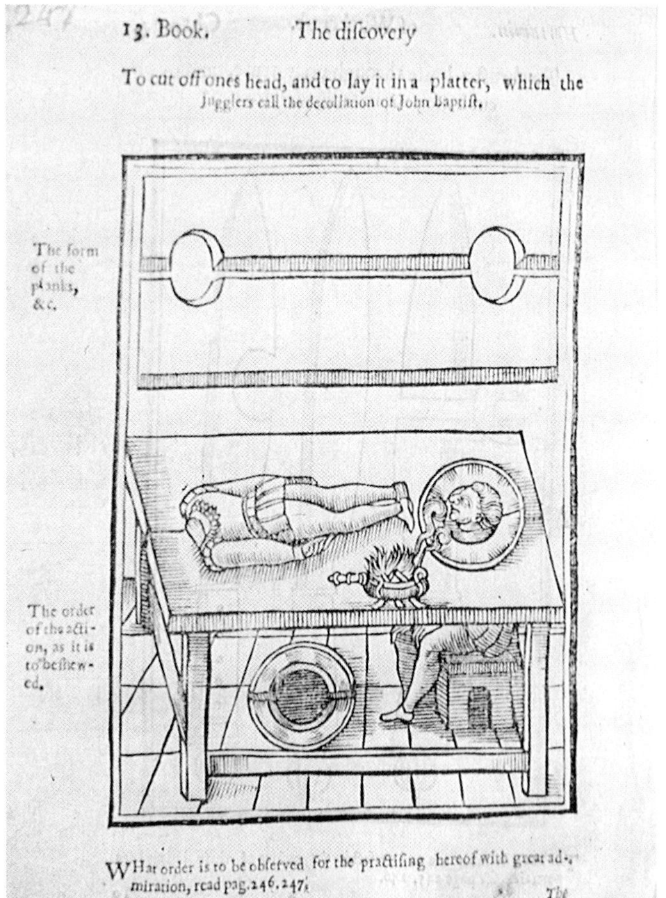
13. Book. The diſcovery

To cut off ones head, and to lay it in a platter, which the Jugglers call the decollation of John Baptiſt.

The form of the planks, &c.

The order of the action, as it is to be ſhewed.

What order is to be obſerved for the practiſing hereof with great admiration, read pag. 246. 247.

The

Above: "Fantasmagorie", the remarkable ghost show produced by Étienne-Gaspard Robertson in the Capuchin Convent, Paris, in 1797. The magic lantern was skillfully employed to project images of ghosts on to gauze screens or smoke rising from incense burned on braziers.

Left: Reginald Scot's seminal book, *The Discoverie of Witchcraft*, published in 1584. One section of the work is devoted to an explanation of natural magic and conjuring and it is the first book in the English language to explain in detail such principles. The cruelty of the witchcraft trials led Scot to write this crusading volume.

Far left: The machinery for opening the doors of a shrine in response to the lighting of a fire on an altar. This phenomenon was achieved through an ingenious underground system. Hot air pressure within the altar forced water into a bucket, the weight of which caused spindles joined to the shrine door hinges to rotate, so opening the doors.

passed through the floor and to which were attached the hinges of the shrine doors. Thus, as the bucket started to descend as it filled with water, the spindles turned and the doors gradually opened. Later, when the fire was extinguished, the air in the altar contracted and water was withdrawn from the bucket which rose, aided by the counterweight. The spindles now revolved in the opposite direction and the shrine doors closed. Urns that poured forth libations operated on a similar pneumatic principle.

"Vocal" statues were made possible by the use of speaking tubes which connected the mouths of the idols with the priests' quarters. The priest, hidden from the crowd of worshipers, used the tube to hear the questions and to supply appropriate answers.

Trumpet sounds were produced mechanically by opening doors that were attached to a funnel-shaped plunger, suspended in a reservoir of water. When the door was opened, the plunger was forced down in the water, displacing air upward through a tube to be emitted, via the trumpet, with an ear-shattering note.

The first-century AD Roman writer Pliny records marvels in the Temple of Heracles at Tyre, in what is now the Lebanon. His account of a seat made of consecrated stone "from which the gods easily rose" is one of several accounts that indicate the use of concave mirrors in conjuring up apparitions. The existence in antiquity of such mirrors is attested by Sir David Brewster in his *Letters on Natural Magic* (1832).

Optical illusions of this kind produced in a religious setting were the forerunners of secular "ghost" entertainments that became popular in the late eighteenth and early nineteenth centuries under the name of Phantasmagoria. These shows employed the magic lantern, an optical instrument invented in the mid-seventeenth century, to produce images by projecting suitable slides on a transparent gauze screen or, preferably, on billowing smoke above a brazier. If projected onto smoke, the figures appeared to move. The lantern was concealed from the spectators and the technique referred to in the modern movie industry as "back projection" was employed. The slides had to be opaque, apart from the figures, so that no stray light was visible to destroy the illusion.

The creator of this style of entertainment was a Belgian physicist, Etienne-Gaspard Robertson, who arrived in Paris after the Reign of Terror and by 1798 had established it as a popular attraction. Robertson assured his audiences that he could bring the dead to life and, after the candles had been extinguished, poured potions on a brazier. Almost immediately, specters were seen in the smoke. These phantoms were identified by spectators as famous French writers and leading figures of the Revolution, such as Marat, Voltaire, Mirabeau, Danton, Jean-Jacques Rousseau and Robespierre. On one occasion, the appearance of a dear departed wife caused the widower to flee the pavilion, apparently convinced that what he saw was not a ghost! Robertson later moved his show from the bright and cheerful Pavilion de l'Echiquier to the sepulchral surroundings of an abandoned chapel in a Capuchin convent, a stroke of genius that ensured his continuing success.

The Phantasmagoria show reached Britain in 1802, when a French magician named Philipsthal presented an entertainment similar to that of Robertson in Edinburgh and

GHOST RAISING

A different technique for ghost-raising was introduced by Henri Robin in Paris in 1847 and by Professor John Henry Pepper at the Royal Polytechnic Institution in London in 1862. The technique involved reflecting a hidden, brightly illuminated figure on a sheet of a plate glass set at an angle and invisible to the audience.

These reflections could be superimposed upon an actor or an object, creating the illusion that both were in the same place. To make an article seem to disappear, the light on that article was turned off. For a slow vanish, the light was gradually reduced. By this means, quite elaborate illusions could be achieved. The technique was featured effectively in various theatrical productions on both sides of the Atlantic.

Below: A dramatic presentation of Pepper's Ghost. A beautiful present-day version can be seen in the ballroom of the Haunted Mansion at Disneyland.

Above: A chosen card is nailed to the wall in this early nineteenth-century performance. The hand-colored engraving is believed to be a variant frontispiece to *Hocus Pocus*, a 38-page booklet published by Thomas Hughes of London in 1826.

London. Ghosts, skeletons and recognizable individuals were conjured up to the accompaniment of thunder and flashes of lightning, and the head of Dr Benjamin Franklin was gradually transformed into a skull. The phantoms advanced toward the spectators, increasing to menacing size, then either receded or abruptly disappeared, much to the consternation of the audience. These effects, long before the invention of the zoom lens, were achieved by mounting the magic lantern on rails so that it could be moved smoothly back and forth. The size of the image was changed by altering the distance between the lantern and the screen.

This kind of entertainment was introduced to America at the beginning of the nineteenth century by Andrew Oehler, a German-born conjurer whose life was a series of misfortunes. These included losing his money in ballooning adventures and being jailed in Mexico in 1806 for sorcery, when his ghost-raising activities proved too much for the superstitious Mexicans. Perhaps wisely, he gave up conjuring completely in 1809.

It is Robertson's Phantasmagoria, however, that may be regarded as the legitimate forerunner of the Midnight Ghost Shows that thrilled audiences in American movie houses during the 1940s and 1950s. With tombstones and graves displayed in the lobby and headless monsters, vampires, ghosts and skeletons roaming the auditorium, these shows were extremely popular for over a decade.

Traveling Showmen

Information about individual performers is not readily available until the advent of daily newspapers. Thereafter, advertisements for conjurers' appearances and reports of their shows provide the kind of detail that had previously been lacking. However, we do know that the principal conjurer in the reign of England's King Henry VIII was called Brandon, while in King James I's time a magician working under the name of Hocus Pocus was

Strange Feats are herein taught by Slight of Hand,
With which you may divert yourſelf and Friend.
The like in print was never ſeen before,
And ſo you'll ſay, when once you've read it o'er.

The whole ART of

LEGERDEMAIN:

OR

Hocus Pocus

In PERFECTION.

By which the meaneſt Capacity may perform the Whole ART without a Teacher. Together with the Uſe of all the Inſtruments belonging thereto.

To which is now added,

Abundance of New and Rare Inventions, the like never before in Print but much deſired by many.

The Seventh Edition, with large Additions and Amendments.

Written by H. DEAN.

LONDON:

Printed for L. HAWES and Co. and S. CROWDER, in *Pater-Noſter-Row*, and R. WARE and Co. on *Ludgate-Hill*. 1772.

Above: Henry Dean owned a bookshop on Tower Hill, London, and is believed also to have sold magical apparatus. His book *The Whole Art of Legerdemain* (1722), and its derivatives, served as manuals for aspiring magicians for over 150 years.

Left: Isaac Fawkes (d.1731) was the most famous and successful English conjurer of the early eighteenth century. This print by James Caulfield shows him with his amazing bag, from which he produced eggs, gold, silver and wild fowl. Beneath him are his posture masters or contortionists.

Overleaf: The delightful hand-colored frontispiece to Fairburn's *New London Conjurer*, published in the 1820s. It shows the Fire King, Ivan Ivanitz Chabert (1792-1859) emerging from his oven, having stayed inside it while a rump steak and a leg of lamb cooked. He is flanked by two conjurers, Philip Breslaw performing the decapitation illusion and Gyngell who has just produced a pigeon from a bottle.

apparently the leading performer. He was so named because, on beginning each trick, he would say "*Hocus pocus, tontus, talontus, vade celeriter iubeo*", a nonsense phrase intended to create a magical atmosphere.

The most successful conjurer of the early eighteenth century was undoubtedly Isaac Fawkes, who appeared in and around London until his death in 1731. His performances were attended by all classes, from royalty to commoner. One of Fawkes' best known feats involved taking an empty bag, displaying it inside and out, and then producing eggs from it, showers of gold and silver coins, and finally some wild fowl. Also he would throw a pack of cards into the air, whereupon they instantly changed into birds which flew about the room. Woodcuts which accompanied his advertisements depict Fawkes performing these tricks. In about 1726 he joined up with Christopher Pinchbeck Senior, a noted maker of mechanically animated figures, and together they exhibited their respective marvels.

A contemporary of Fawkes was the extraordinary twenty-nine-inch-high German, Matthew Buchinger. He did not have any legs, and instead of arms had two fin-like appendages. Despite these tremendous handicaps, Buchinger was an expert exponent of the Cups and Balls, with the climax of live birds being produced from beneath the cups. He was also an accomplished player of the flute, dulcimer, trumpet and bagpipes, and was capable of writing and drawing to a high standard. Nor were these the limits of his virtuosity, for he married four times and fathered eleven children.

BRESLAW

URN'S
UROR
GYNGELL
RT THE FIRE KING.

Later in the eighteenth century, the German conjurer Philip Breslaw performed with cards, dice, money, rings and watches and advertised his ability to make a fresh egg fly out of any person's pocket into a box on the table, before flying back again into the pocket; he excelled, by all accounts, at sleight-of-hand.

An entirely different character was Gustavus Katterfelto, a quack doctor, conjurer, lecturer and pseudo-scientist, who arrived in London in 1781. He sold quack cures during the great influenza epidemic which swept the capital in 1782 and, as well as making a great deal of money, became a target of contemporary cartoonists. Katterfelto's entertainments began with an hour-long philosophical lecture, followed by experiments, demonstrations and finally a conjuring performance. The principal scientific feature of his show was the solar microscope, which he (misleadingly) claimed to have invented. Since its effective operation depended upon sunlight, Britain's cloudy skies often ruined his performances. However, Katterfelto was not lacking in modesty, describing himself as "the greatest philosopher in this kingdom since Sir Isaac Newton". Advertisements proclaimed "Wonders! Wonders! Wonders!" and the sight of this tall, gaunt individual, wearing a long black coat and a square velvet cap being accompanied by a black cat and two black servants, must have created a suitably mysterious atmosphere. His conjuring tricks were standard for the day, resembling those of his compatriot Breslaw, Gyngell in England and other contemporary magicians, employing cards, dice, money, watches, caskets and mechanically animated figures. After a period of affluence Katterfelto's fortunes declined precipitously and he died in poverty at Bedale in Yorkshire in 1799.

A conjurer who had a more legitimate claim to a scientific background than Katterfelto was Jacob Philadelphia. He was the earliest known magician to have been born in North America although, paradoxically, he never performed on that continent. Born Jacob Meyer in Philadelphia, he adopted the name of his native city when he sailed for England in the mid-1750s. He took with him a letter of introduction from his teacher, the Rosicrucian mystic Dr Christopher Witt, to the Duke of Cumberland. With the financial support of the duke, Philadelphia carried out experiments and further studies. In 1765, after the duke's death, he traveled all over Europe, lecturing and displaying conjuring feats, some of which were based on mathematical and physical principles. Sleight-of-hand was combined with apparatus effects, including a figure of Bacchus holding a barrel of water, which turned to wine when the tap was turned, and a magic inkstand, which furnished inks of different colors on command. He also performed the decapitation illusion with a dove and two boys. A contemporary witness, Ludwig Boclo, recorded that while the beheading of the two boys was certainly an illusion, the resuscitation of the dove, whose body he held in his hand while the head was passed round the assembled company, remained "an unsolvable mystery".

Philadelphia was adept at securing publicity and one of the stories that was widely told was of his simultaneous departure by carriage through each of the four gates of Berlin. It is not known whether this story was simply invented or whether he used doubles to achieve the desired effect. At Göttingen in Germany in 1777, however, the tables were turned on him by the German physicist and satirist Professor Georg Christoph Lichtenberg, who issued anonymously a satirical broadsheet that so ridiculed Philadelphia's performance that the conjurer hastily left town.

Above: A cartoon of Gustavus Katterfelto, the Prussian quack doctor, published by H. Humphrey of London in 1783. Titled *The Wonderful Most Wonderful Dr Kat-he-felt-ho*, it shows him carrying his solar microscope on his back, clutching in his left hand a bag containing 5000 guineas mulcted from his gullible audiences, and in his right the "Gentle Restorer", which allegedly ensured virility. Katterfelto's wife and children are depicted as devils.

Pinnacle of Popularity

The nineteenth century witnessed a significant change in the presentation of conjuring skills. With the advent of more theaters, there was a move by the more successful performers from the fairgrounds and taverns to the minor theaters and subsequently to the new vaudeville shows where, in the years leading up to the First World War, magic attained a pinnacle of popularity.

Nineteenth-century magicians were also great travelers. The development of railways and steamships brought greater opportunities for travel and European performers visited America, Australia and the Far East. Nor were American, Australian and Oriental conjurers slow to make reciprocal journeys.

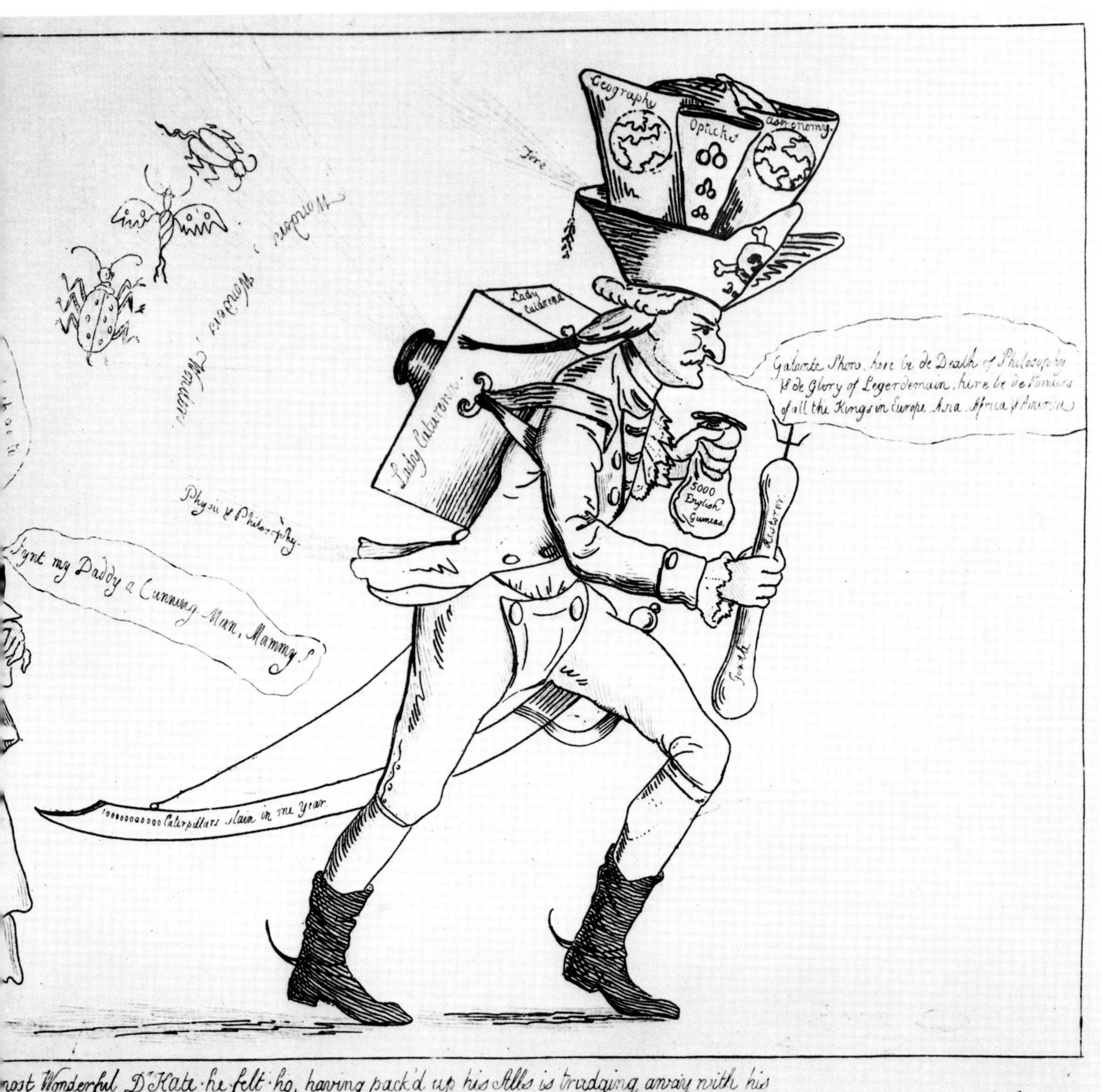
Geography
Opticks
astronomy
Fire
Lady Caldorona
Lady Caldorona
Wonders! Wonders! Wonders!
Physic & Philosophy
Galante Show, here be de Death of Philosophy & de Glory of Legerdemain, here be de Wonders of all the Kings in Europe, Asia, Africa & America
5000 English Guineas
Electrical
Isynt my Daddy a Cunning-Man, Mammy!
100000000000 Caterpillars slain in the Year
most Wonderful Dr Kate-he-felt-ho, having pack'd up his Alls is trudging away with his
necessary Appendices to his own Dear Countrey —Weep England! Weep! Oh!
Pub 31 March 1783, by H. Humphrey, No 51 New Bond Street

Left: Okito (Theo Bamberg, 1875–1963) was of the fifth generation in a dynasty of Dutch magicians. He presented a graceful oriental act, one of the highlights being The Floating Ball, which moved mysteriously around the stage with no visible means of support.

THE HOTTEST SHOW IN TOWN

The first American-born conjurer to win acclaim in his own country was Richard Potter, a mulatto and possibly the son of Sir Charles Frankland, the British Tax Collector for Boston, Massachusetts, and his black slave Dinah. Potter was born in 1783 and, after growing up on the Frankland estate, traveled to Britain. There he joined a circus, spent some time in France and then returned to Boston in 1801 as assistant to the Scottish conjurer and ventriloquist John Rannie. Ten years later, Rannie retired and Potter launched his own show, entitled "Evening's Brush to Sweep Away Care; or, a Medley to Please".

The show was so successful that for over twenty years he toured the United States and Canada with magic, ventriloquism and occasionally a salamander act, in which he passed a red-hot iron bar over his tongue, drew it through his hands and afterwards bent it into various shapes with his naked feet. For good measure, Potter then immersed his hands and feet in molten lead, demonstrating a remarkable invulnerability to heat. He died in 1835 and was buried on his estate at Andover, New Hampshire, which is now known, in his honor, as Potter's Place.

Above: A nineteenth-century poster advertising a performance by the magician Professor John Henry Anderson. The illustrations depict Anderson performing items from his repertoire, including the Magic Scrap Book and the Inexhaustible Bottle.

Foremost amongst the widely traveled magicians of the last century was Scotland's John Henry Anderson, self-styled Great Wizard of the North, who combined his conjuring with a love of acting. He was born in 1814, the son of a tenant farmer, was orphaned at an early age and joined a troupe of traveling players, with whom he saw his first magician, the Austrian Signor Blitz. He was so impressed that he decided to become a magician himself and joined the company of a showman called Scott who, somewhat fancifully, called himself The Emperor of All the Conjurers. Scott did, however, teach the young Anderson some magic, including the Gun Trick which subsequently featured prominently in Anderson's repertoire.

Around 1837, Anderson made his debut as The Great Caledonian Magician in theaters in Scotland and the north of England. By 1840, he was appearing in London as The Great Wizard of the North, with a spectacular show that involved "Gorgeous and Costly Apparatus of Solid Silver" and a presentation of Second Sight, in which he divined the nature of articles placed into a mother-of-pearl case by members of the audience. Later in his career, assisted by one of his daughters, he performed the more usual version of Second Sight as practised by modern conjurers, namely the blindfolded medium on stage who divines objects handed to her partner as he moves about the auditorium.

Anderson was a tremendous advertiser and a great traveler. In the course of his career he visited the USA, Russia, Sweden, Denmark, Prussia, Canada, Australia and Hawaii, as well as covering the length and breadth of Britain. But he was dogged by accidents, particularly those caused by fire, which seemed to pursue him relentlessly. The City Theatre on Glasgow Green, Scotland, which he built in 1845 out of his profits, was gutted by fire later that year and he sustained considerable financial loss. There was a minor fire at one of the US theaters he played in the early 1850s and then, in March 1856, came the major tragedy at the Covent Garden Theatre in London. It is unclear precisely what happened but fire enveloped the stage area, the theater quickly became an inferno and the roof fell in. Mercifully no lives were lost but the financial consequences for the under-insured Anderson were dire.

Thereafter, Anderson's fortunes declined: he still traveled the world but expenses and creditors devoured his profits and he died at Darlington, England, in 1874, in rather straitened circumstances.

A contemporary of Anderson in Europe and the United States was Carl Herrmann, a German-born conjurer who was expert at sleight-of-hand and created a sensation in both New York and London. Carl's younger brother, Alexander, decided in 1876, at the age of twenty-seven, to settle in the USA. Alexander Herrmann became the foremost

Below: Adelaide Herrmann (1853-1932), widow of a famous American magician, the Great Herrmann, continued to present her husband's show for thirty years after his death in 1896. The Flight of the Favorite was the transposition of a girl from one raised cabinet to another.

American large-scale illusionist of his day, with a mansion and estate at Whitestone Landing on Long Island and a steam yacht for recreation.

Alexander's wife Adelaide, who assisted him with his show, carried it on in her own right after his death in 1896. Initially, she had a partnership with Alexander's nephew, Leon Herrmann, but this did not work out so after three seasons they parted. The indomitable Adelaide carried on and made her mark in vaudeville with beautifully staged magic and gorgeous stage sets. An example of her repertoire is "Noah's Ark – Where Do They Come From?" An ark-shaped cabinet was shown empty and then filled with water. From it were produced, "two by two", pigeons, hens, ducks, cats, "lions" and "tigers", the last two species being dogs wearing appropriate heads. Adelaide, who was called the Queen of Magic, performed to the age of seventy-five, and died in 1932, four years after her retirement.

Uncrowned King of Magic

Another American performer whose name proclaimed "magic" until his retirement in 1908 was Harry Kellar. He had a big traveling show and took the place of Alexander Herrmann as the uncrowned king of American magic after Herrmann's death. The Kellar show was later taken over by Howard Thurston, who toured American theaters with his "Wonder Show of the Universe", bringing joy to generations of youngsters who looked forward eagerly to his annual visits.

France's greatest conjurer, widely hailed as the father of modern conjuring, was Jean Eugène Robert-Houdin, born the son of a clockmaker at Blois in 1805. He began as an apprentice watchmaker, but one day received, by mistake, an encyclopedia of amusements that included a section on conjuring. He was completely absorbed by this new discovery and later stated that it had given him one of his most joyful experiences.

Robert-Houdin's skills as a mechanician and conjurer lent themselves to the construction of various "automata", including a writing figure and the Mysterious Clock which, with a transparent dial and mounted on an equally transparent column, nonetheless kept perfect time. He was such a successful pioneer in the application of

Below: Jean Eugène Robert-Houdin (1805-71), France's most famous conjurer, who is widely regarded as the "Father of Modern Magic". On the centenary of his death in 1971 the French government issued this commemorative postage stamp which shows the suspension illusion and his magic clock.

Above: The Indian Trunk Trick, in which the conjurer's assistant disappears from the locked and corded trunk, as explained to readers of *The Picture Magazine* in 1893. One end of the trunk revolves upon a central pivot, enabling the assistant to escape via a trapdoor in the stage when the trunk is upended.

electricity and magnetism to conjuring and other devices, that he received honorary medals in 1844 and 1855. He also opened his own theater of magic at the Palais Royal, Paris, in 1845. Robert-Houdin became a national figure and on the centenary of his death (1971), the French government issued a commemorative postage stamp.

The Egyptian Hall in Piccadilly, London, which stood from 1812 until its demolition in 1905, started out as a museum but within seven years had become a suite of exhibition and sale rooms that attracted an incredible array of artists, lecturers, freaks, showmen and entertainers. For the last thirty-one years of its life it was the headquarters of the most famous magic show in Britain, which carried on for almost another three decades at St George's Hall – Maskelyne and Cooke, subsequently Maskelyne and Devant, and finally simply Maskelyne's. England's Home of Mystery, as it was affectionately termed, was the Mecca for generations of schoolchildren and their parents and on its small stage some of the most incredible illusions ever created were presented.

Presiding Genius

The presiding genius and founder of a dynasty of English magicians was John Nevil Maskelyne (1839-1917). With his boyhood friend George Alfred Cooke, he created a style of intimate magical entertainment that lasted for sixty years. It embraced magical sketches or playlets, a number of which included the famous Box Trick. In this trick, the performer escapes from a mahogany trunk in which he has been placed, and which itself has been enveloped in a canvas cover before being tied up.

Maskelyne was also known for his plate spinning, a form of juggling in which six dessert plates were kept spinning on a table top while another plate was spun down an inclined plane only four inches wide, then up a spiral and down again to the table.

Maskelyne, like Robert-Houdin, had started life as a watchmaker and used this skill to

VICTORIA ROOMS, CLIFTON.

Tuesday, Nov. 16th, to Saturday, Nov. 20th; each Evening at 8.

Day Performances, Wednesday and Saturday, at 3.

MASKELYNE & COOKE'S.

MARVELLOUS ENTERTAINMENT, FROM THE EGYPTIAN HALL, LONDON.

construct automata. The most famous of these was Psycho, a whist-playing automaton, conceived jointly with a Lincolnshire farmer, John A. Clarke. The diminutive figure of a Hindu, seated cross-legged on a small box which, in turn, rested upon a clear glass cylinder (to prove there were no wires or tubes to the stage), played whist with three members of the audience and almost invariably won. Three other automata also featured — Zoe the drawing girl, and Labial and Fanfare, who respectively played euphonium and cornet — but Psycho was undoubtedly the main attraction.

Maskelyne's two sons, Nevil and Edwin Archibald, both became part of the company, as subsequently did three of Nevil's sons, Clive, Noel and Jasper. After the closure of Maskelyne's Mysteries in 1933, Jasper toured the British music halls with a smaller show. He served as a major in the British Army during the Second World War and his magical talents were put to good use in the Camouflage Experimental Section, as related in his book, *Magic – Top Secret* (1949).

The performer widely acclaimed as Britain's greatest conjurer was David Devant (1868-1941), a man of great personal charm who brought a refreshingly new approach to the art. He was the inventor of some startling illusions (which are described in Chapter Four), was an expert shadowgraphist and also specialized in sleight-of-hand. He had already appeared in vaudeville when Maskelyne engaged him in 1893, and created for the occasion a brand new illusion called The Artist's Dream. Although a stage performer, he invested his presentations with the intimacy of a home entertainer and captivated his audiences with his whimsical patter.

Devant's pre-eminence was recognized in 1912, when he was the only conjurer to be included in the very long list of performers for the first-ever Royal Command Performance at the Palace Theatre in London. On that auspicious occasion, he was assisted by his daughter Vida and the nine-year-old Jasper Maskelyne in the trick known as A Boy, a Girl and Some Eggs, in which a seemingly endless supply of eggs was taken out of an empty hat and given to the children to hold. Their increasingly desperate attempts to hold on to the growing number of eggs, without dropping and smashing them, created a perfect situation comedy that complemented the mystery.

Sadly, at the zenith of his career, Devant was stricken with a progressive paralysis which forced him into retirement in 1920. He ended his days in the Royal Home for Incurables at Putney, London, where he died at the age of seventy-three.

Above: Vonetta (originally Von Etta), "the Only Lady Illusionist, Protean and Quick Change Artiste" flourished on the British Music Hall stage during the period 1906-14.

Far left: A lithograph poster proclaiming "Marvellous entertainment" from the English illusionists and anti-spiritualists, Maskelyne and Cooke.

Koins and Cards

The twentieth century opened with a blaze of magical glory as young, aspiring magicians vied with each other to present the most spectacular show and patrons of variety theaters throughout the world were nightly mystified and entertained by a succession of novel acts. The London music halls resounded to applause for an influx of wonder-workers, many of them Americans. Audiences were astounded by the manipulative skills of T. Nelson Downs from Iowa, The King of Koins, and of Howard Thurston from Ohio, The King of Cards; by the breathless whirlwind of wizardry of Horace Goldin's topical illusions and by the startling transformations of the great German illusionist, Lafayette. They applauded the Oriental marvels of Chung Ling Soo (the stage name of William Ellsworth Robinson of New York City) and were thrilled by the incredible ability of Ehrich Weiss, alias Houdini, to extricate himself from every conceivable type of restraint that his challengers could devise.

Illusions aplenty were also provided by the international team of Le Roy, Talma and Bosco, the beautiful Talma being also a skilled manipulator of coins, and by the inventive genius of Selbit, an Englishman who created some of the most ingenious illusions of all time.

These innovators are just a few of the forerunners of modern magic, from whom today's star performers derive the basic principles of their repertoires. In the following chapters, a detailed look at particular specialties will illustrate how much can be learned from past masters of the art – and how many of their techniques are still shrouded in mystery.

Stark realism characterizes this French poster purporting to show how a performer, grandiosely named the British Circus Imperator, presented the decapitation illusion.

MAGIC MADE EASY.

BY

PROF. HARRY HOUDINI

KING OF CARDS

AND

HANDCUFFS.

PRICE . . . 25 CENTS.

THIS BOOK CONTAINS

Magic Tricks, Illusions, Second Sight Acts, Secrets of Money Making, Etc, Etc.

VAN FLEET, Printer, Clipper Building, New York.

2

THE GREAT ESCAPE

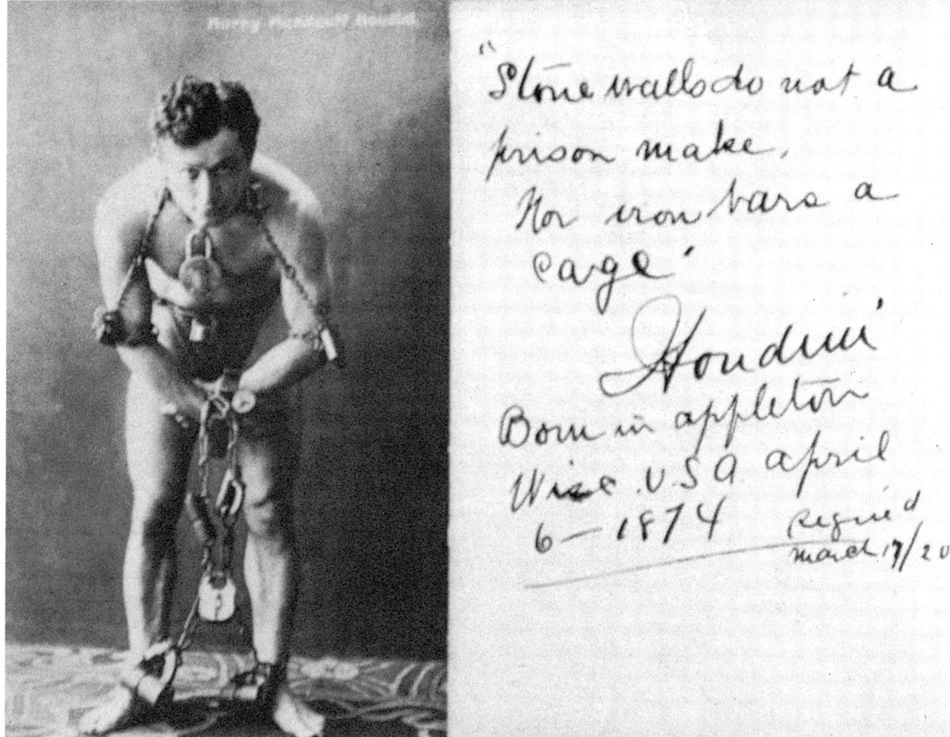

Above: "Houdini and the Mrs", a favorite photograph of Harry and Bess taken in London in 1909.

Left: In 1898 Houdini's affairs were at a low ebb and, unable to secure engagements, the struggling entertainer published this 16-page booklet *Magic Made Easy*. It explained some simple tricks and even offered for sale some of the secrets of the tricks that he featured in his own show, including the Handcuff Act.

Above right: Houdini delighted in inscribing and signing books, photographs and even valuable playbills and conjuring ephemera. This inscription is particularly interesting since it proclaims his adopted date and place of birth, April 6, 1874 at Appleton, Wisconsin. Houdini was, in fact, bornErich Weisz(Ehrich Weiss),the son of a rabbi, on March 24, 1874 in Budapest and was later brought to the United States as an infant.

For years, people have been fascinated by the skill and daring of the escape artist, who attempts to free himself from ropes, chains or handcuffs placed upon him by volunteer spectators trying their best to ensure that escape is impossible. Yet time and again, despite their best efforts, the performer releases himself — often in even less time than it took to secure him.

The acknowledged master of the great escape was Harry Houdini, who not only became a legend in his own lifetime but is still remembered more than half a century after his death. In the early twentieth century he topped the bill at theaters and vaudeville shows throughout the world, presenting dangerous and sometimes bizarre feats of escapology, many of which had never been seen before.

He was born in Budapest, on March 24, 1874, the son of a rabbi, Samuel Weiss, and his wife Cecilia, who named him Ehrich. When he was a few weeks old, the family left Hungary and emigrated to the United States, where they settled for a while in Appleton, Wisconsin.

Weiss became interested in magic in his teens and gave shows around the neighborhood, but it was the book *Memoirs of Robert-Houdin* that stirred his imagination and prompted him to become a professional magician. Robert-Houdin became his idol and, by adding the letter "i" to the French magician's name, he created the name by which audiences throughout the world would recognize him – Houdini.

Like most small-time entertainers, he had periods of work and long stretches of unemployment. He worked in beer halls, dime museums and amusement parks. While working on Coney Island he met Beatrice (Bess) Rahner, one of the Floral Sisters, a song and dance act. They married after a whirlwind courtship, and she became an important part of the act.

Houdini's magic act, in which he used small apparatus such as playing cards and silk handkerchiefs, was average with the exception of one illusion with which he concluded his performance. This was Metamorphosis, a transposition of two persons which, when slickly presented, never fails to astound.

In Houdini's presentation of this mystery, Bess's wrists were tied before she stepped into a sack which was securely fastened. Harry then lifted her, and placed her inside a trunk, which he locked and tied with ropes. Placing a draped cabinet around the trunk, he closed the drapes from within.

An instant later the drapes opened again to reveal Bess, wrists free and standing upright beside the trunk. She untied the ropes, unlocked the trunk and unfastened the ropes securing the sack, from which stepped Houdini, with his wrists securely bound. Variants of this trick are still performed, and it is still delighting and baffling audiences.

Right: The youthful Harry Houdini appeared as a manipulator of playing cards before finding fame as an escape artiste. At this time, in the 1890s, there were several performers who all advertized themselves as "The King of Cards".

Below: The American Davenport Brothers, Ira (1839 1911) and William Henry (1841-77), allegedly made spirits appear while bound hand and foot and locked in a cabinet. They created a London sensation when they arrived there in 1864, but their methods were soon exposed by conjurers. In 1910 Houdini became friendly with Ira who revealed to him their methods. In this photograph are, *left to right*, Ira, William Fay (the Brothers' manager), author Robert Cooper and William Henry.

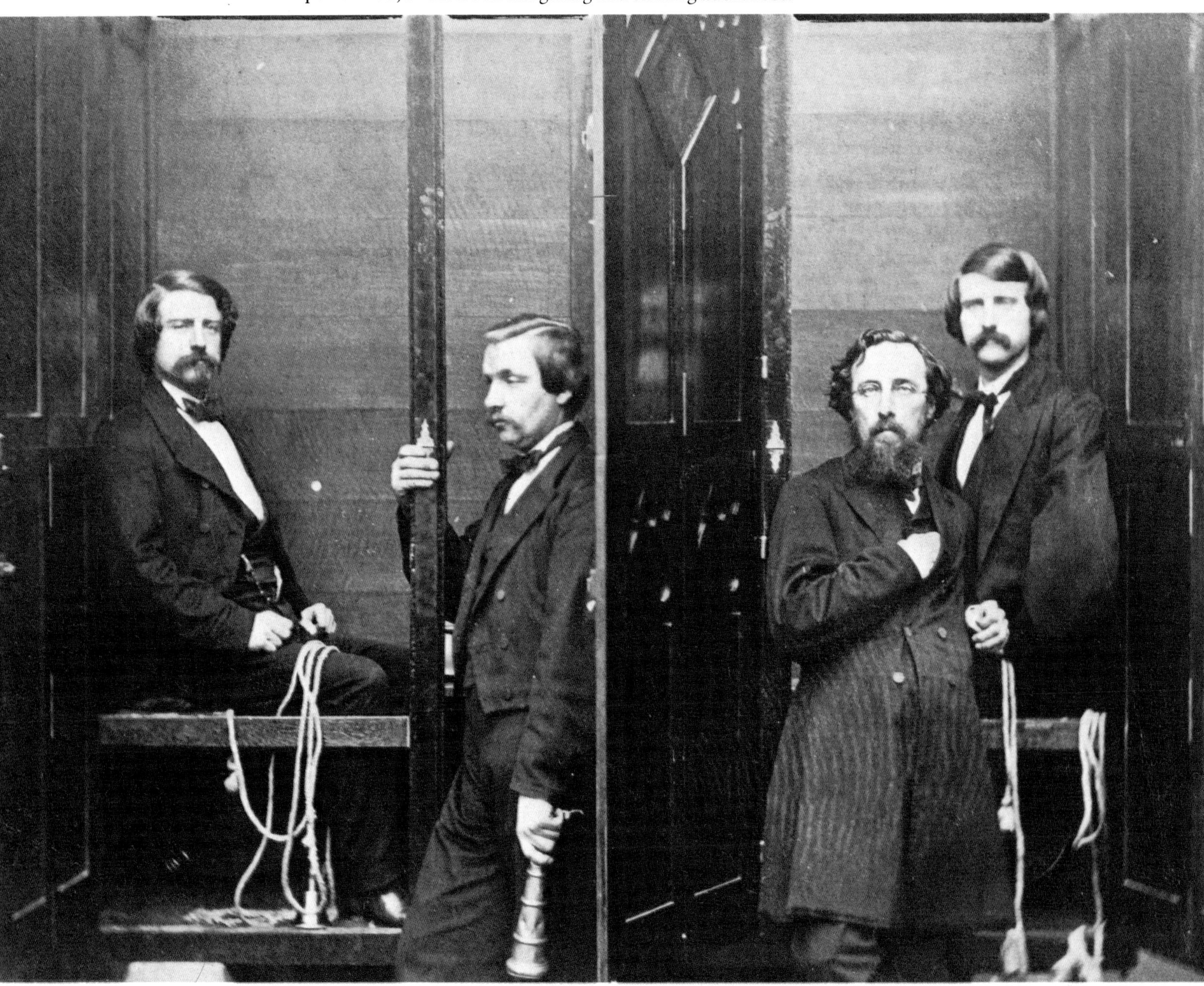

HARRY
HOUDINI
KING
OF CARDS
NATIONAL PR.& ENG. CO. CHICAGO
1838

CHALLENGE

TO

HOUDINI

Mr. H. HOUDINI, Tivoli Theatre, City. Sydney, April 12th, 1910.

Dear Sir,

The undersigned Expert Carpenters and Joiners, **Herebv Challenge You** to allow us to construct a **Large and Secure Packing Case** from One Inch Timber, and making use of Two and Half to Three Inch Flat Headed Wire Nails.

We believe we can so nail you in this box, rope it up and then nail the ropes to the box, that it will be **impossible for You to make Your escape.**

If you accept we will send the box along for examination, but demand the right to re-nail each and every board before the test so as to guard against preparation on your part. Awaiting your reply, we beg to remain, yours truly,

JOHN ANDERSON, "Lynton," Mansion Road, Strathfield.
JAMES WILLIAMSON, Balfour Street, Bellevue Hill.
WILLIAM ELPHINSTONE, 4 Church Street, Camperdown.

On behalf of the firm of E. THORNTON, Contractor and Builder, 42 Castlereagh Street, City.

HOUDINI ACCEPTS THE ABOVE CHALLENGE

FOR

FRIDAY NIGHT, APRIL 15

TEST TO TAKE PLACE ON THE STAGE OF

MR. HARRY RICKARDS TIVOLI THEATRE

The Box when finished will be placed in Theatre Vestibule for Public Examination.

The Handcuff Challenge

In his spare time, Harry became interested in police regulation handcuffs. He studied their mechanism and devised ways in which he could escape from them. He decided to include a challenge handcuff act in his program, inviting members of the public to supply the handcuffs.

The act was seen by and greatly impressed a booker of the Orpheum vaudeville circuit, Martin Beck. At a subsequent performance he arranged for some handcuffs that Houdini had not seen before to be offered in the challenge. They were accepted and Houdini escaped from them without any trouble.

Beck saw a great future for what, at that time, was a novelty and offered the young couple a series of bookings on the understanding that they abandoned the silk handkerchiefs, the playing cards and the pigeons. Houdini agreed to devote all his attention to the handcuff challenge and Metamorphosis. Martin Beck's idea of specializing in escapes was the turning point in Houdini's career and his Challenge Act became a sensation. He spent countless hours familiarizing himself with the working of every type of handcuff, gaining extra knowledge by visiting locksmiths, police stations, museums and second-hand shops. He devised various types of keys and picklocks which he could use to escape from practically every kind of restraint. This knowledge and preparation enabled him to achieve apparently impossible feats.

Recognizing the value of publicity, he arranged to escape not only from handcuffs but from police leg-irons and from prison cells. He found that some of the police authorities were co-operative but others refused to assist in what they considered to be a cheap publicity stunt. When carrying out his jail-breaks, Houdini was stripped naked and carefully examined by a doctor. The handcuffs or shackles were supplied by the police, who led him to a prison cell, fastened them on him, securely locked the cell door and left. To the great astonishment of the police officers and the amusement of newspaper reporters, Houdini later joined them, fully clothed and free of his restraints. Houdini was, naturally, very secretive about the methods he used. Some of his critics said that a dollar bill inserted in the right palm provided an easy means of escape from any prison cell!

Once Houdini became an established escapologist, he widened the scope of his escapes, challenging businesses and organizations to devise their own particular kind of restraints with which to shackle him. Joiners, metal workers, sailors, carpenters, brewers and even suffragettes all took up the offer.

He was asked to escape from packing cases, steel boilers, many different kinds of handcuffs, leg irons and shackles, an especially made giant football, a burglar-proof safe, and even from inside a dead whale!

Safe Escape

The attempt to escape from a burglar-proof safe took place on Friday, December 4, 1908 at the Euston Palace Theatre, London. Handbills were distributed to the public in the form of a printed letter from the challenger, Mr J.R. Paul, a locksmith, with an acknowledgment by Houdini.

> Houdini,
>
> Dear Sir,
>
> I have in my possession a genuine old burglar-proof safe, weighing about eight hundredweight, which will easily hold a human being.
>
> I would like to know whether (you being locked up inside this safe) there is any subterfuge by which, with your knowledge of locks, you could discover a method of escaping therefrom, without destroying or injuring the lock or safe.
>
> If you would care to make this escape in private you can do so at any time at my works, but should you wish to do so publicly I will bring the safe to the Euston, or any other place you may designate, at your convenience.
>
> I am, sir,
> Yours faithfully,
> J.R. Paul

Far left: Houdini appeared in Australia in 1910 under the banner of impresario Harry Rickards. This poster advertises a challenge escape from a packing case at the Tivoli Theatre, Sydney.

Below left: One of Houdini's favorite publicity stunts involved escaping from a prison cell in whichever town he was playing, having been first stripped and medically examined for concealed keys.

Below right: A special challenge feature was an escape having first been securely chained to a ladder which, along with the chains, were supplied by the challenger.

HARRY HOUDINI THE JAIL BREAKER

INTRODUCING HIS LATEST & GREATEST

PRISON CELL & BARREL MYSTERY

HOUDINI is strapped & locked in a barrel placed in a police cell which is also locked and in less than 2 seconds changes places.

£100. WILL BE PAID TO ANYONE FINDING TRAPS, PANELS OR FALSE DOORS IN THE CELL

Houdini accepted the challenge, which had created a good deal of attention, drawing a full house at the Euston Palace. The safe was inspected by members of the audience and a representative from the firm of locksmiths.

Houdini stepped into the safe and the locksmith closed the heavy door, manipulating the lock to make sure that the safe was secure. This escape was different to most of the others undertaken by Houdini, because although cell doors and handcuffs can be opened with duplicate keys or picklocks, a safe does not have a keyhole on the inside of the door. The mechanism is covered by a heavy metal plate.

Houdini's assistants placed a screen in front of the safe while the orchestra struck up a waltz. The safe looked so formidable that the audience prepared themselves for a long wait. The question that was uppermost in their minds was, how long could a man last in that confined space with only a limited amount of air?

As the minutes ticked by, people rather anxiously began to look at their watches. Suddenly, the screen was pushed aside. It crashed to the stage revealing Houdini in front of the burglar-proof safe, breathing heavily, with streams of perspiration running down his face. Rather wearily, he acknowledged the shouts, cheers and applause from the audience, while the locksmith walked around the safe in disbelief. The escape had taken less than fifteen minutes.

When the safe was returned to its owner the following morning, he and his workmen would obviously check it to try and discover how the escape had been accomplished. These men were experts but so were Houdini's "back room boys", who were responsible for many of the escape artist's spectacular feats. They were responsible not only for preparing the apparatus – replacing long nails with shorter ones, strong springs with weaker ones, and so forth – but also for preventing anyone from interfering once an escape was underway. Houdini's most faithful "backroom boy" was Jim Collins, who stayed with him for most of his career. Franz Kukol and George Vickery were his other main assistants, without whom many of Houdini's most flamboyant escapes might have proved impossible.

In this case, the preparation of the safe was particularly important. The safe had been delivered to the Euston Palace on the afternoon of the performance, giving Houdini and the members of his staff time to examine the locking mechanism and to make some adjustments. Strong springs were removed and replaced with weaker ones. Minor alterations were made to Houdini's satisfaction, and then the back plate was screwed in position. Now the safe could be opened from *within*, even after it had been securely locked and tested. No evidence of trickery would be discovered.

The escape now depended upon showmanship and no-one could equal Houdini in "selling" an escape to the public. The escape took just a few seconds but if Houdini had immediately leapt out from behind the screen he would have ruined the act as a piece of theater. Instead, he sat behind the screen reading a magazine while the audience became increasingly tense and restless, worried that he was going to run out of oxygen and could never escape in time. When the suspense neared its height, Houdini made his dramatic appearance, suitably "tired" from his apparently exhausting efforts to escape.

The Straitjacket Escape

During his travels, Houdini was always on the lookout for items that could be used in his program. While touring the Canadian provinces in 1894, he met a doctor who was in charge of an asylum for the insane. He visited the institution, where he was fascinated by the attempts of a patient to free himself from a canvas and leather jacket which had been fastened around him with heavy leather straps. It was the first time Houdini had seen a straitjacket.

The jacket was made of heavy canvas and had a leather collar and cuffs. The sleeves were sewn up at the ends, to which were attached two leather straps. The jacket opened at the back, where there were more buckles and straps.

When a straitjacket was put on a patient, the arms were inserted into the sleeves and the

Left: An unusual Houdini lithograph. The macho image that the escapologist liked to project would not be enhanced by a fairy, and the red devils were virtually the trademark of the American magician Harry Kellar (1849-1922) and his successor Howard Thurston (1869-1936).

straps at the back were tightly fastened. The patient's arms were then crossed over his chest and the straps attached to the cuffs brought around to the back, where they also were firmly secured.

Watching the man struggling and throwing himself around the padded cell trying to get out of the jacket, Houdini decided that a dramatic straitjacket escape could become a feature of his act. He obtained a jacket from the doctor and, for the next week, concentrated on finding ways of effecting an escape. The considerable physical effort required resulted in plenty of bruises but, by working repeatedly on certain parts of the jacket, he was able eventually to free himself.

When the escape was first performed before an audience, two or three men fastened him in the straitjacket and his assistants then hid him from view behind a curtained cabinet. Minutes later, when he reappeared, holding the jacket in his hand, the audience's response was a complete disappointment. The onlookers had no idea just how much sheer physical effort had been necessary to escape from the jacket, thinking that Houdini had relied on trickery while out of sight. Consequently, his brother Theo advised him to dispense with the cabinet and perform the escape in full view of the audience, whose positive response now matched the tremendous physical effort required in making the escape.

The most difficult escape from a straitjacket attempted by Houdini took place during his tour of Germany. A Chief of Police challenged him to escape from a jacket provided by Police Headquarters and secured by some of his officers. The challenge was accepted. Some picked men strapped Houdini into the jacket, pulling the straps so tight that he thought his ribs would break, and which made breathing very difficult. When the police chief was satisfied, the men left and Houdini began an ordeal that was to last for ninety unpleasant minutes, an experience which he later described as "painful, agonizing and miserable".

Below left: Theodore Hardeen (1876-1945), Houdini's brother, who showed Harry his first trick. They worked together as The Brothers Houdini in 1891. Subsequently, after Houdini's great success as an escapologist in Europe, Hardeen set up in friendly "competition" with him. He also pioneered the Straitjacket Escape in full view of the audience, rather than in a curtained cabinet, at Swansea, South Wales, in 1905.

Below: A rear view shot of Hardeen strapped into a straitjacket; despite the securely fastened buckles and straps, he still managed to escape.

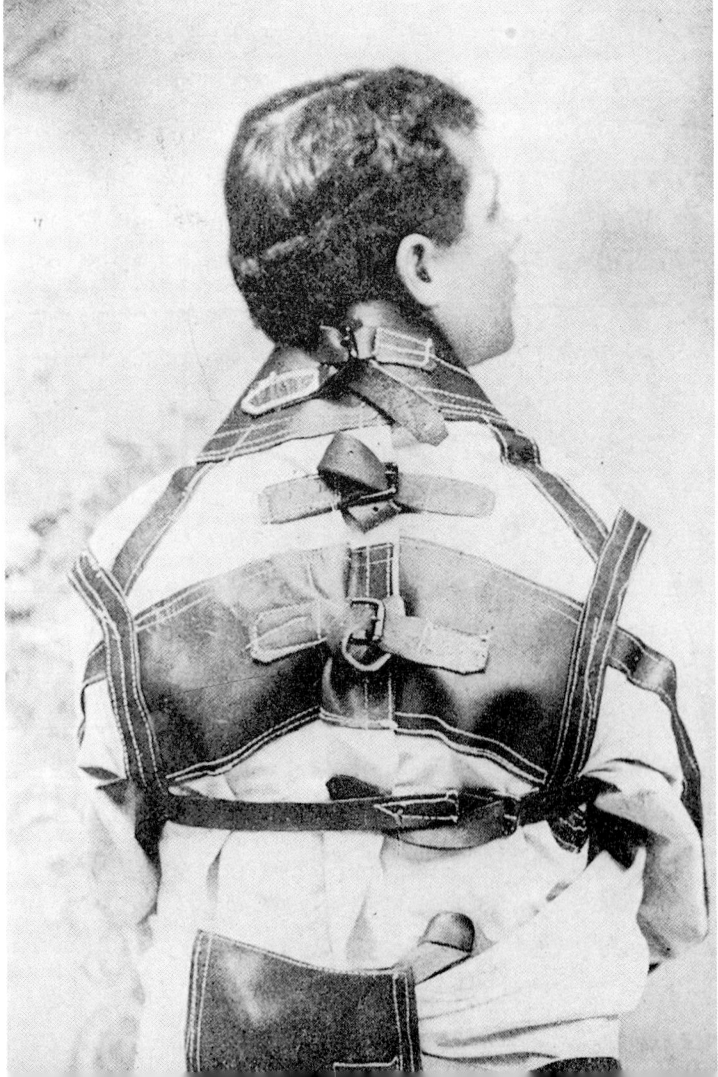

Underwater Escapes

Houdini won a great deal of newspaper publicity when he carried out his underwater escapes. There were many challengers who were ready to supply a wooden packing case, into which Houdini, after being handcuffed, was securely fastened. The case was lowered by a crane into the murky depths of a river, from which he eventually emerged, holding the handcuffs. One of Houdini's great assets was his ability to hold his breath for an unusually long time, so that he was able to remain submerged longer than the audience thought possible. When the crowds of onlookers were fearing the worst, he broke the surface, waving his hands in triumph.

For many of these escapes, he was dependent on his backroom boys "gaffing" the box; that is, rearranging crucial parts of its structure. Sometimes, concealed catches held wooden planks in place and on other occasions, shorter nails were substituted for long ones. Whatever method was used, it had to be failsafe. Also, when the case was returned to its manufacturers, it was essential that no clue remained as to how the escape had been achieved.

Despite the apparently easy methods used in this type of escape, danger was never far away. The shock from immersion in freezing cold water, a strong wind or fierce undercurrent were some of the difficulties faced by Houdini. One popular story about Houdini was included in the film (featuring Tony Curtis and Janet Leigh playing Houdini and Bess) about his life. The story concerned the daring leap from Detroit's Belle Isle Bridge, into the cold waters of the river some twenty-five feet below.

It took place on a cold November day with a large crowd of curious sightseers, well wrapped-up against the biting wind, watching incredulously as Houdini stripped down to his trousers. Two pairs of police regulation handcuffs were snapped around his wrists, and an involuntary gasp was heard from the crowd as he plunged into the near-freezing water. Yet minutes later he resurfaced, holding aloft the handcuffs.

Below: Houdini being bound by chains and manacles moments before the Bridge Leap, in which he jumped into a river, disappeared beneath the water and then reappeared, free of his bonds.

This page: Randi performing the Houdini Milk Can Escape. This sequence shows the manacled escapologist being submerged in a can full of water, with football stars Joe Green and Franco Harris helping his assistant to force down and padlock the lid. Finally, a curtained canopy is drawn around the can. Randi freed himself within just two and a half minutes!

THE BREWER'S CHALLENGE

Not all Houdini's escape attempts were successful. Although he managed with great difficulty to escape from the German straitjacket, he was not so fortunate when appearing at the Empire Theatre, Leeds, England, where he accepted a challenge from Joshua Tetley and Sons, Brewers, to escape from a galvanized container filled with beer.

Houdini had, for the past three years, featured his Water Can Escape. The galvanized can was like a large, old-fashioned milk churn, with padlocks securing the lid. Houdini climbed inside, the can was filled with water and the lid locked into position by volunteers from the audience. A draped cabinet was placed around the can and the assistants, wearing waterproof clothing, stood by with axes to smash the padlocks in case Houdini got into difficulties.

When trying to escape from the beer-filled can, Houdini had trouble with an unforeseen problem: he was overcome by the alcoholic fumes. His chief assistant, realizing that something was wrong, wrenched the lid from the can and saved the unconscious Houdini from drowning.

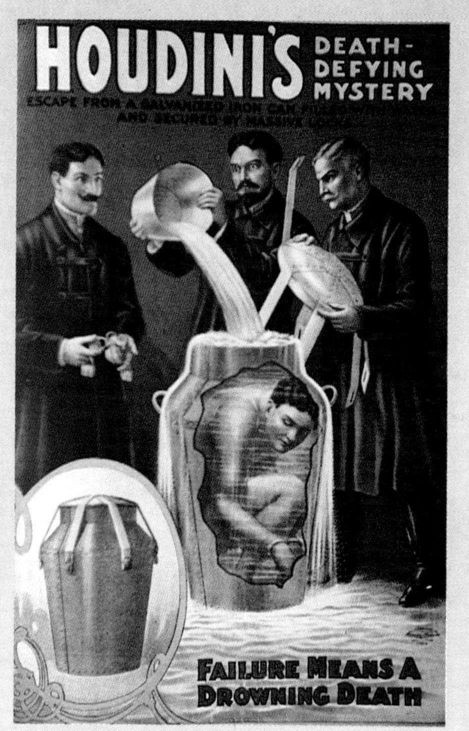

Houdini's Milk Can Escape, was first performed in 1908. Three years later tragedy almost struck at Leeds, England, when he accepted a challenge from a firm of brewers to escape from the beer-filled can. The teetotal Houdini was so overcome by the alcoholic fumes that he had to be rescued by his assistant, Franz Kukol.

When later recounting this experience to journalists, Houdini made certain additions to and omissions from the story. He vividly described his ordeal, claiming that the river had been frozen over with several inches of ice, into which a large hole had had to be cut before he could attempt the escape.

He added that, as he entered the water, a dangerous undercurrent dragged him downstream, and that only his quick thinking and calmness in a crisis had saved him from a watery grave. By lying on his back, he claimed, he had been able to draw air from the small space between the water level and the ice above. With great difficulty, and almost superhuman strength, he had struggled back to the hole in the ice, where relieved friends pulled him, exhausted, to safety.

He omitted to tell the gentlemen of the press that, before taking the plunge, he had made sure that a safety rope was fastened around his waist to prevent possible accidents – but why spoil a good story over mere details?

The Hippodrome Handcuffs

Possibly the most famous of Houdini's handcuff escapes, which caught the imagination of the public bringing a vast amount of newspaper publicity – with some papers devoting a full page to the event – occurred during one of his English tours. It took place on March 17, 1904 at the London Hippodrome, where 4,000 people crowded into the theater for the challenge that had been the talk of London for several days.

During the Saturday performance of the previous week, Houdini challenged anyone to provide a restraint from which he could not free himself. A reporter from *The London Illustrated Mirror* stepped forward to accept the challenge, saying that he had a pair of handcuffs which, he believed, would defeat "even Houdini".

The journalist had been introduced to a blacksmith, who showed him a pair of handcuffs of his own design, the lock of which had taken him five years to perfect. The newsman, recognizing the possibility of a good story, borrowed the cuffs and took them to some of London's leading locksmiths. They were unanimous in their praise of the workmanship and, encouraged by their comments, the man from the *Mirror* accepted Houdini's challenge. Houdini agreed to attempt the escape during a special matinee on the following Thursday, St Patrick's Day.

The audience sat impatiently through the first six variety acts which, under normal circumstances, would have been well received. On this particular occasion, they had come to see one man – Houdini.

When he appeared, soberly dressed in a black frock coat, stiff collar and dark tie, cheers and applause echoed around the theater. He began with a short speech before asking the newspaperman to join him on stage, where the two men shook hands.

Members of the audience and some of Houdini's friends came on stage to check that there was fair play on both sides. These forty men watched closely as the representative from the *Mirror* fastened the handcuffs around Houdini's wrists and turned the key in the lock six times. They agreed that the cuffs were securely fastened. Before retiring to the small, black cloth cabinet, to which he humorously referred as his "ghost house", Houdini addressed the audience.

> "Ladies and gentlemen, I am now locked up in a handcuff which has taken a British mechanic five years to make. I do not know whether I am going to get out of them, or not, but I assure you that I am going to do my best."

Amid great applause, he entered the small cabinet. The time was 3.15p.m.

The theater orchestra struck up a rousing military march and the audience settled down for a long wait. There was hardly any conversation as they looked anxiously for his reappearance.

As the minutes slipped by the man from the *Mirror* paced backward and forward, occasionally glancing at his watch. His eyes hardly left the entrance to the small black cabinet. He waited for his scoop, "Houdini defeated".

Suddenly there were cries of "He is free!", as Houdini's head appeared from the top of the cabinet. But the hopeful cries died when it was realized that the handcuffs were securely in place. Houdini merely wanted to examine them more closely in the powerful stage lighting. The orchestra drifted into a dreamy waltz number as he disappeared back into the cabinet. The time was 3.37.

Right: Houdini presenting the Chinese Water Torture Cell escape, which he first featured regularly in 1912. With his ankles locked in stocks that formed the lid of the tank, he was lowered head-first into the water and the lid padlocked in position. A curtained cabinet then enclosed the cell. Houdini escaped in two minutes.

Inset right: Miss Undina presented a copy of Houdini's Water Torture Cell under the sponsorship of two German impresarios, but she had to stop performing it when Houdini took successful legal action against them.

Below: The famous Russian dancer, Kosloff, putting the finishing touches to the Russian Transport Tie. Houdini waits patiently, before trying to escape.

MISS UNDINA
in ihren neuen sensationellen ·
· Entfesselungs-Act aus der Fussfolter ·
(unter Wasser!)

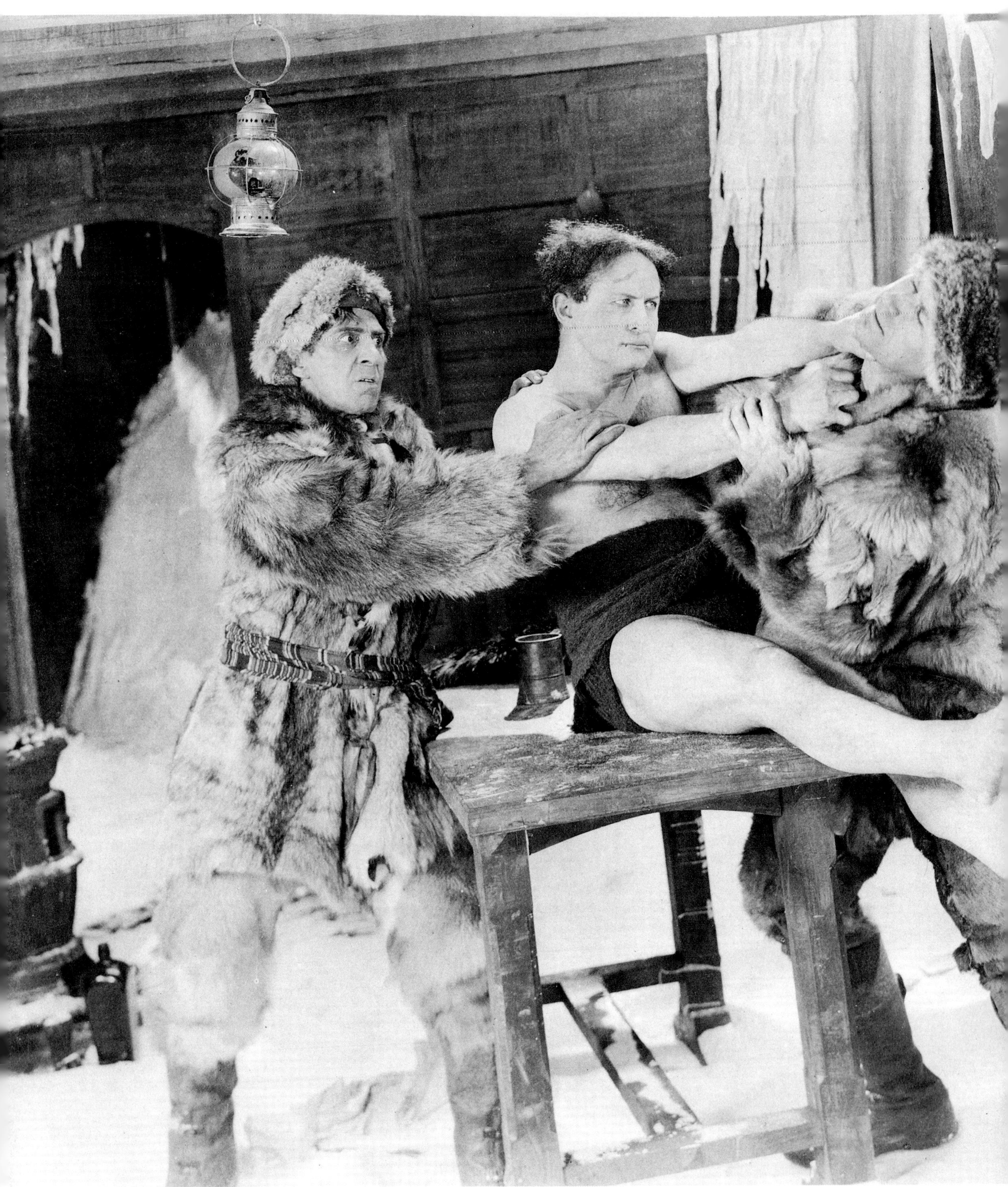

At 3.50 he emerged once more, with perspiration running down his face and his stiff collar wilted and broken. He explained that his knees were hurting but added, "I'm not finished yet". While the crowd cheered the journalist had a word with Mr Parker, the theater manager, who ordered a pillow which the reporter placed in front of the cabinet, and which was gratefully accepted by Houdini.

Twenty minutes later, he reappeared but again the premature cheers were stifled when he was seen to be still manacled. Houdini approached his challenger to ask if the handcuffs could be removed, in order to allow him to take off his coat. The request was denied because it was rightly thought that there was an ulterior motive in asking for the removal of the cuffs. Houdini had seen the cuffs being fastened, but if he could see them being unlocked he might be provided with a clue that would help him to escape.

Accepting the refusal without argument, Houdini maneuvered his manacled wrists until his fingers were able to reach into his waistcoat pocket, from which he took a pocket knife. Opening the blade with his teeth, he brought the coat over his head and dramatically slashed it into pieces, which he threw aside, before returning to his cabinet.

The man from the *Mirror* suffered some verbal abuse for not acceding to Houdini's apparently innocent request but once the storm of disapproval had passed he continued his pacing, occasionally checking the time by his pocket watch.

Ten more anxious minutes had gone by when, taking everyone by surprise, Houdini leapt from the cabinet holding the handcuffs which, their owner had proudly claimed, "no mortal man can pick". It had taken him just over one hour.

A roar went up from the audience and the observers rushed forward to congratulate him. Some of them hoisted Houdini on to their shoulders and carried him around the auditorium, amid shouts, cheers and stamping of feet.

The journalist sportingly shook hands, offered his congratulations and told the audience that his newspaper would shortly be pleased to present Houdini with a silver replica of the Birmingham Handcuffs, as a souvenir of the memorable occasion. This brought more cheers and applause. Harry, ever the showman, always ready to take advantage of whatever a situation offered, burst into tears at the "kindness, sympathy and consideration" shown during his long and arduous struggle.

Some critics have attempted to provide solutions to how Houdini escaped from the Birmingham 'cuffs, one of the most popular being that his wife, Bess, seeing that her husband was in difficulties, pleaded with his challenger to let her have the key to the handcuffs which she dropped into a glass of water and carried to Houdini. Houdini is said to have drunk the water and retained the key in his mouth, removed the cuffs and waited for the appropriate moment to show himself, free from the restraint. It is not a bad theory, but why would a journalist who had a scoop on his hands have given the key to Bess? More importantly, according to a newspaper report describing the challenge, Bess was not in the theater at the time, having left earlier in the afternoon through illness.

Anyone who is acquainted with Houdini's methods and his ways of dealing with difficult restraints knows that he would have devised an infallible way of escaping, long before the challenge took place. This, however, was one secret that he kept to himself.

Houdini Tricked

The Hippodrome Handcuff Challenge was reported in many daily newspapers, describing the grim struggle that had taken place in the confines of the small cabinet. Harry was jubilant at the resulting publicity. He was not so pleased with one report that appeared about a past failure in opening a pair of handcuffs provided by a police officer.

Left: Houdini the film star, featured in *The Man from Beyond*, which had its premiere at the Times Square Theater, New York, in April 1922. He is flanked by Erwin Connolly and Frank Montgomery. This was the first film produced by the short-lived Houdini Picture Corporation and told the improbable story of Houdini being hewn out of a block of ice in which he had been incarcerated for a hundred years.

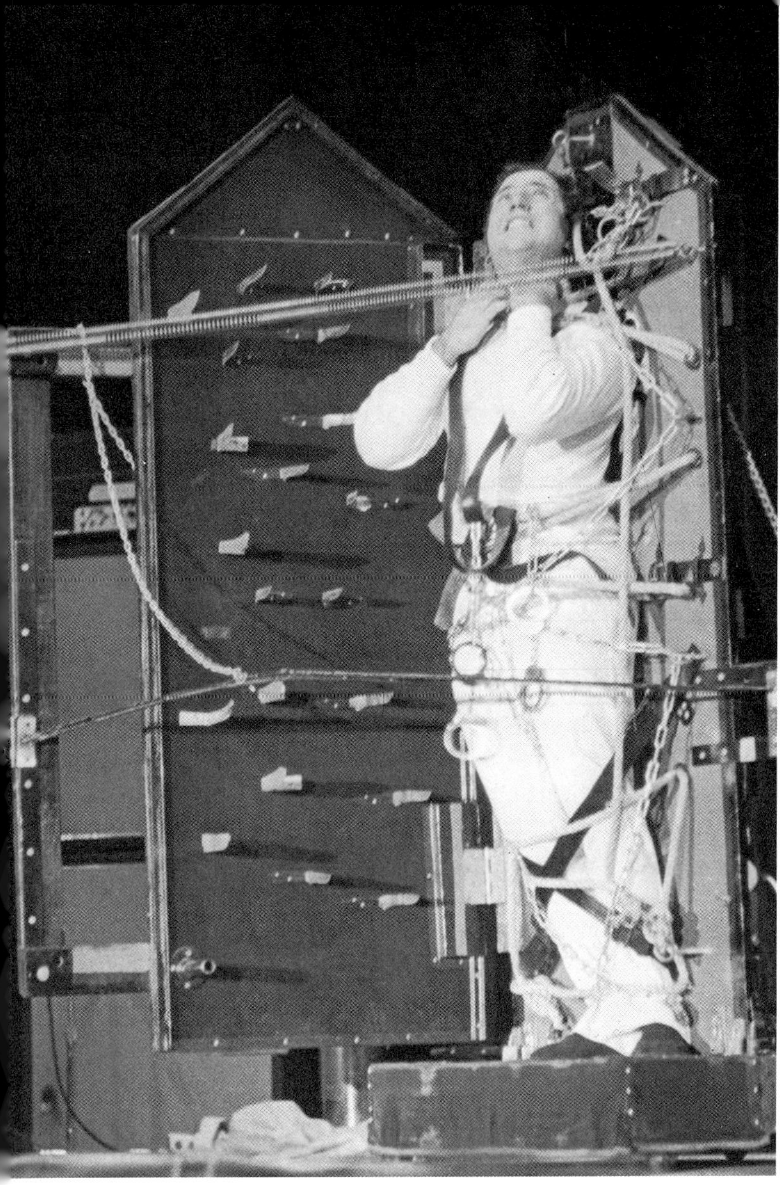

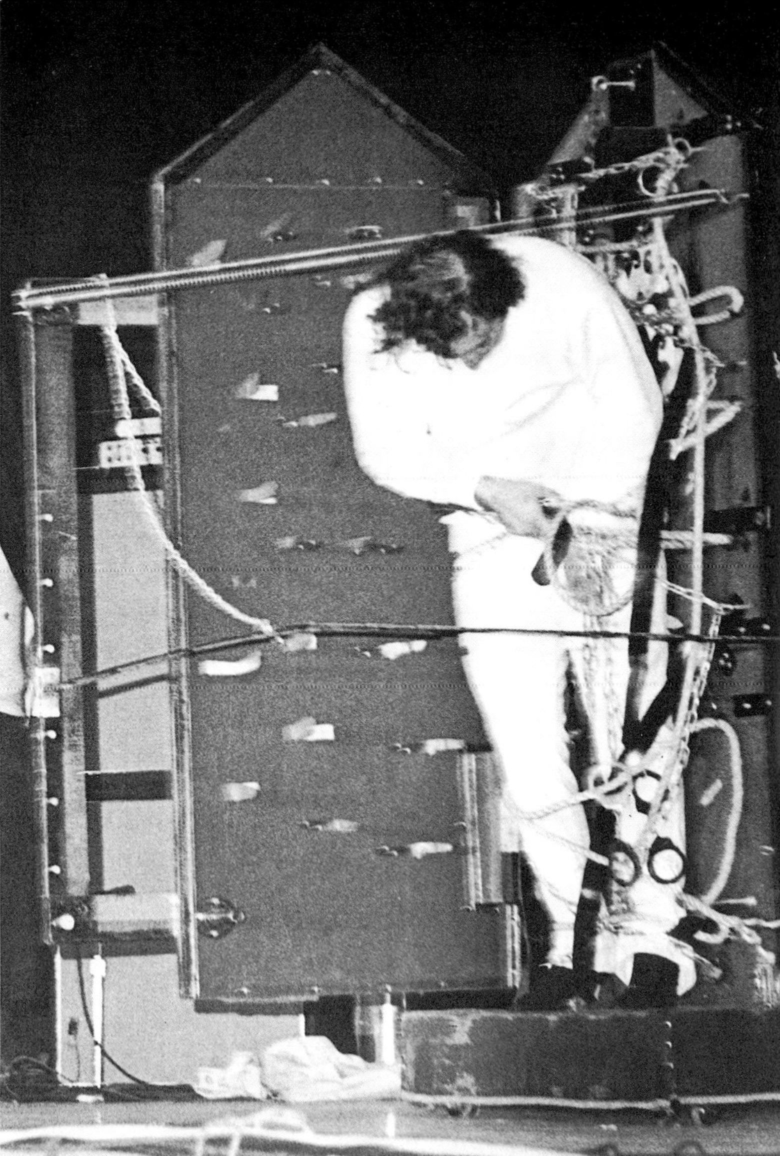

Above left and right: Norman Bigelow, who calls himself "Houdini Reincarnated", spends much of his time touring America's college campuses with his spectacular show. The "Death Chamber" seen here is a box-like contraption that snaps shut in precisely three minutes. The door of the box carries eight-inch razor-sharp knives pointing inward – the performer has to free himself from the chains, ropes and handcuffs within the tight time limit or be impaled.

It happened early in his career and, although the public have short memories, Houdini had not. He remembered for a long time the unfairness of the challenge. A report in the *Chicago Journal* described how he had managed to release himself from manacles provided by the local police force. The following week, Sergeant Waldron of the Evanston Police visited Kohl and Middleton's Museum, where the escape artist was appearing. From his pocket he took a pair of handcuffs, which he locked around the young man's wrists and challenged Houdini to escape.

A few seconds later, one of the 'cuffs swung open. The other proved more difficult and Houdini eventually had to admit defeat. He was furious when he learned that the police officer had dropped pellets of lead shot into the mechanism, causing the cuff to jam. Although he felt humiliated, Houdini learned from this experience and, in future, whenever a challenger brought a pair of handcuffs or a similar restraint, he checked it carefully to make sure it was in working order.

Despite his long association with the escape business and his recognition as the world's leading escape artist, Houdini very rarely referred to himself as an "escapologist" and this title never appeared on his theater bills. The word "escapology" to describe the "art of escaping" was made popular by an Australian magician, Murray Carrington Walters, who featured his magic and escape show in many countries around the world and became known as Murray the Escapologist.

He carried out many escape stunts for publicity purposes and provided many good stories for the newspapers. In the 1930s, the straitjacket escape had become one of the standard items in any escape artist's repertoire. The Australian escapologist decided to go one better and approached Bertram Mills, the proprietor of a famous circus, to suggest a stunt that would provide a great deal of publicity for the circus and for himself.

Lions and Race Tracks

The Bertram Mills Circus was playing a Christmas season at Olympia, London, a place of entertainment where spectacular, large-scale displays and military tournaments are held. At the close of one of the evening performances, an invited audience of film, radio and newspaper reporters watched as Murray was securely strapped into a straitjacket and taken across the sawdust ring, where stood a large animal cage in which seven African lions moved restlessly, occasionally snarling.

The escapologist was bundled into the cage and the door slammed behind him. To free himself, he had to pull the jacket over his head, a very dangerous move because for a few seconds he could not see the beasts, or what movements they were making. Now free, and being very careful not to draw attention to himself or make any quick movements until the very last moment, he suddenly leapt for the door of the cage, which was slammed behind him as a lion sprang to attack.

Murray received worldwide publicity for this daring feat and was booked by Bertram Mills to repeat the stunt, three times daily, for the remainder of the season.

Just over fifty years later, this escape was re-enacted by a young English escapologist, Karl Bartoni, at the Hippodrome Circus, Great Yarmouth, England. Watched curiously by five 550lb lions, he released himself from a straitjacket and leg irons in four and a half minutes.

Below: Escapologist Karl Bartoni defying death with his 1985 version of Murray's 1933 straitjacket escape from a lions' cage.

Castrol GTX - Liquid Eng
CHAMPION
BP BP BP
FRAGILE
B690 CEV

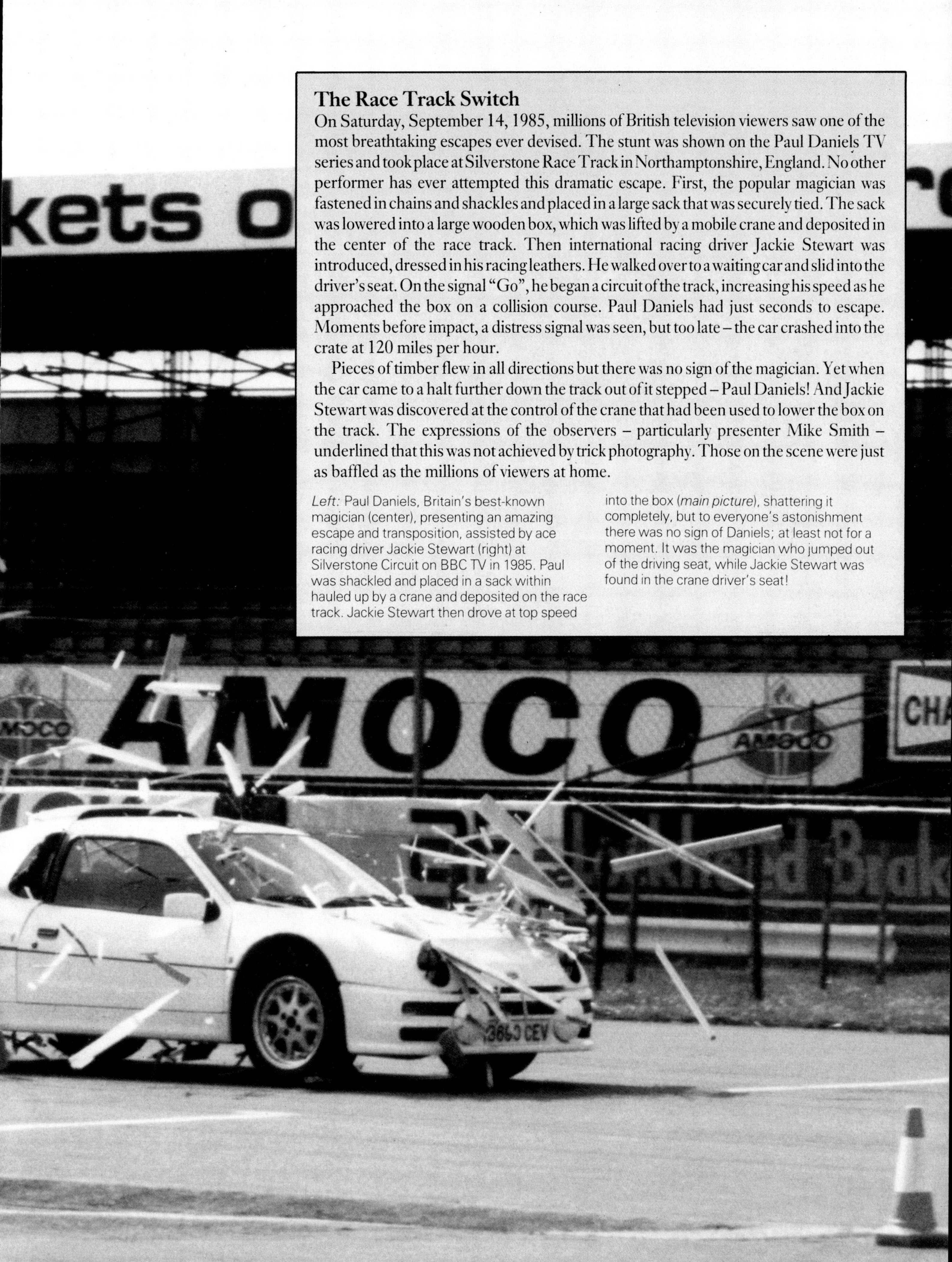

The Race Track Switch

On Saturday, September 14, 1985, millions of British television viewers saw one of the most breathtaking escapes ever devised. The stunt was shown on the Paul Daniels TV series and took place at Silverstone Race Track in Northamptonshire, England. No other performer has ever attempted this dramatic escape. First, the popular magician was fastened in chains and shackles and placed in a large sack that was securely tied. The sack was lowered into a large wooden box, which was lifted by a mobile crane and deposited in the center of the race track. Then international racing driver Jackie Stewart was introduced, dressed in his racing leathers. He walked over to a waiting car and slid into the driver's seat. On the signal "Go", he began a circuit of the track, increasing his speed as he approached the box on a collision course. Paul Daniels had just seconds to escape. Moments before impact, a distress signal was seen, but too late – the car crashed into the crate at 120 miles per hour.

Pieces of timber flew in all directions but there was no sign of the magician. Yet when the car came to a halt further down the track out of it stepped – Paul Daniels! And Jackie Stewart was discovered at the control of the crane that had been used to lower the box on the track. The expressions of the observers – particularly presenter Mike Smith – underlined that this was not achieved by trick photography. Those on the scene were just as baffled as the millions of viewers at home.

Left: Paul Daniels, Britain's best-known magician (center), presenting an amazing escape and transposition, assisted by ace racing driver Jackie Stewart (right) at Silverstone Circuit on BBC TV in 1985. Paul was shackled and placed in a sack within hauled up by a crane and deposited on the race track. Jackie Stewart then drove at top speed into the box (*main picture*), shattering it completely, but to everyone's astonishment there was no sign of Daniels; at least not for a moment. It was the magician who jumped out of the driving seat, while Jackie Stewart was found in the crane driver's seat!

Two examples of the range of problems with which escapologists must contend.

Left: David De-Val (David Frederick Littler), the expert locksmith and escapologist who has hit the headlines with prison escapes, including one from highwayman Dick Turpin's condemned cell in York Castle, Yorkshire.

Below: James Randi (James Randall Zwinge), a Canadian magician and escapologist in the best Houdini tradition, is heavily manacled before trying to make his escape.

SOME DOS AND DON'TS OF ESCAPOLOGY

It is clear from the stunts described in this chapter that an escapologist faces some danger, despite the cynical view that "It's only a trick". To be successful, the performer must keep danger at a minimum or, if possible, eliminate it altogether.

- Every item used must be checked and re-checked, particularly if it is a restraint provided by a challenger.
- The apparatus owned by the escape artist must be kept in good working order, as accidents can occur if equipment has been neglected.
- Nothing must be left to chance. An escapologist must know his craft thoroughly, for the confidence which this gives enables him to act swiftly and correctly when difficulties arise.
- Challengers and audience observers must be watched to ensure that they cannot sabotage the equipment after it has been examined and found to be in working order. This is one of the functions of the escapologist's assistants. Arrangements must be made to have one or more persons standing by to protect the escape artist, because once he is locked up, or tied, he is at the mercy of all comers.
- Finally, he must learn to stay calm when the unforeseen occurs, since panic will not resolve an emergency, but only make it worse.

Despite the dangers and discomforts which are occupational hazards in the escape business, new generations of performers continue to appear on the showbusiness scene, with new and more daring stunts, each trying to outdo the rest.

So long as the public wants thrills and excitement, there will be artists who are willing to satisfy their needs like Alan Alan and Shahid Malik who escape from a straitjacket while dangling in mid-air from a blazing rope, or Nick Janson, who, having freed himself from shackles, escapes from his "flying bomb", before it explodes. Howard Peters appears in outdoor galas, and David de Val is still receiving newspaper reviews for his jailbreaks. The most prominent American escapologist is James Randi, famous for his Niagara stunt.

Danger holds a fascination for the man-in-the-street, and these professionals are happy to supply it, since danger is their business.

Left, top to bottom: Magician and escapologist Shahid Malik presents a sensational escape from a packing case suspended from the 100-foot jib of a crane. He is securely chained and imprisoned in the crate which then is hoisted into the air; after a short while the crate crashes to the ground, leaving Shahid, who has made his escape, suspended by his ankle from the crane.

Above: The Indian magician, Sorcar, presenting the "Asrah" illusion, in which he makes his assistant, draped in a sheet, float in mid-air. When he snatches away the sheet, she has vanished!

3

DISAPPEARING ACTS

Above: Horace Goldin (Hyman Goldstein, 1874-1939) presented *The Tiger God*, subtitled *A Moorish Mystery*, a magical play in three scenes, produced in 1911. It undoubtedly originated from Lafayette's magical playlet, *The Lion's Bride*.

There are many tricks and illusions in which objects, animals and human beings mysteriously disappear, only to reappear some moments later. For example, audiences are amazed when water is poured into a glass tumbler which is then covered with a silk handkerchief and suddenly disappears, or watch incredulously as a large bowl of water, standing on a thin tray, seems to vanish into thin air. They are fascinated when a white rabbit, the magician's symbol, is placed in a box on a table which is covered with a large cloth. After a clap of his hands the magician dismantles the box, which is empty. The audience think they have outsmarted the conjuror, believing the rabbit to be hidden within the table. With a smile, the magician removes the cloth, revealing a skeleton frame incapable of concealing anything.

Two masters in this field of magic are Doug Henning and David Copperfield, who demonstrate what dramatic effects can be achieved with the application of ingenuity to the basic principles used for the simplest trick. Making large objects vanish is invariably more impressive than vanishing smaller items. When making a person disappear, the magician is confronted with a number of difficulties, due to the size and weight and the problem of compressing the human frame into a small space. Despite these handicaps, magicians have created some startling mysteries.

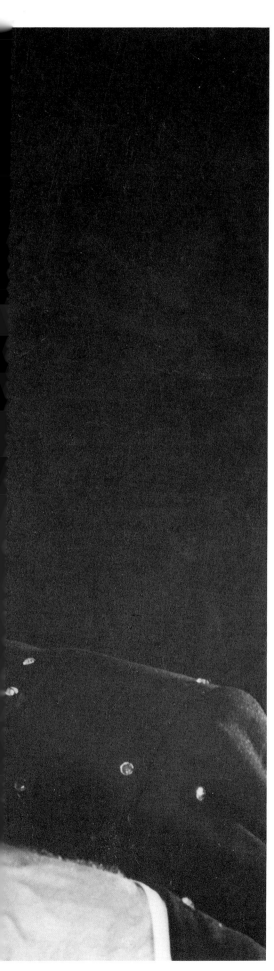

The Black Bag Mystery

This mystery is a favorite of some performers because it does not require large cabinets or boxes.

A young lady steps into a large black bag, which is tied at the neck with thick cord. Two members of the audience make sure that the bag is securely fastened. Next, two long ropes are tied to the top of the bag and a rope is handed to each of the assisting spectators. A large screen is placed in front of the bag and the volunteers are asked to pass the two ropes over the top of the screen but to retain their hold of them.

The magician informs his helpers that on the count of three they are to pull on the ropes. He counts "One – two – three" and, when the two men pull on the ropes, the empty bag flies over the top of the screen, which is removed to show that the young lady has mysteriously disappeared.

As the two men inspect the bag and make sure that the knots are still securely tied, a pistol shot is heard at the back of the theater. The young lady runs down the aisle and onto the stage where she takes her bow.

This mystery is popular with magicians because it uses a minimum of apparatus, can be presented quickly, is simple to carry out, and gets a good response from the audience. The only items required are two identical black bags, large enough to contain the girl. One of the bags is folded and placed inside the other.

To present the illusion, the magician introduces his assistant, who comes forward holding the bag. Two gentlemen from the audience are invited to assist. The girl steps into the bag, which is drawn up over her, and the magician holds together the top of the bag, before the spectators tie the cord. Inside the bag, the girl takes the concealed bag and, unfolding it, pushes the top of it through the neck of the sack which is being held by the magician. Taking a piece of cord, he winds it around the neck of the sack, then allows the two men to complete the tying. The performer makes sure that the couple of loops he has made trap the outer bag, to hold it in place. He then covers the top of the outer bag with his hand. The spectators tie above his hand, so that only the inner bag is secured.

When the tying is completed, two long ropes are handed to the assistants and attached to the top of the bag. The ropes are passed over the top of the screen and tightly held by the two men.

Behind the screen, the girl separates the two bags by releasing the outer bag from the cord and, taking that bag with her, she moves silently through a break in the back curtain and makes her way to the back of the theater. As she lets go of the inner bag, the tension on the ropes slackens and the bag flies forward.

At the appropriate time, she makes her appearance from the back, firing a pistol or shouting "I am here!" and running down the aisle to the stage where she receives her applause.

Even a supposedly simple disappearing trick can sometimes be a problem as, according to an old theatrical legend, a magician's assistant discovered to her embarrassment in the course of this trick. She had been able to make her "disappearance" without any trouble but when she arrived at the back of the auditorium and ran down the center aisle, shouting "I am here!", she realized that she had taken a wrong turning and was in an adjoining theater, where the audience was absorbed in a serious drama.

The Vanishing Rabbit

A rabbit and a top hat have been the symbol of the magical profession for many years and

Faust (Granville Taylor) putting his audience under the "fluence". Faust, who has presented spectacular illusion shows in Japan, acquired many of the illusions of the late Cecil Lyle, for whom he once worked as an assistant.

audiences of earlier generations, perhaps more than audiences of today, expected a mystery featuring a rabbit to be included in a magician's program.

Many performers responded to the public's demand and used a rabbit in their acts, usually sticking to tradition and producing a rabbit from a top hat. A new slant is to make the rabbit disappear instead.

The magician walks on stage, reading a newspaper, and his assistant enters from the opposite side, carrying a white rabbit on a tray. She draws the magician's attention to the fact that he is there to perform magic, not to read a newspaper.

Suitably admonished, he walks over to his table and covers it with the newspaper. Taking the rabbit from his assistant, he places it within the pages of the newspaper and makes up a parcel.

Walking to the front of the stage, handling the parcel carefully, he suddenly brings his hands together and squashes the newspaper, which he tears into pieces, allowing them to fall to the floor. The audience is astounded. The rabbit has vanished.

The secret of the vanishing rabbit is audacious but effective. The table has a six-inch gold-fringed drape, which conceals a hidden trap in the top of the table. The newspaper, although apparently carelessly handled, is cleverly faked. A piece, a little larger than the area of the trapdoor in the table, is cut out of the last three pages.

The magician enters at the left side of the stage, reading the newspaper with the front page facing the audience. The cut pages are concealed. The magician opens the newspaper, being careful to ensure that the faked pages are not seen.

His assistant enters with the rabbit and the performer lays the newspaper on the table, the cut-out in the pages fitting perfectly over the trap. Without moving the newspaper, he opens the front few pages and, while apparently placing the rabbit on the paper, actually lowers it into the trap.

Below: "The Flying Visit" was a transposition illusion invented by Belgian illusionist Servais Le Roy (1865-1953) who, together with his wife Talma and comedy magician Leon Bosco, comprised the Comedians de Mephisto company. Talma and the performer exchange positions in a bewildering manner.

Above: The Great Lafayette (Sigmund Neuberger, 1871-1911), showman extraordinary, as he appeared in his magical one-act drama "Dr Kremser – Vivisectionist". Tragically, Lafayette died in a fire that broke out on stage at the Empire Palace Theatre, Edinburgh on May 9, 1911; nine other members of his company also lost their lives in the fire.

Carefully folding the newspaper, as though it contained the rabbit, he carries it to the front of the stage, then crushes the newspaper and tears it into pieces, showing that the rabbit has vanished and at the same time destroying the evidence of the cut-out pages. While he was bringing the mystery to a successful conclusion, the assistant carried the table off-stage.

Again, even this apparently straightforward trick can cause problems for the unwary or just unlucky performer. One magician forgot to tell his assistant to remove the table and, as he tore the newspaper into pieces and declared that the rabbit had completely disappeared was met with roars of laughter instead of the usual gasps of amazement from the audience. Puzzled, he turned around to see the head of the rabbit showing above the top of the table, peering curiously at the audience.

A ROYAL MYSTERY

One of the most remarkable disappearance mysteries was performed by the French magician, Jean Eugène Robert-Houdin (1805-1871), at a Royal Command Performance for King Louis Philippe of France in 1846. Robert-Houdin was highly regarded as a magician, had opened his own theater of magic at the Palais Royal in Paris, and received his greatest accolade by being invited to present his program of mysteries at the French court. He was determined to present mysteries that his royal patrons would always remember. One trick which he had created especially for the occasion proved to be the highlight of his program.

He collected a number of handkerchiefs from members of his audience, which he folded neatly into a small "parcel". Taking an opaque, bell-shaped dome, made of glass, he showed it to be empty and placed it over the handkerchiefs. The magician then approached the king and showed him some cards, bearing the names of various locations. The card selected by Louis Philippe read, "The chest beneath the last tree on the right, in the orange grove".

Before the magician could continue, the king dispatched some servants to the orange grove to make certain that no-one approached the tree until the mystery was concluded.

The magician then lifted the glass dome to show that the handkerchiefs had vanished and requested that a servant should be sent to dig up a chest he would find under the selected tree in the orange grove. Minutes later, to the astonishment of the court, the servant returned carrying a small wooden chest, which he placed before the king.

Taking a key, proffered to him by Robert-Houdin, Louis Philippe unlocked the chest and discovered a letter, allegedly written by the famous Italian magician, Count Cagliostro. With it were the borrowed handkerchiefs which, amid an excited buzz of conversation, were returned to their owners.

Robert-Houdin had made careful preparations for this mystery well in advance of its presentation. He decided which location to use and made sure that the chest was in place, ready to receive the handkerchiefs.

Before the handkerchiefs were placed under the glass dome, a secret exchange was made for a similar "parcel". One of Robert-Houdin's assistants took the original handkerchiefs to the orange grove, put them in the chest with the letter and, locking it, put it in the hole, already dug. Covering it over with soil, he then made himself scarce.

The king, in taking the card with the orange grove location, thought that it was his own selection but it was not. The magician had decided which card would be taken and had "forced" it on Louis Philippe. A description of how to "force" a card is given in Chapter Six.

The Bewildering Ball

A child's colored play ball about 4 inches in diameter is placed in a wooden box that stands on a table. A magic pass is made, or the chosen word said, and when the box is opened it proves to be empty. Inviting a boy and girl to assist him, the magician closes the lid. The children say the magic word and the ball reappears in the box. The children are thanked for their help and return to their seats.

The disappearance depends upon the wooden box, the bottom of which is fixed to hinges, positioned at the lower inside front of the box. A piece of wood of the same size and shape is fastened to the bottom of the box, at a right angle.

When the box is tipped forward, this "L"-piece remains stationary, with the bottom piece lying flat on the table. When the box is stood upright, the vertical piece of the "L" is parallel with the front of the box.

To present the mystery, the box is shown to be empty and the ball bounced a few times before placing it in the box (**1**). Tipping the box forward (**2**), the magician opens the lid and the box appears to be empty (**3**). The audience thinks that it can see the bottom of the box, but it is looking at the upright of the "L" that has "replaced" the bottom and hides the ball.

The lid is closed and the box turned to its original position (**4**). The children are invited to assist, the lid is opened and the ball can be seen (**5**).

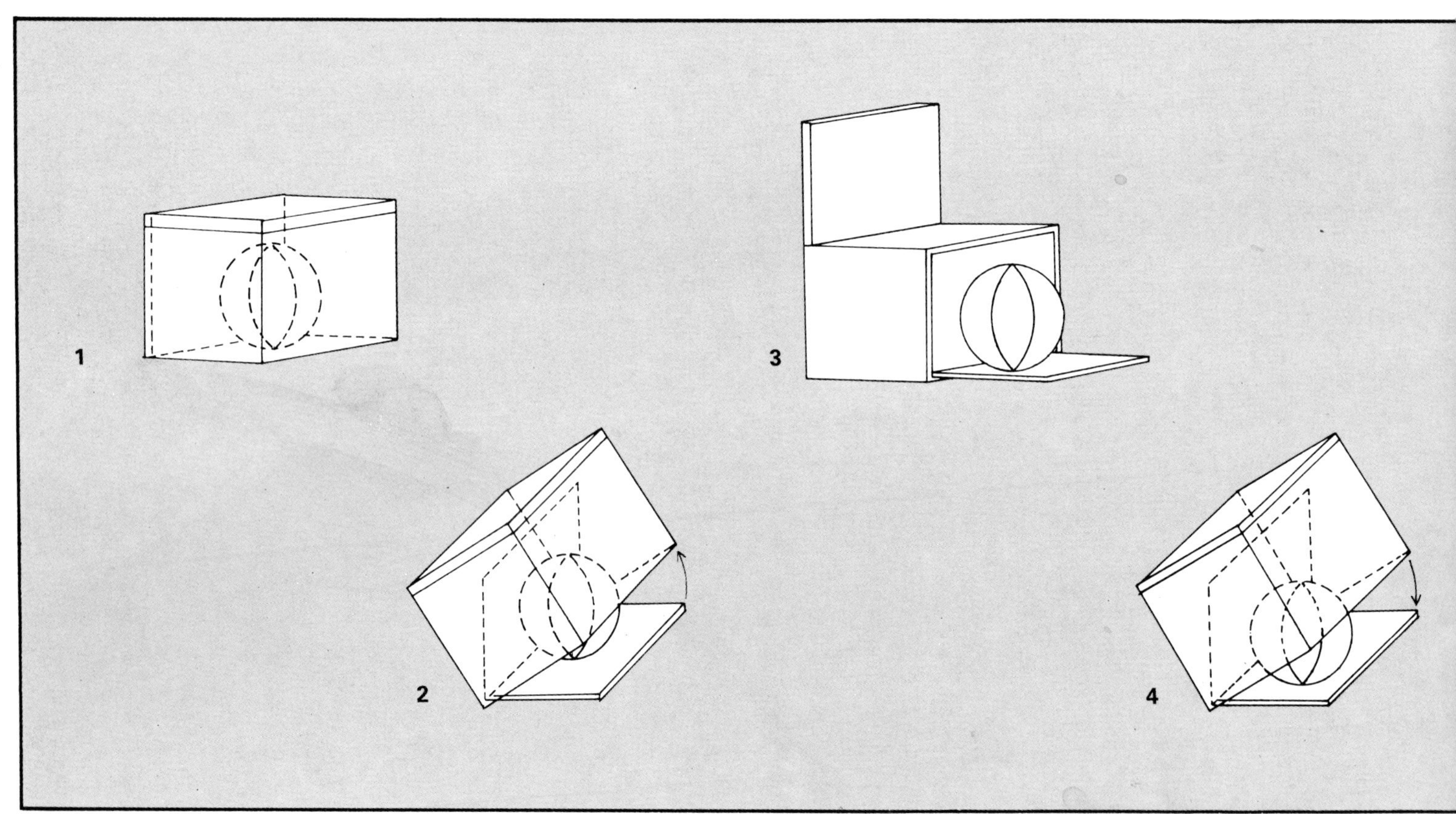

This box can be used in many ways; for instance, after being shown to be empty, a large production of various items could be made. Care must be taken regarding the viewing angles, otherwise the ball or other items may be seen behind the box.

The Baffling Banknote

There are various pieces of conjuring apparatus available from magic dealers in which an item can be made to vanish but special equipment is not always necessary. To make a small article – such as a ring, a coin or a banknote – disappear, the simplest method is one using an ordinary pocket handkerchief. For the purpose of describing this trick, it will be assumed that a banknote is being used.

The borrowed note is placed under a draped handkerchief and held by a member of the audience, who, feeling the note through the material, assures everyone that it is still there. Taking one corner of the handkerchief, the magician suddenly pulls it away, leaving the assistant empty-handed. The handkerchief is shown back and front and is seen to be empty.

A piece of paper the size of the banknote is folded until it is small enough to be concealed in the hem of the handkerchief, near one of the corners. To make the banknote disappear, the handkerchief is held at its center between the left thumb and forefinger. The handkerchief hangs down.

The banknote, which has been folded to the same size as the paper in the hem, is placed under the handkerchief, with the right hand. As the hand moves upwards under the handkerchief, the folded paper in the hem is pushed up under the center of the handkerchief, where it is held through the material. The real banknote is concealed in the right fingers and disposed of when it is convenient.

The spectator is asked to hold the "banknote" through the handkerchief but is in fact holding the paper. Taking the handkerchief by one corner, the magician pulls sharply and the note seemingly disappears. The handkerchief is shown back and front, to convince the spectators that the money is not concealed there. While this is being done, the performer's fingers cover the paper in the hem.

The Bewildering Ball
1 The ball is placed in the box.
2 Although the box is tipped forward, the "L" piece stays in position.
3 What the audience takes to be the bottom of the empty box is, in fact, the face of the "L". The ball is hidden from view, on the far side of the box.
4 The box is closed and tipped back to the starting position.
5 Members of the audience open the box to find the "missing" ball.

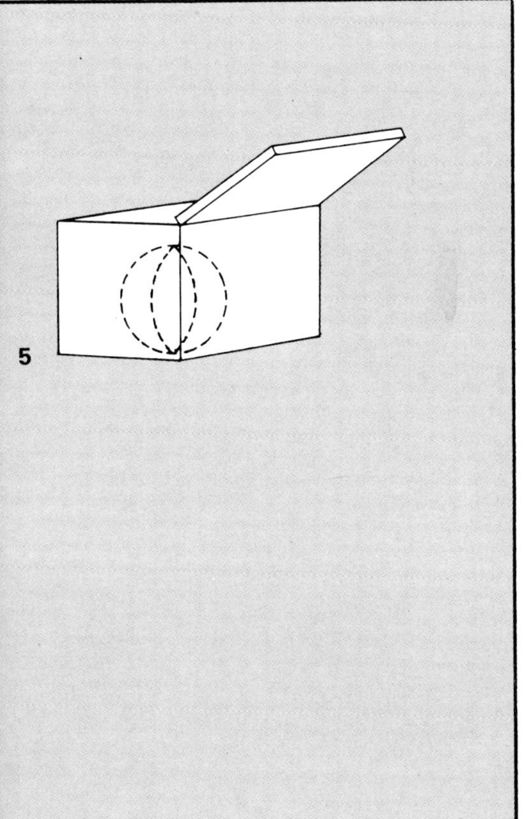

THE DISAPPEARING ELEPHANT

"Make it big" was the motto of The Great Lafayette, whose spectacular show drew thousands of people to the theaters where he appeared. It was his friend, Harry Houdini, however, who presented the most spectacular disappearance of his time at the New York Hippodrome, in 1918. Before a packed theater, he made a full grown elephant vanish. To say that the audience was dumbfounded is putting it mildly. How could an elephant vanish on a brightly lit stage? Because of its immense size and weight, trapdoors were out of the question and, in any case, beneath the stage was a large pool used for aquatic shows.

The keeper brought the huge beast onstage and walked it around, confirming that it was the real thing. A large flimsy cabinet was then placed in position on the stage. The end doors faced the audience and, when opened, revealed the empty interior. The elephant entered the cabinet and the doors were shut. When the doors were opened a few moments later, the cabinet was empty.

The sensational disappearance baffled not only members of the public but also members of the magical fraternity, who knew how to make a dove or a rabbit disappear – even a donkey – but who, when questioned by their fellow magicians, admitted that they did not know how the elephant vanished. There were many guesses but some of them were made by people who had not witnessed the disappearance, so their solutions did not always fit the facts.

A popular suggestion was that the long cabinet had, at the far end, a second set of doors to which springs were fitted. The elephant passed through the main part of the cabinet and into a small enclosure, the spring doors immediately closing once the animal had passed through.

Some cynics suggested that four men brought the cabinet on but eight men were required to push it off!

Journalists found plenty to write about and, as a result of the tremendous publicity, Houdini was booked by the Hippodrome management for a further six weeks, on condition that he presented the Vanishing Elephant at each performance. The act became so successful that it played at the New York Theater for almost five months.

When questioned about how the elephant disappeared, Houdini's stock answer was, "Even the elephant doesn't know".

The Indian Basket

The magic and mysteries of India have long been a vital ingredient of travelers' tales. There are many stories of the marvelous feats of the fakirs who seemed to be immune from fire, could thrust daggers through their flesh without injury, or cause a fruit-bearing tree to grow within seconds of planting a tiny seed in the ground. One of the most sensational of these mysteries is the Indian Basket Trick.

Grasping the wrist of a loudly protesting girl, the Indian magician drags her to a large, oblong basket and, brandishing a dangerous-looking sword, forces her to lie in the basket. The lid is fastened and, waving the sword, the magician thrusts the blade into the basket from every angle. At each sword-thrust, the girl screams, until there is a sudden, ominous silence.

Withdrawing the bloodstained weapon, the magician casts it aside, then tips over the basket so that the lid faces the audience. Throwing back the lid, he reveals that the basket is empty and the girl has vanished.

The basket is based on the same principle as the box used to vanish the ball, described earlier in this chapter. The girl climbs into the basket and lies towards the far side, while the magician thrusts the sword through the sides of the basket. Knowing where she is lying, the magician thrusts upwards, avoiding her. The bloodstains are applied to the sword either by the girl or by the magician, who releases a quantity of crimson fluid which has been concealed in the hilt of the sword. When the magician tips the basket, the fake bottom of the box hides the girl from the audience's view.

Although the principle of the tip-over box has been used in many different ways, there is no doubt that the most sensational presentation is that used in the Indian Basket Mystery.

The Trick That Never Was

The mystery usually associated with India is the Rope Trick, a mysterious happening that never took place. Lots of people who have been to India claim that they have seen it but, when closely questioned, admit that they have not seen it themselves yet know someone who has.

Some magicians have traveled to India for the express purpose of discovering the secret and have offered large sums of money to see a presentation of the Rope Trick, but no-one has come forward to claim the money. A well-known circus proprietor and The Magic Circle, London, have challenged anyone to present the trick in the open air, away from trees or buildings, and have set aside financial rewards to be handed over to the successful person.

The money is safe. The Indian Rope Trick is a legend, built on fantasy. There are many variations of the legend but the most straightforward, and the one attempted by the stage illusionists, is where a coil of rope lies on the ground or in a basket. One end of the rope slowly rises to a great height and remains suspended. A small Indian boy climbs the rope and, when he reaches a certain height, the music which has been playing throughout the proceedings stops. The magician claps his hands, the rope falls to the ground and the boy vanishes in mid-air.

A number of famous illusionists have included a version of the Rope Trick in their programs, including the American magician Carl Hertz, who was better known for his vanishing of a canary in a cage; Horace Goldin, the Polish-born inventor of many fine illusions; Howard Thurston, who succeeded Harry Kellar as America's premier magician, and the German magician, Kalanag.

It should be said, however, that few of the stage presentations of this famous mystery were convincing. The main reason for including them in the program was for publicity. The legend always provided good copy for the newspapers, thereby attracting customers to the theater where the trick was being shown.

Howard Thurston (1869-1936) included a version of the Rope Trick in his "Wonder

Left: The Indian Rope Trick, as performed by Karachi and his son Kyder, outdoors in England in 1934.

Show of the Universe" but when it had served its purpose – attracting attention to the show – it was withdrawn. The method used by Thurston was both costly and, at times, unreliable. It required considerable rehearsal, well-drilled assistants and split-second timing. If the timing was out, the mystery was ruined.

The Rope Trick was presented before an Indian-style backdrop, in the center of which there was a tall archway. From a basket standing in the archway, a rope slowly ascended and stopped just below the top of the arch. A boy, dressed in an Indian costume, climbed the rope and remained motionless at the top.

Smoke from an eastern-style brazier began to rise upward, enveloping the boy. When the smoke thinned, the audience could still see the boy on the rope. The music suddenly stopped and Thurston waved his hands in the direction of the rope. To the astonishment of the audience, the boy vanished in mid-air.

The rope was drawn upwards by two thin steel wires that were invisible against the dark background. The boy climbed the rope and waited for the smoke that was to be used as a screen. The "smoke" from the brazier was actually steam and, as it billowed upward to cover the boy, he was drawn up and out of the view of the audience.

Meanwhile, a transparent screen had been lowered in the archway and, from a projector worked behind the screen, a life-size picture of the boy was thrown onto it. As the "smoke" thinned, it appeared that the boy was still on the rope. At a signal from the magician, the music stopped and, when he waved his hands, the projector was switched off so that it appeared that the boy had vanished into thin air.

When everything synchronized, the effect was startling, but there were times when it was not so effective. The weakness of the illusion lay in the timing of the projector. If it was switched off too soon, while the "smoke" still enveloped the boy, the audience assumed that he had been pulled up into the flies, which was true. If the picture was held too long, the audience realized that it was not a real person on the rope.

When the Indian Rope Mystery had served its purpose in obtaining publicity, it was put into store with all the other illusions that would not be used again.

The Flying Birdcage

A magician who gained a great reputation, as both a performer and inventor, was the French-born Buatier de Kolta (1847-1903), who toured Europe and the USA showing some of his most original mysteries, which were appreciated by the public and copied by many magicians.

He was invited by John Nevil Maskelyne to appear at London's Egyptian Hall,

Right: Charles Bertram (James Bassett, 1853-1907) seen here in an 1886 cartoon, showing Buatier de Kolta's Vanishing Lady illusion. Mademoiselle Patrice, the lady who vanished, looks round the curtain while John Nevil Maskelyne peeps over the screen, wondering "how it's done".

Left: The highly inventive French magician Buatier de Kolta (Joseph Buatier, 1847-1903), who created some marvellous illusions, including the Expanding Die. A small die, placed on the table, instantaneously expanded to a large-sized die from out of which stepped a female assistant.

Above: A 1905 cartoon of American magician Carl Hertz, presenting his Clock Dial trick in which the clock hand stops at any hour called for by the audience.

Far right: The Danish-American illusionist Dante (Harry Jansen, 1883-1955) toured a spectacular magic show that made a tremendous impact when he first came to Britain in 1936. Dante appeared with Laurel and Hardy in the 1942 film *A-Haunting We Will Go.*

"England's Home of Mystery", and met with immediate success. One of his smaller mysteries, yet one of the most baffling, was The Flying Birdcage. He brought on a cage containing two canaries. Without covering the cage, he caused both cage and birds to disappear. Versions of this trick are still being performed today.

One of de Kolta's imitators who featured this mystery was the American Carl Hertz (1859-1924), who captured valuable newspaper publicity when he presented the trick before a Select Committee of the British Parliament, which was discussing the Performing Animals Bill. The reason for Hertz's appearance was to show that no harm came to the birds used in his show.

The Flying Birdcage was a featured item in the Blackstone Show, too. The famous American magician Harry Blackstone vanished the cage, then went off-stage and returned with another cage with which to repeat the trick. He invited some members of the audience to come on stage and watch the mystery close-up. They were asked to place their hands on the top and sides of the cage. Nevertheless, the cage vanished, leaving the helpers empty-handed and as mystified as the rest of the audience.

The Birdcage is currently being presented by Harry Blackstone Junior, who is still mystifying audiences over a hundred years after de Kolta first showed the trick to the theater-goers of Paris. It is a highlight of Harry Junior's show as, surrounded by upward of twenty children, all endeavoring to place a hand on it, the cage nonetheless dissolves into thin air.

A larger version of the vanishing canary, also devised by de Kolta, was an illusion which he called The Captive's Flight. A cage about three feet high was placed on a small wooden platform and a girl dressed in a yellow canary costume entered the cage. The magician covered the cage with a large cloth and counted to three. Removing the cloth with a grand flourish, he revealed an empty cage. The "bird" had flown.

The Vanishing Lady

The illusion with which de Kolta's name will always be associated is The Vanishing Lady, a mystery that is relatively simple to present and baffling to the spectators. The trick is still a popular part of several magicians' programs. Audiences know that traps in stages are used by magicians in their illusions, and de Kolta knew that they knew. To allay any suspicions that he might resort to this method, he spread a newspaper on the stage. He placed a chair on the newspaper and introduced his female assistant, who sat on the chair. Holding up a large silk shawl, he covered the young woman, making sure that no part of her was visible. He lifted the lower part of the shawl to show her feet, then almost instantaneously he whipped away the cloth, revealing the empty chair. His assistant had completely disappeared. A few moments later she reappeared on stage, to tremendous applause.

The act was first staged in 1886, creating a public sensation and arousing the envy of other magicians, who flocked to de Kolta's shows to try to figure out how he managed it. Soon magician's assistants were vanishing with varying degrees of success throughout London and Paris, although none could match the finesse of the original.

An English magician, Charles Bertram, had the distinction of being the first to present The Vanishing Lady in England because the inventor was still busy performing his act in Paris. Bertram's "first" took place on Maskelyne's stage at the Egyptian Hall in London, where the vanishing lady was the magicienne Mademoiselle Patrice. The act so caught the public imagination that a cartoon featuring Bertram, Patrice and Maskelyne appeared in the periodical *Judy*, while the British satirical magazine *Punch* used the illusion to make a political point: Russia vanishing Bulgaria through the Treaty of Berlin, by covering her with the shawl of diplomacy.

For many years after this, The Vanishing Lady was not seen in magicians' programs but then the late Richiardi Junior revived it during the 1940s and it remained a striking feature of his show. More recently, Doug Henning has presented an updated version of the illusion on one of his TV spectaculars.

The mysterious

DANTE

and his own BIG American company

Presenting the Worlds greatest

MYSTERY-SPECTACLE

A Space Age Mystery

This illusion, based on an old idea, was especially created for an audience of young people who were interested in space exploration.

A solid, square base was laid in the center of the stage and an astronaut, dressed in a space suit, was introduced to the audience. He took up his position on the wooden base. Technicians dressed in white overalls came on stage, carrying some large cylinders which were placed over the astronaut. A nose-cone was put in place and the "rocket" was complete, except for a few minor adjustments which were carried out by the technicians, after which they left, taking their tool kits with them.

The audience was invited to join in the countdown to "blast-off". When the count was completed, there was a huge flash and the technicians rushed on stage and began to dismantle the rocket, rolling the empty cylinders across the stage to waiting colleagues who took them away. The astronaut had disappeared.

The wooden base, made of thick plywood, was used to eliminate any suspicion regarding escape traps in the stage. The cylinders used in building the "rocket" were made of heavy cardboard, suitably decorated. The cylinder being placed at the bottom had a small door, which was positioned at the back of the rocket.

The cylinders were placed over the astronaut and the technicians made "adjustments" to the rocket. Inside, the astronaut removed his space suit and helmet. Underneath, he was dressed in white overalls. One of the technicians placed his box of tools near the rear door, while pretending to make various adjustments, and the astronaut put his space suit and helmet in the box, which the technician eventually took away.

As the other technicians were gathered around the rocket making final preparations for the "blast-off", the astronaut crawled through the door, fastening it behind him, and joined them. When they left the stage, he went with them.

The technicians had placed flash boxes around the rocket and, at the end of the countdown, the flashes were set off, bringing the mystery to a successful conclusion with the disappearance of the astronaut.

The Real Secret

Although the disappearances described in this chapter have all been the result of relatively simple techniques, they have mystified and delighted thousands over the years. John Gaughan, a famous builder of illusions for some of the greatest names in magic today, sticks to the principle of "keep it simple". The simpler a mystery is to carry out, the more the magician can concentrate on presentation, which is all important.

The real secret of success in magic is not to be found in the tricks themselves but in the personality of the magician. As the famous Danish-American magician Dante (Harry Jansen, 1883-1955), who toured the world with his full evening magic show, said in a newspaper interview: "There are thousands of violinists throughout the world, but only one Heifetz." There are thousands of magicians throughout the world, who are performing the same tricks as the master magicians, but there was only one Dante.

The Vanishing Automobile, starring the German illusionist Kalanag (Helmut Schreiber, 1893-1963). After a farewell wave from his wife and assistant Gloria, the car and occupant disappear in a puff of smoke.

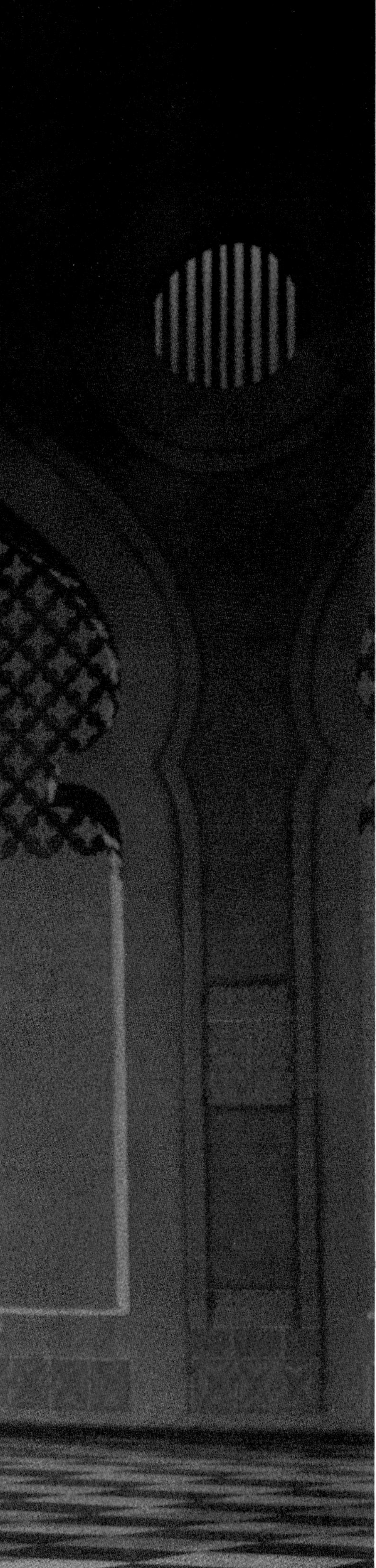

4

ACTS OF ILLUSION

While all conjuring may rightly be deemed illusion, the term "illusion" holds a special connotation for practitioners of the art. It refers specifically to *large magical effects*, involving people or animals, in contrast to tricks that employ smaller apparatus or sleight-of-hand. The apparent decapitation of an ox by Dedi about 2600 BC and the beheading of John the Baptist, as described in Scot's *Discoverie of Witchcraft* in 1584, are the earliest recorded example of such illusions.

Illusions in the grand manner emerged in the nineteenth century, by which time magic had found a home in theaters. Now the full range of stage machinery could be harnessed to new ingenious inventions, creating some exhilarating effects – female assistants appearing and disappearing, floating in mid-air, apparently being dismembered, crushed, dissected, restored and transformed. Animals too were made to vanish and reappear, while motorcycles and automobiles also found a place in these extravagant presentations. Illusions really are "big time" magic, the preserve of professionals; here are some of them for interest and for inspiration.

Past and present: Mark Wilson (*left*), one of the leading magicians in the world today, presents his lovely version of the Broomstick Suspension illusion. Harry Kellar (1849-1922) (*above*), at the time of his retirement in 1907, was staging the greatest magic show in America. Here he is shown presenting his magical sketch, "The Witch, the Sailor and the Enchanted Monkey".

Find the Lady

"Positively the most amazing illusion ever conceived". So claimed the program for the Great Lyle's stage presentation of the old race course swindle, the Three Card Trick (see Chapter Six). It had been invented by the English magician Amac (R.W. MacFarlane), who featured this trick, The Elusive Lady, in his US and British tours of the 1920s and 1930s.

The curtains parted to reveal three giant cards hung side by side from a batten, which was suspended from the flies and stabilized by wires anchored to the stage. Beneath each card the audience could see the chrome legs of a stool. The cards were now taken down and a female assistant, dressed as the Queen of Hearts, was introduced. She mounted a stool and one of the cards was placed in front of her. A second card was now maneuvered suspiciously by sliding it across the front of the card covering the lady before hanging it over the second stool. Finally the third card was placed in position. The impression created was that the lady could have shifted from one stool to the next as the second card was moved across. However, despite the fact that the audience had an unobstructed view through the legs of the stools and behind the cards to the backdrop, the lady was found behind the third card, to which no suspicion had been directed. The trick was repeated twice, and even with a foot dangled from behind one of the cards, but the audience only became more confused by their inability to "Find the Lady".

Lyle then offered to dispel any remaining audience suspicions. The backdrop was removed, giving a clear view to the rear wall of the stage. The lady mounted the center stool and was covered by a card. A cloth was handed to her behind the card. The card was then removed to disclose the lady standing on the stool, holding up the cloth in front of her. Lyle approached the stool and put his hand momentarily behind the cloth, which then collapsed on his arm, the lady having apparently dissolved into thin air. It is an astounding illusion that never fails to bring audible gasps of amazement from the audience.

After Lyle's death the illusion was acquired by Faust (Granville Taylor), who continues to feature it in his theater shows.

Below: Faust performing Amac's bewildering stage illusion "Find the Lady", which is based on an old racecourse card-trick swindle.

Above: British magician and illusionist Van Buren presents "The Vanishing Motorcycle and Rider" in the center of a circus ring. The rider drives into the container, and when the sides collapse both vehicle and rider have amazingly disappeared.

The Artist's Dream

David Devant (David Wighton, 1868-1941) was a prolific inventor of illusions. For his first appearance under the banner of Maskelyne and Cooke in 1893, he devised The Artist's Dream, for inclusion in a playlet. The scene is an artist's studio, where the grieving artist is observed painting his young, recently deceased wife Ellaline, seated on a garden swing. Tired, he draws a drape across the easel, sits at a table and falls asleep. The Angel or Spirit of Mercy appears and, taking pity on his plight, draws back the drape to disclose that the painting has come to life. Ellaline steps down from her swing, approaches her sleeping husband and kisses his hand. The Angel then beckons her back to the swing, draws the curtain and exits as the artist awakens. Recalling the vivid images, the artist goes to the easel and opens the drape. Alas, the painting is just as he had left it. It was only a dream.

One of the most charming and inexplicable of Devant's illusions, The Mascot Moth, was itself inspired by a dream. Devant dreamed that he chased a moth, actually a human being with wings, with a candle before it shriveled and disappeared; this was the illusion that he then created. His assistant, dressed to resemble a moth with wings attached to her arms, "fluttered" around the stage while Devant approached her, holding a candle in a large candlestick. The "moth" halted, closed her wings in front of her face and then suddenly vanished completely, without any covering whatsoever being used. It was a difficult illusion to stage, requiring split-second timing, but well worth the necessary rehearsal and Devant always regarded it as the best he had ever done.

Subsequently, the Mascot Moth vanish was introduced into The Artist's Dream sketch to make the Angel of Mercy disappear, the angel's wings replacing those of the moth. In this modified version, the artist dashes to the picture and takes it down, then turns to see the Angel. He approaches her cautiously but, as he reaches out to touch her, she vanishes immediately and he falls to the floor insensible.

Vanishing Motorcycles

In the years leading up to the First World War, when there was much talk of spies and of invisible rays being used to annihilate one's enemies, Devant incorporated such ideas into an original illusion called Biff, in which a Royal Enfield motorcycle, with its engine running and complete with rider, vanished.

In this presentation, a large wooden packing case was placed center stage, supported by legs about eighteen inches high. A ramp led up to a door at one end of the case and the motorcyclist, after a couple of laps around the stage, drove up the incline and into the case. The door was shut behind him and the packing case then hoisted into mid-air by the four ropes attached to its corners. The engine was still noisily pounding away and the case visibly vibrating. Devant now directed his imaginary "DD" (David Devant) ray upon the case and, suddenly, the engine stopped; simultaneously, the case literally fell to pieces, showering planks upon the stage, leaving only a skeleton framework still suspended. Of the motor cycle and rider, there was no trace.

The English illusionist Van Buren currently features a version of the Vanishing Motorcycle in his shows and, interestingly, it can be worked surrounded in a circus ring, which emphasizes the versatility of this remarkable illusion.

A very spectacular development of Biff has been incorporated into the magnificently staged shows of Siegfried and Roy at Las Vegas. The scene opens with a stage showing of a short film of Siegfried and Roy driving a jeep down the Las Vegas Strip with a tiger seated between them. The screen is raised, to disclose the same jeep on the stage, with its passengers aboard. Siegfried descends and Roy drives the jeep up a ramp into an open-framed cabinet. After Siegfried has demonstrated the isolation of the cabinet from the stage and backdrop, blinds are raised from the base of the cabinet to hide Roy, the tiger and the jeep from view. There is a sudden puff of smoke, the blinds are dropped and the denouement is totally unexpected, for while many of the audience anticipate the disappearance of jeep and passengers, they are amazed to see in their place a midget-sized Roy holding a miniature jeep in one hand and a small tiger in the other – an incredible shrinking effect!

The tiny Roy now mounts a small motorcycle and, after driving it around the stage and theater runway, speeds up a ramp at the back of a paper target, bursts through it and is instantaneously transformed into the life-size Roy mounted on a standard-size motorcycle. The combination of incongruity and strong illusion used here is irresistible but, as noted, this is simply the lead into another motorcycle illusion.

The stage is now set with two large boxes, one completely assembled and the other only partially so. Siegfried puts on a safety helmet while Roy rides his motorcycle to center stage and then dismounts. Together they complete the assembly of the open box by raising the sides into place and then they position it on the left, ready for the next step. Roy remounts his motorcycle and drives it into the other, assembled box at the right of the stage, where he is joined on the cycle by Siegfried. Both are visible by means of a screen-like front to the box and remain so as the box is hoisted into mid-air. The climax comes with a sudden explosion, accompanied by billowing smoke, as the magicians vanish in clear view of the audience. Simultaneously, the sides of the first box, which has remained on the stage, collapse to reveal Siegfried and Roy astride the motorcycle. This stunning transposition is an extension of the original Devant illusion, dressed in an ultra-modern manner.

Whippet Car

If you can vanish a motorcycle, why not an automobile too? So reasoned the astute, publicity-conscious showmen for, by ensuring the co-operation of a local automobile salesman, tremendous interest would be generated in every town the show played. The size of the object to be vanished, surpassed only by Houdini's Vanishing Elephant (Chapter Three), was guaranteed to arouse curiosity and generate box-office appeal. The illusionist did not even need to use his own automobile. Of course there *were*

Right: A poster advertising The Vanishing Whippet Car, one of the featured acts of Howard Thurston (1869-1936), whose magic show was an annual treat for generations of American youngsters.

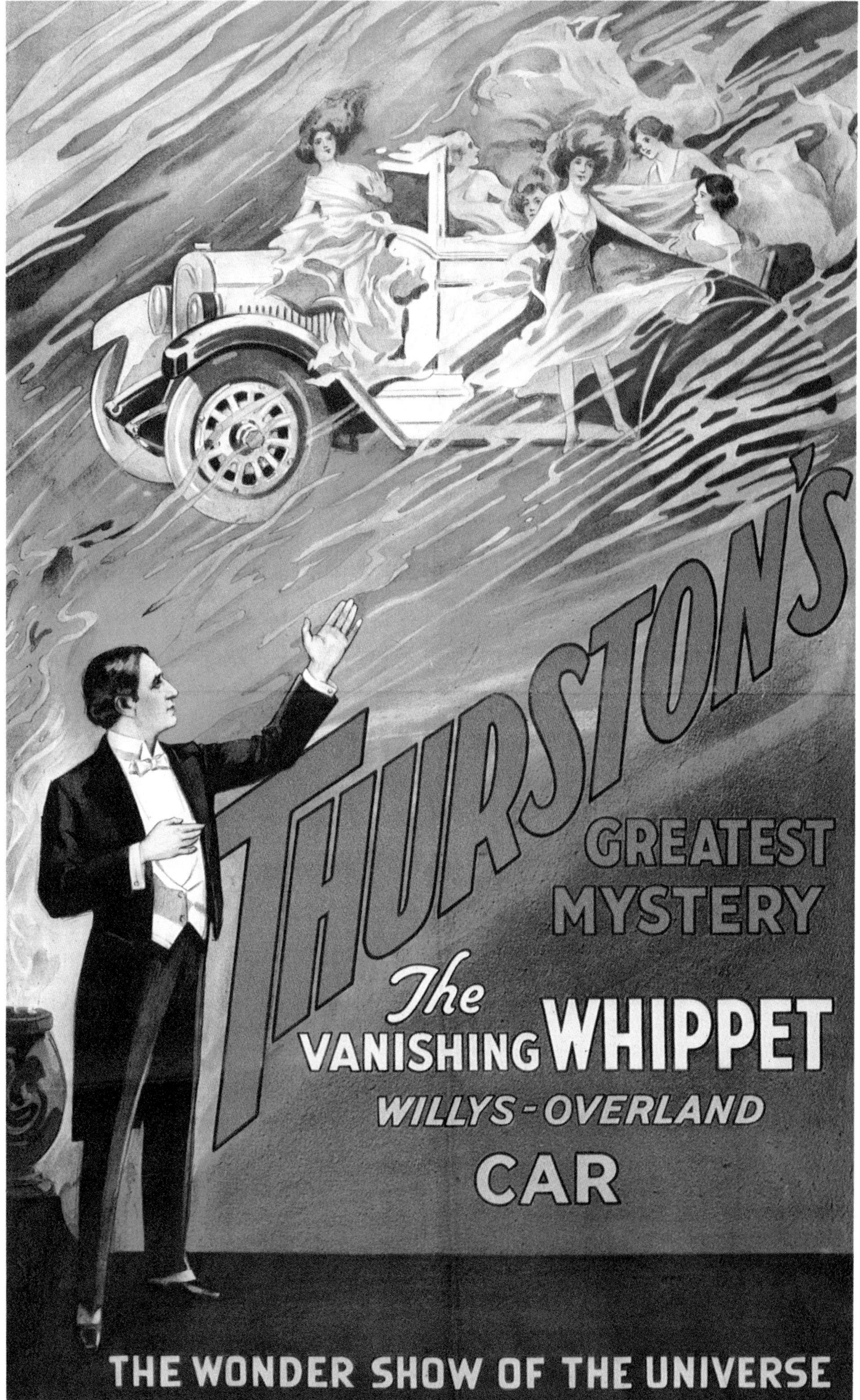
THURSTON'S
GREATEST
MYSTERY
The
VANISHING WHIPPET
WILLYS-OVERLAND
CAR
THE WONDER SHOW OF THE UNIVERSE

drawbacks, namely the scale of apparatus needed to effect the disappearance, although this was, in fact, comparatively light and portable.

Howard Thurston featured The Vanishing Whippet Car for three seasons in the USA and over twenty years later it became a popular item in the European shows of the German illusionist Kalanag (Helmut Schreiber). Thurston experimented with several presentations of the illusion and his final version was substantially the same as that used subsequently by Kalanag.

This is how it appeared to the audience. The curtains parted on a full stage hung at the back and sides with horizontally striped drapes. At the rear was a "garage" composed of two large, vertically slatted gates, through which the backcloth was clearly visible. The gates met at right angles, the V-corner so formed projecting towards the audience. The gates were opened, and the automobile was brought on stage and driven into the garage. The gates were then closed and the car, with its occupants gaily waving, was plainly visible through the slatted openings. The illusionist then fired a pistol, there was a flash, a puff of smoke, and the car vanished instantaneously, allowing the audience an unobstructed view of the backcloth.

There was no covering of any kind and it was, in magicians' parlance, a "visible vanish". Trapdoors were clearly out of the question and it was a puzzling rather than a baffling illusion, for audiences reasoned that the car must still be there, camouflaged in some way so they could not see it. They were right and it was, in fact, a modern mechanized variant of a nineteenth-century illusion, The Sphinx, that had stunned London in 1865 when Colonel Stodare (1831-1866) first presented it at the Egyptian Hall.

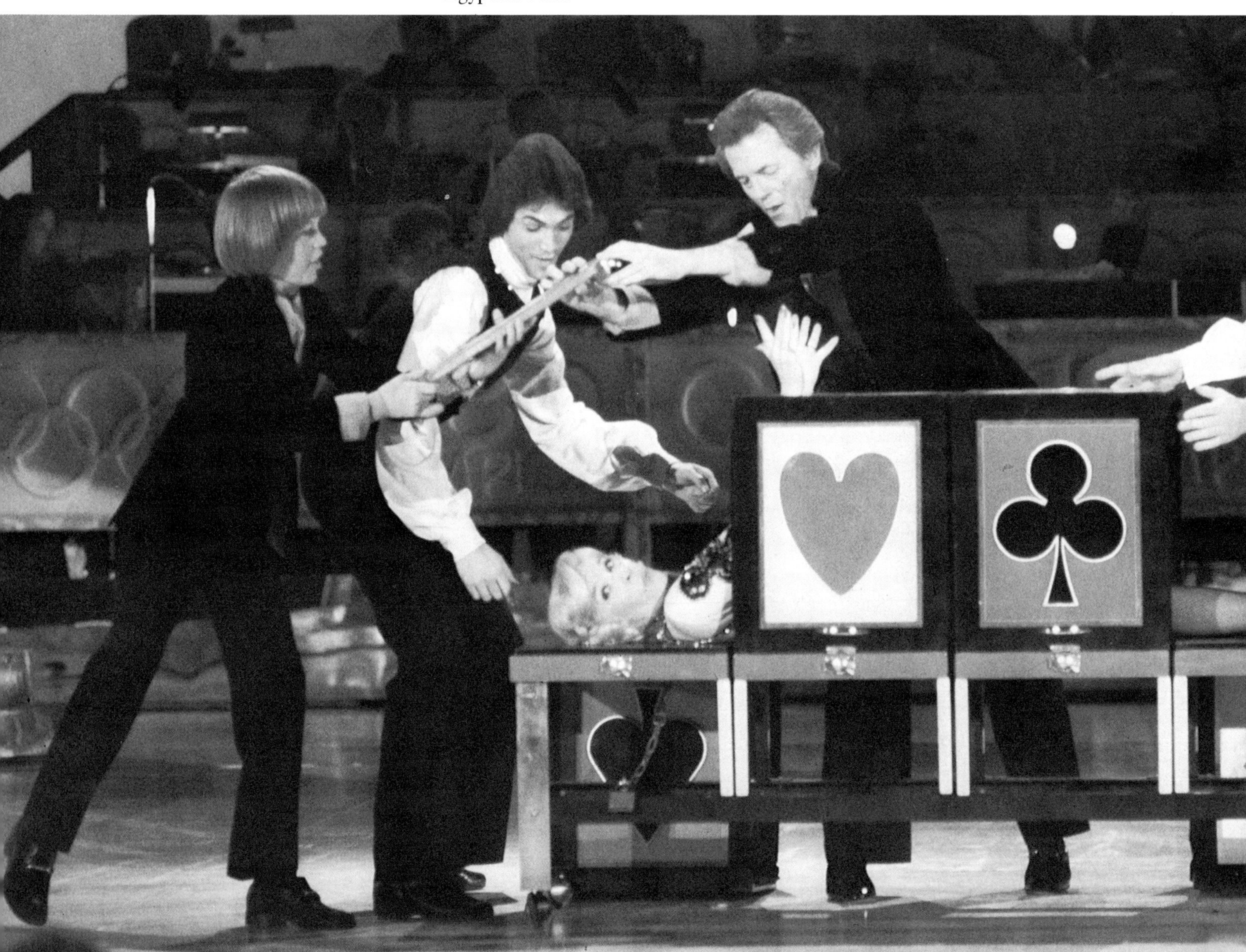

The Colonel used to enter carrying a small, square box which he placed on an undraped three-legged table. He told his audience that the box contained the head of an ancient Sphinx and lowered the front door of the box to display what seemed to be exactly that – an Egyptian-style head with closed eyes. Stodare then moved to a position at the side of the stage, to obviate any possibility of ventriloquism being suggested as an explanation of what followed. He bade the Sphinx open its eyes, which it did, to smile and to make a speech. Compliance was total and some twenty lines of verse (in English) were uttered. Stodare then closed the box, lifted it from the table and informed the audience that the charm used to revivify the ashes of the ancient Egyptian, who had lived and died many centuries ago, lasted but fifteen minutes. That time had now expired and the head had returned to its original state. The box was opened and all that remained of the formerly voluble head was a pile of ashes.

Contemporary critics hailed the Sphinx as one of the most extraordinary illusions ever presented to the public. Truth be known, it was based on an optical device originated by Thomas W. Tobin of the Royal Polytechnic Institution, London, for a series of lectures by Professor Pepper and patented by them as the Cabinet of Proteus. "It's all done by mirrors" is an explanation for illusions frequently offered by audiences. This is normally as inaccurate as "It's up his sleeve" for sleight-of-hand performances. In this instance, however, they were right!

It is of more than passing interest that New York magician Milbourne Christopher used the method devised for vanishing an automobile to vanish an elephant when he emulated Houdini with this feat on CBS TV's program, "The World's Greatest Magicians" in 1967.

Below: Mark Wilson at Las Vegas in 1980, dividing his wife into four parts, aided by his assistants. In the 1960s, Wilson presented a very popular American TV series for children, *The Magic Land of Allakazam*. Later, in 1971, he did a series of television shows entitled *The Magic Circus* and subsequently made many other TV appearances. He is an expert in creating magic themes and entertainment packages for amusement parks, and trade and industrial shows.

Dissected Ladies

Selbit (Percy Thomas Tibbles, 1879-1938) was a talented illusionist and inventive genius who devised a number of wonderful effects that are still featured in many modern shows. Undoubtedly the most famous and talked of is Sawing Through a Woman, first presented in 1921 in London. Selbit introduced a vertical wooden box, flanked by two male assistants.

The victim came on stage and four members of the audience assisted in tying lengths of cord around her neck, wrists and ankles, each cord being identified by luggage tags. She then entered the box, and through holes in the sides and back the ropes were threaded, pulled tight and knotted on the outside. The lid was closed and padlocked. The assistants then lifted the box and placed it horizontally on supports. The four men from the audience were asked to hold the ends of the ropes tightly. Sheets of plate glass were thrust down through slits in the lid and back of the box, effectively dividing it into four compartments; the glass apparently met with no resistance from the lady.

To compound the mystery further, two steel blades were now pushed through the box from front to back, one left of center and the other to the right, dividing the box into eight parts. A two-handed, cross-cut saw was introduced, the central sheet of glass withdrawn from the box, and then the two assistants, standing on opposite sides, proceeded to saw through the middle of the box. It was a dramatic moment. After the saw had passed completely through the box, the steel blades and remaining glass plates were removed, the ropes cut close to the knots, the padlocks unlocked and the lid opened. The ends were pulled apart, revealing Selbit's assistant none the worse for her adventure. The knots with their attached tags were examined and the helpers from the audience were presented with them as souvenirs of the occasion.

The new illusion attracted great publicity, which was played up by Selbit offering £5.00 per night for volunteers willing to be sawn through; he had no takers! It also attracted the attention of other illusionists, principally Horace Goldin (1874-1939) in the USA. The Polish-born Goldin claimed that he had invented the illusion himself and introduced a version in which a shorter box rested on a special table stand. The assistant climbed into the box, from which her head and feet projected at opposite ends, where they were secured by stocks. The lid was closed and the box sawn through. Steel plates were then pushed into grooves on either side of the saw cut and the two halves of the box pulled apart sufficiently to allow the performer to walk between them. The lady had been "sawn in two". The halves of the box were pushed together, the plates withdrawn and the lid opened to allow the assistant, once again intact, to emerge and take her bow.

Goldin was even more publicity-conscious than Selbit. He arranged for suitably garbed morticians to walk the street outside the show and for ambulances to wait at the stage doors of the theaters he played, "lest anything go wrong". Other illusionists copied the trick and recriminations and litigation were rife.

Below: "The Buzz Saw" performed by Ravisoud, the Swiss illusionist, during a Magic Circle Christmas Show.

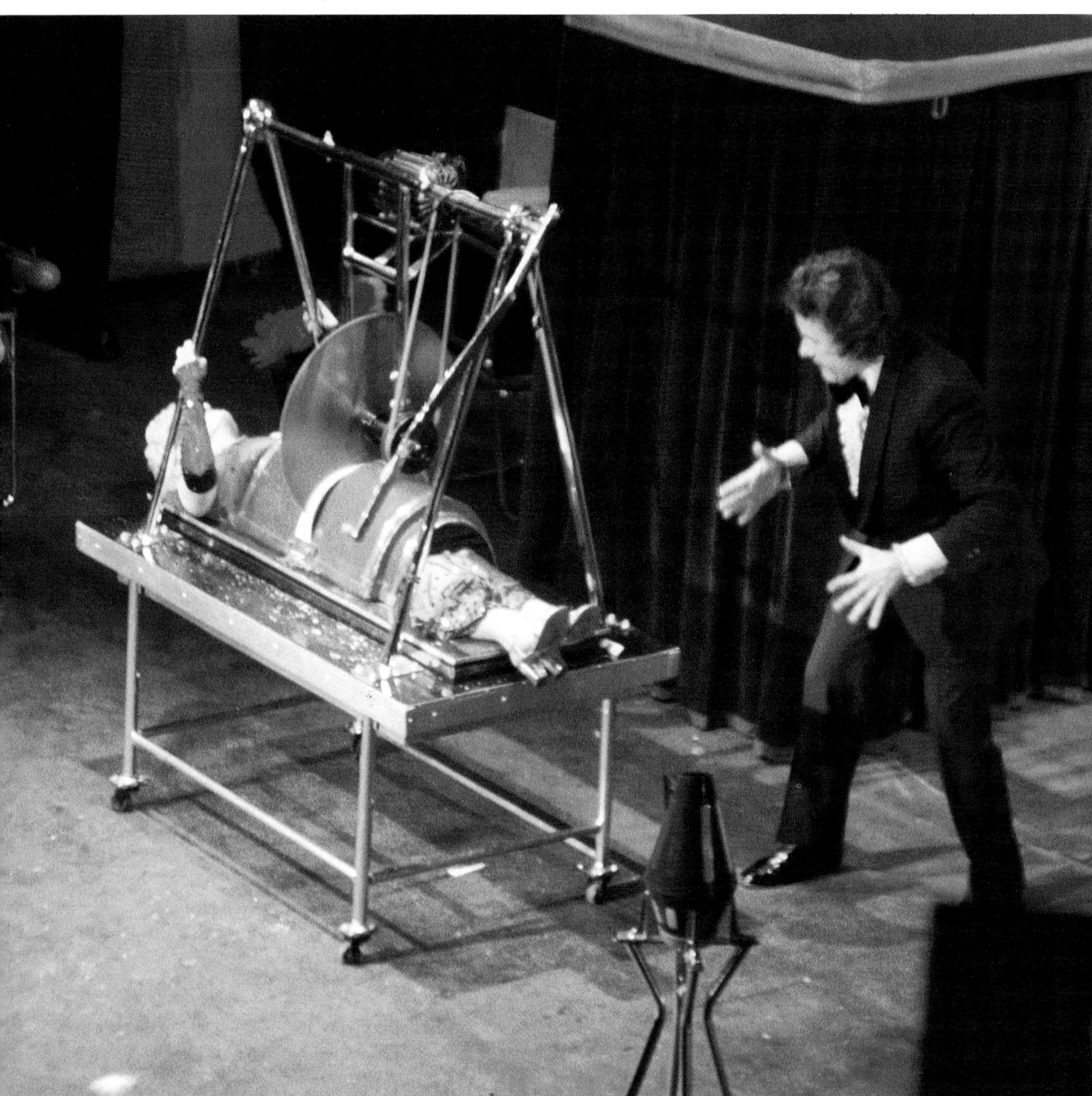

Ten years later, Goldin produced a new version which dispensed with the box, employed a circular saw, and was titled The Living Miracle. The audience saw the circular blade apparently rip bloodlessly through the girl assistant's midriff, without any covering whatsoever. In the USA, this style of "sawing through" became known as The Buzz Saw and a number of performers were soon featuring it, including Harry Blackstone Senior. In his presentation the girl was severed face-down instead of the more usual, face-up position. Blackstone Junior continues the family tradition with this most impressive of sawing illusions.

Gory Routine

The Buzz Saw has not always been presented in a bloodless manner, however. The Peruvian magician Richiardi Junior (1923-1985) followed in his father's footsteps with a gory routine that delighted South American audiences but had a more squeamish, albeit fascinatedly morbid, reception in the USA. The noisy, motor-driven saw ripped through the blond assistant and blood spurted everywhere, cascading onto the stage. Entrails were displayed and audiences filed across the stage to view first hand the apparent mayhem. This last touch guaranteed that the show became a box-office success.

Without doubt, though, the greatest impact ever made by the Sawing Through illusion was achieved by the Indian magician, Sorcar Senior (1913-1971), when he appeared on British television on April 9, 1956. He had sawn through his seventeen-year-old assistant, Dipty Dey, with the buzz saw, inserted a metal cleaver into her body to "prove" that she really had been sliced, when time ran out. The program was faded out before Sorcar had had the opportunity to revive his assistant. Presenter Richard Dimbleby's worried expression fueled the concern of millions of viewers who were convinced that they had just witnessed the demise of Sorcar's assistant. Frantic viewers jammed the BBC switchboard for an hour or more, to have their anxieties allayed with the reassurance that Dipty Dey was alive and well. Sorcar could not have wished for better free publicity to herald his opening at the Duke of York's Theatre, London!

With the trend to cabaret and club work, the search for a more portable method for performing Sawing Through a Woman led the brilliant South-African-born magician Robert Harbin (1909-1978) to devise the ideal apparatus. It could be carried in a suitcase and enabled the performer to use any lady from his audience who was willing to be the victim. She was invited to lie down across the seats of suitably placed chairs and a small rectangular frame, hinged to a narrow baseboard that passed beneath her, was placed over her waist. The gap between her waist and the opening in the frame was packed with a cloth, "to prevent any mess", and short wooden pegs were inserted into several holes that perforated the vertical sides of the frame.

The saw, which had a detachable blade, was inserted into the top of the frame and the sawing commenced with horizontal cuts. As the blade traveled relentlessly downward, it cut through the wooden pegs which, severed, dropped out of the frame, until the blade touched the baseboard beneath the girl. She had, apparently, been sawn right through and, to prove the fairness of the proceedings, the blade was released from the saw and withdrawn from beneath the girl's spine. Sadly, as with all good illusions, this one was quickly pirated and Harbin did not get his just recognition. It is some kind of accolade, however, that this is still one of the most widely practised illusions in the entire magic repertoire.

It was Robert Harbin, too, who invented the finest, most bewildering and most widely-copied illusion of modern times, the Zig-Zag Girl. The apparatus, as can be seen from the accompanying illustration, consists of an upright cabinet with four cut-outs, for face, hands and a foot, respectively, and three doors opening at the front. A lady from the audience is invited to inspect the cabinet and the cut-out holes before the illusionist's assistant, in stockinged feet, enters the cabinet. The two lower doors are closed as one and fastened and the assistant pushes her foot through the lower hole.

There is a small door in the center section which is opened and the assistant presses her belly against it; the audience volunteer feels and confirms its genuineness. The small

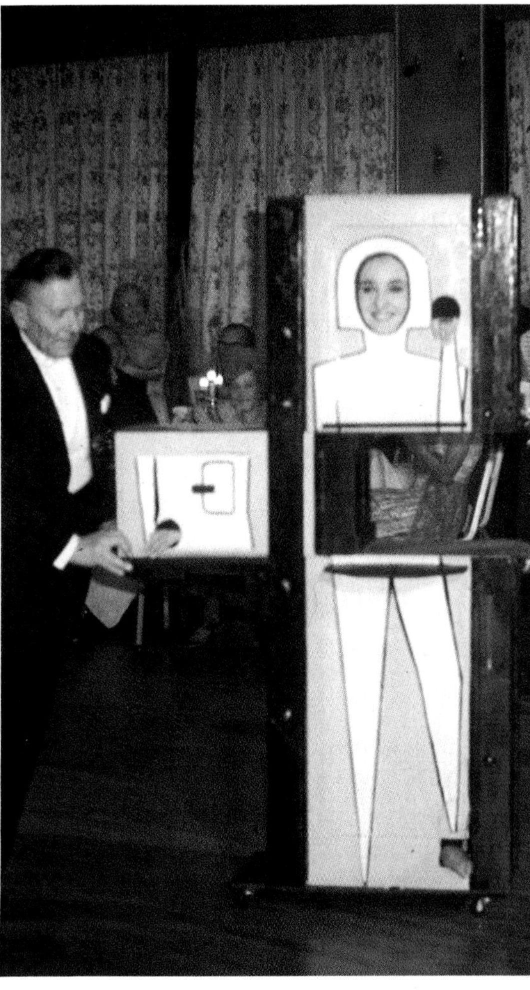

Above: Robert Harbin (Edward R.C. Williams, 1909-1978), who possessed one of the most inventive magical brains of all time, performing the Zig-Zag Girl illusion which he invented. It is one of the most baffling and popular illusions of modern times.

door is closed and the assistant puts her right hand through the hole in the center section. Finally, the top door is closed, the assistant presses her face against the large opening and pushes her left hand through the remaining hole, adjacent to her face.

The center section of the cabinet is designed to move sideways and this the performer now attempts to do; however, because of the assistant's protruding right hand, it can travel only a short distance before the hand strikes the main upright. A handkerchief is borrowed from the volunteer and placed in the assistant's fingers, which withdraw with it into the cabinet. Even with the hand withdrawn there is still a snag. The assistant's body now impedes the movement of the center section. But the performer has a solution to that problem.

Two metal blades are introduced and pushed through slots in the cabinet from front to back, where they protrude. The assistant has apparently been dissected into three pieces and, in consequence, her mid-section slides readily with the center section of the box to its fullest extremity. Incredibly, the girl has no middle – above is the face and hand, below, the foot. The audience volunteer is invited to walk all round the cabinet and to shake hands with the illusionist through the gap between the upper and lower sections. Then the little door in the center section is opened and the assistant is asked to breathe in and out while the spectator feels her belly. The hand, with the handkerchief, is pushed through the hole and the handkerchief returned to the owner.

Announcing the reassembly of his assistant, the performer closes the small door, she withdraws her hand and the center section is pushed back into position. The blades are removed and the cabinet opened to show that the victim is fully restored in one piece.

Harbin regarded the Zig-Zag Girl as his best illusion – and rightly so. It appears impossible and even magicians, when they eventually learned the secret, could still watch and marvel that it was achieved by the means adopted. Unfortunately, this illusion was pirated to an even greater extent than Harbin's Sawing Through, a form of flattery that he would willingly have foregone.

Another dissection illusion that is both amusing and amazing is the Mis-Made Girl, from which Doug Henning extracts much entertainment. A vertical cabinet, large enough to take a girl standing erect, has four doors at the front, one above the other, numbered 1 to 4 downward. After the assistant has entered and the doors have been shut, three steel blades are inserted into the cabinet, front to back, effectively dividing it – and, presumably, the girl – into four sections. The cabinet cubes thus formed are now lifted off, one at a time, by assistants and placed about the stage. The dissection is clearly complete.

To conclude she must be reassembled but, by an unfortunate oversight, the cubes are restacked in the wrong sequence. When the four doors are opened, a highly comical situation is revealed – the assistant's head is where her legs should be and her feet and midriff sections are haphazardly around it! Amidst much consternation, the cubes are reshuffled into their correct numerical sequence and, with a sigh of relief, the girl steps out of the cabinet correctly reassembled.

Right: Emerson and Jayne with their brilliant Flying Carpet act.

Up in the Air

One of the larger, sensational illusions seen in the youthful David Copperfield's show at Las Vegas and on television was performed with a $60,000 Ferrari. The automobile was driven on stage and up a small ramp to a structure resembling a low bridge. Copperfield observed that automobiles were normally intended to travel in two directions but that on this occasion it would go in a third direction – upward. The Ferrari was then covered with a large cloth and, in response to the performer's gestures, it slowly ascended high into the air. This took place against a glittering backdrop, with a silhouette of skyscrapers. Assistants waved long poles bearing streamers around the floating automobile, to disprove the possibility of any attachments. Then the automobile floated downward sufficiently to enable Copperfield to take hold of the covering cloth. With a sharp pull, the cloth came away and, to everyone's amazement, the Ferrari had vanished.

Above: Servais Le Roy, the Belgian illusionist who settled in the USA in 1918, levitates his wife and assistant Talma. She was a magicienne herself, presenting her own act, "Talma, Queen of Coins", around the turn of the century.

Left: Mark Wilson suspends his wife and assistant, Nani Darnell, in front of Hollywood's exclusive Magic Castle club, where stage, parlor and close-up magic are performed each night. This West Coast institution, created by the brothers Bill and Milt Larsen, is one of the most important magic centers in the world.

Below: Faust and "The Bride of the Air". His assistant is covered with a sheet before rising mysteriously into the air. After a hoop has been passed over her to demonstrate that there are no supporting props, the sheet is suddenly pulled away to reveal . . . nothing. She has completely vanished.

This was a striking, new version of an old illusion created by the great innovative Belgian magician, Servais Le Roy (1865-1953). It was called Asrah and in its original form Le Roy apparently hypnotized his beautiful wife, Talma, who fell into a trance. She was caught by an assistant as she fell, and carried to a couch. Talma was covered by a sheet, her arm dropping limply into view. It was placed back under the covering and Le Roy motioned for the inert form to rise. Slowly the covered Talma rose in the air and the couch was removed to allow Le Roy to stand beneath while he passed a hoop completely over her recumbent form, thereby disproving the presence of supports. Then, reaching for the sheet, he whipped it away and Talma had dissolved into thin air. It is a beautiful illusion and has been featured in the repertoires of many famous magicians.

An earlier form of the levitation illusion was invented by John Nevil Maskelyne, in which the assistant was not covered and did not vanish in mid-air; this is described in Chapter Five. The first form of this effect had been produced in response to accounts of the floating up to the ceiling of a well-known spiritualist medium, Daniel Dunglas Home; conjurers had repeatedly been challenged to perform this feat. Maskelyne did so at the Egyptian Hall, and in his Levitation Extraordinary he stood erect on the stage, floated up and above the audience's heads to the dome of the Hall, where he turned to a horizontal position and then descended, equally gracefully, to the stage.

The Arabian Nights fantasy of flying carpets has been brought very convincingly to stage and cabaret in the beautiful presentation of the British partnership Emerson and Jayne. These former dancers with the Ballet Jooss have created a poetic Oriental spectacle that combines humor with mystery. Sheer wonder is evoked as Jayne, seated cross-legged on a carpet that ripples beneath her, floats up in the air, across the stage and even out over the orchestra pit.

The motive power defies detection and magic initiates who recognize deployment of the so-called Black Art Principle, invented over a century ago by Max Auzinger, can still give themselves up entirely to the delightful cameo. (The Black Art Principle is based on the fact that anything black becomes invisible if placed in front of something else that is also black. This is because it not only blends in but, with the correct form of lighting, casts no shadow.) Whether in variety shows, cabaret or Christmas pantomime, Emerson and Jayne's specialty act always intrigues, mystifies and entertains and it has done so even in the mythological home of the flying carpet in the Middle East.

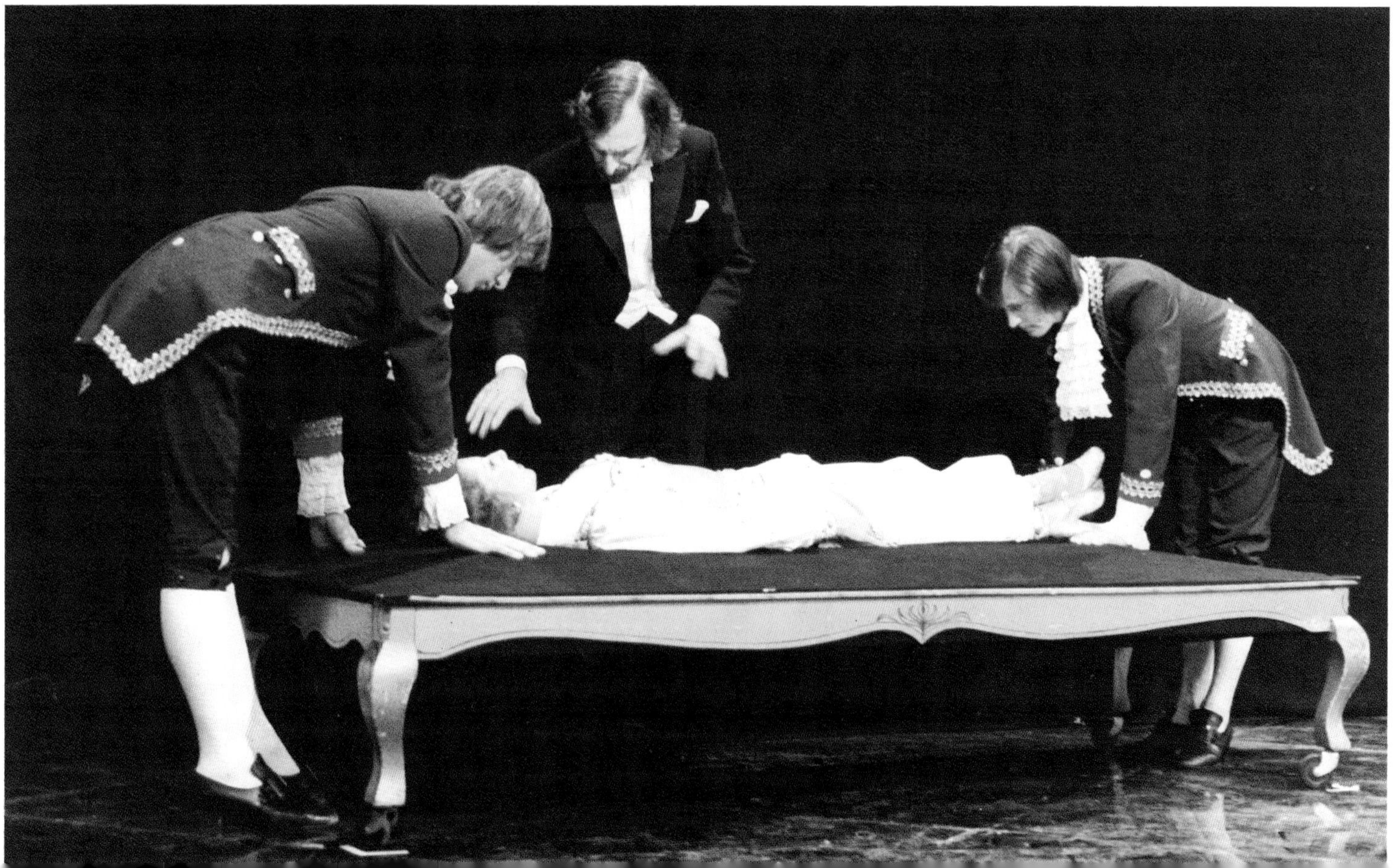

Above: The Egyptian Hall, in London's Piccadilly, was, from 1873 until its demolition in 1905, England's Home of Mystery, where Maskelyne and Cooke presented magic, illusions and automata. Their most famous automaton was Psycho, the Whist Player.

Right: Siegfried and Roy, the German-born magical superstars who have dominated the Las Vegas entertainment scene for years, specialize in using wild animals in their lavish spectacle "Beyond Belief".

HOMES OF ILLUSION

For sixty years, London had its unique Maskelyne's Home of Mystery where most of the finest illusions could regularly be seen. After Maskelyne's theater closed in 1933, there was no other recognized "home" of magic for the theater-going public until, in comparatively recent times, the USA fairly laid claim to two such theatrical venues, in widely contrasting environments. The first is at Las Vegas, where Siegfried and Roy, the superstars of magic and the ultimate in professional showmen, have their lavish Ziegfeld-style extravaganza "Beyond Belief" at the Frontier Hotel.

The other, perhaps more suprising, venue is the Cabot Street Theatre at Beverly, Massachusetts. Since 1977 a company of over sixty enthusiasts, welded together by the charismatic Cuban magician Marco the Magi (Cesareo Pelaez), have presented "Le Grand David and His Own Spectacular Magic Company" here at weekends and holidays. Color, spectacle, gorgeous costumes and immaculate apparatus allied to magical skills bring life to classic illusions in a memorable theatrical setting. This venture by a troupe who are not full-time professional entertainers is unique. So successful has it proved that after 1,000 performances they now present a second show, "In Concert", at the Larcom Theatre in Beverly.

Although it is a private club and not open to the general public, the Magic Castle in Hollywood is certainly another "home of magic". It is a Mecca for top-flight professional and amateur magicians, containing three different settings – the Close-Up Room for intimate performances, the Parlor, where small-scale magic is displayed and the Palace of Mystery theater for stage magic.

It's All Done by Lasers

Lasers are one of the most dramatic forms of modern technology to have become part of the magician's act. Their use in The Spiker illusion, where the victim is apparently impaled with lasers instead of steel spikes, is an obvious application which Siegfried and Roy have used to striking effect.

The two performers enter from left and right, carrying transparent plastic shields on which are mounted five laser spikes. They fire beams over the heads of the audience before turning their attention to the framework of a cubical box mounted on a low table. Their principal assistant, Lynette Chappell, enters the box to which front and rear panels are attached. The front panel has a small central aperture, through which Lynette pushes a silk handkerchief, which she keeps in motion with her hand throughout the ensuing action.

Siegfried and Roy then approach the box from opposite sides, bearing their laser shields, and push the laser spikes in through appropriately spaced holes in the box sides, apparently transfixing Lynette in the process. The front and back panels are removed, there is a flash, and Lynette has vanished; only the ten laser spikes and their penetrating beams remain.

Another laser illusion which has been created in the USA although seemingly, at the time of writing, not yet performed in public, is breathtaking in its conception. A laser beam is directed at, and apparently passes right through, an assistant. The beam is then slowly elevated and the transfixed assistant is taken up into the air, impaled on the laser beam. This is certainly space-age magic and in every sense a refreshingly new angle on the levitation illusion.

Left and *above:* David Copperfield treats Catherine Bach to a new type of "assistant's hazard" as she is placed in a cabinet, hoisted up into the air upside down, and then subjected to a Star Wars style laser bombardment with remarkable results. Standing on your head with ankles and feet immediately above, and your midsection missing, may not be everyone's ideal position, but it's certainly different!

David Copperfield hit international headlines as a result of his TV spectaculars which included such seemingly impossible feats as making the Statue of Liberty vanish, levitating himself across the Grand Canyon, and walking through the Great Wall of China.

Transformations

Transformations of identity or of form have long been part of the stock-in-trade of the illusionist. The Great Lafayette included an Arabian Nights pantomimic playlet called The Lion's Bride in his show. Disguised as his sweetheart and wearing a yashmak, Lafayette was thrown into a lion's cage. The lion roared and leaped out of the cage, rearing on its hind legs to whip off a false head, revealing Lafayette himself – a startling, unexpected transformation.

Siegfried and Roy perform a similar exciting transformation illusion. Siegfried presents a huge tiger in a cage that rests on top of a table fitted with four hinged panels. The cage is covered with a cloth and then the four table panels are raised to form an open-topped box around the draped cage. The cage containing the tiger is then hoisted

Below: Mark Wilson's version of "Sawing Through" is one of the best in the business, for Nani is placed in a locomotive and tender which is then divided on its track. The resulting halves are turned round so that Nani can inspect the soles of her feet!

into the air by means of chains attached to each corner. When it is high above the stage, Siegfried whips the cloth away – the tiger has vanished. At the same moment as the cloth falls to the stage, the sides of the box collapse and Roy leaps into view. Audience attention is then directed to a trunk that has been in full view on the stage throughout. Siegfried opens it and out jumps the missing tiger. The trunk is drawn off stage with Roy and the tiger perched on top.

Other illusionists use the theme of human/animal transformations with great effect. Blackstone Junior has a spectacular production number based on a lively circus theme. His wife, Gay, is placed in a cage, which is then covered. When the cloth is whipped away, Gay has vanished and in her stead is a 450lb Bengal tiger.

5

MINDREADING AND LEVITATIONS

People are curious about subjects which seem to be beyond the limits of natural laws. Topics such as hypnotism, mindreading and levitation have been discussed, criticized and have, for many years, been regarded as controversial. Hypnotism, which two centuries ago was steeped in mysticism, has become almost respectable now that it has been accepted by some medical authorities. Levitations are generally regarded as part of an illusionist's act, but mindreading is still thought of, by many people, as something apart from a feat of conjuring. It remains a mysterious force which they cannot fully understand. Yet there is nothing supernatural about these apparently other-worldly powers – just a great deal of skill and ingenuity.

Because so little is known about the powers of the mind, and so much remains to be explored, "psychics" – like the Israeli, Uri Geller – can claim that it is possible to bend metal objects by the power of thought or duplicate a drawing contained in a sealed envelope. Ted Serios in the States can demonstrate his apparent ability to take "thought" photographs and the man in the street takes him seriously, believing that these things are possible.

Left: Doug Henning puts the "fluence" on his assistant, enabling her to balance horizontally on top of a microphone stand in a modern version of the Broomstick illusion.

Above: Henri Robin, the French magician, presenting his version of Second Sight with a blindfolded female assistant.

Mindreading acts were well established in theaters and vaudeville shows during the second half of the nineteenth century. Newspaper advertisements informing the public of amazing demonstrations were frequent. Here is an example:

MINDREADER EXTRAORDINARY
TO MYSTIFY
THEATER-GOERS OF FARLINGTON

Mysterioso, the man who draws aside the veil of the hidden mysteries of the East, appears on the stage of the Hippodrome Theater, Farlington, this week. He will demonstrate his remarkable ability to glimpse into the future, and reveal the events that await you.

Scientists have delcared themselves mystified by Mysterioso's amazing, and uncanny, powers. He answers questions put to him by members of the audience, who will leave the theater baffled because they will know that they have witnessed a demonstration of genuine mindreading.

This advertisement is a sample of the type of publicity used to attract curiosity-seekers, believers in the supernatural and those looking for something different in entertainment.

Partner Acts

Some mindreaders prefer to work alone while others include a partner, usually their wives or sisters, to assist them in their demonstrations of second sight.

The Danish team of Julius and Agnes Zancig were one of the most famous man and wife acts, billed as "The Zancigs – Two Minds with but a Single Thought". It was usual at this period, when presenting a second sight act, for the lady to remain on the stage, blindfolded, while her partner moved around the auditorium accepting articles handed to him by members of the audience, which the lady would eventually describe in great detail.

If, for instance, a pocket watch had been given to her partner, she would describe the metal of which it was made, the hours and minutes to which the hands were pointing and details regarding any inscription to be found on the casing, including the maker's name. To inject some humor into the act, she might tell the audience the number of times the item had been pawned.

Some of the pioneer two-person second sight acts depended upon a verbal code with which to communicate the names of articles to their partners. Here is a simple basic code, as an example:

One	Two	Three	Four	Five	Six	Seven	Eight	Nine	Zero
I	Go	Can	What	Quick	Please	Will	Now	Now then	Right

The performer might ask "What is this number?". The answer would be "Four".
"I want you to tell me this number, please."
"Sixteen."

A date on a coin would be transmitted as:
"I want you, now then, to tell me what this date is, please."
One Nine Four Six.
"1946."

If a verbal code act is presented today, most of the coins offered will have been minted in the present century, therefore the first two figures can be omitted and the sentence shortened to:
"What is the date, please?"
Four Six
Answer: "1946."

Above: The Zancigs, a Danish thought-transference act that created a sensation when it opened at the London Alhambra in 1905 and subsequently became famous throughout the world. Zancig (Julius Jensen, 1857-1929) and his wife Agnes developed an intricate code system that they could use at incredible speed. The results they obtained appeared impossible without genuine telepathy. Even Sir Arthur Conan Doyle, author of the Sherlock Holmes detective stories, was convinced they were psychic. After Agnes's death in 1916 Julius married Ada (seen in this poster) and continued with the act, although it did not regain its previous heights.

Right: David Devant (David Wighton, 1868-1941) demonstrating thought transmission with his sister Dora. Devant was acknowledged to be the greatest English magician of his time by virtue of his charm, conjuring ability and magical creativity. From 1905 to 1915 he partnered J.N. Maskelyne to form the famous team of Maskelyne and Devant.

Although the basic code words given above are not difficult to learn, memorizing lists of articles is far from easy. If one group is comprised of coins and banknotes, think of how many of these are in everyday use, excluding foreign coins and old coins, such as a Lincoln penny, or a silver dollar. Remember, also, the different varieties of metal and materials used in the manufacture of these items.

There is no doubt that the need to memorize thousands of articles and the constant rehearsals required to keep the performance up to scratch are the reasons for the decline in second sight acts which use verbal codes as a means of communicating information.

The act presented by The Zancigs was in a class of its own and in 1906 they were invited to perform in the presence of Britain's King Edward VII and Queen Alexandra.

Left, above and below: Frances Willard presenting the famous Willard Spirit Cabinet act, assisted by her husband, Glenn Falkenstein.

First her wrists are tied behind her back with strips of cloth, and another strip is tied round her neck, and then she sits on a stool in a curtained cabinet. The ends of the cloth strips are now securely nailed to the floor and to the wooden board behind her by spectators and then she is apparently put into a trance. The curtains are closed and immediately bells and horns, which had been placed on the table beside her, are heard and are then thrown out of the cabinet. Glenn flings the curtains open but Frances is still in a trance and securely bound.

A spectator is then blindfolded, and invited to sit in the cabinet with Frances. The curtains are closed, yet again the instruments play and the cabinet shakes. The curtains are then pulled open, revealing the hilarious sight of the spectator with a pink bucket on his head and his trousers rolled up to the knees! Frances is still securely bound and entranced.

Finally, the curtain is closed once more and a gentleman's jacket is borrowed and hung over the cabinet top. Glenn commands the spirits to take the jacket, which quickly disappears from view. A second later the curtain is ripped open – Frances is now wearing the jacket, despite still being securely nailed to the boards. The curtains are closed and the jacket is immediately flung out. It is an electrifying performance.

Left: The Mentalist Peter Zenner (Peter Estyn Jones), demonstrating his remarkable ability to "see" with his finger tips. Securely blindfolded, he is describing accurately an article that has been proffered by a spectator.

Another team of thought-readers who appeared before royalty were Mr and Miss Tree, who asked members of the audience to suggest tune titles and pieces of music, instead of articles. Their appearance before King George V of Britain and Queen Mary took place in 1925 during the Royal Variety Show held at the Alhambra Theatre, London.

Leo Tree asked spectators to whisper the name of a tune to him and Myra, sitting some distance away at a piano, played the requested tune. The piece of music asked for by the King was "The Merry Widow Waltz".

When King George met the couple after the performance, he asked them to entertain at another function and this led to many more appearances at social gatherings held at royal residences. The Trees described themselves in their brochures as "The Famous Royal Command Personalities".

Mindreading on Radio

Not all acts use simple verbal signaling systems. A young Australian couple, Sydney and Lesley Piddington, became famous for their thought-reading demonstrations in the late 1940s, which relied on a far more sophisticated system. Sydney, a former accountant, had been a prisoner of war in Changi, a Japanese prison camp. While there he read a book about experiments in thought transmission. He and a fellow prisoner, Russell Braddon (who later became a famous author), gave demonstrations of mentalism, which became the talk of the camp.

When he was released in 1945, Sydney married Lesley Pope and together they presented a mindreading act, first on Australian radio and later, in 1949, on British radio. Famous personalities were invited to appear on the programs to act as a panel of judges and a number of different locations were used during the series. In one test, Lesley was driven around London in a taxi cab, accompanied by a member of the panel. In the radio studio someone selected a song title and, on her return, Lesley showed the title of the song which she had written on a pad during her journey. This was confirmed by the judge. When checked with the studio selection it was found to be correct. During another broadcast Lesley, under close supervision in the Tower of London, was able to reveal words from a book chosen by a member of the studio audience.

Below: The Great Masoni (Eric Mason, d. 1977) and Shan presenting the Giant Memory feat. Twenty articles were specified at random by members of the audience and written alongside the numerals 1 to 20 on the blackboard. The blindfolded Shan, with impressive rapidity, then called out the appropriate article in response to a given number, or vice versa, and ran through the complete sequence, backwards or forwards.

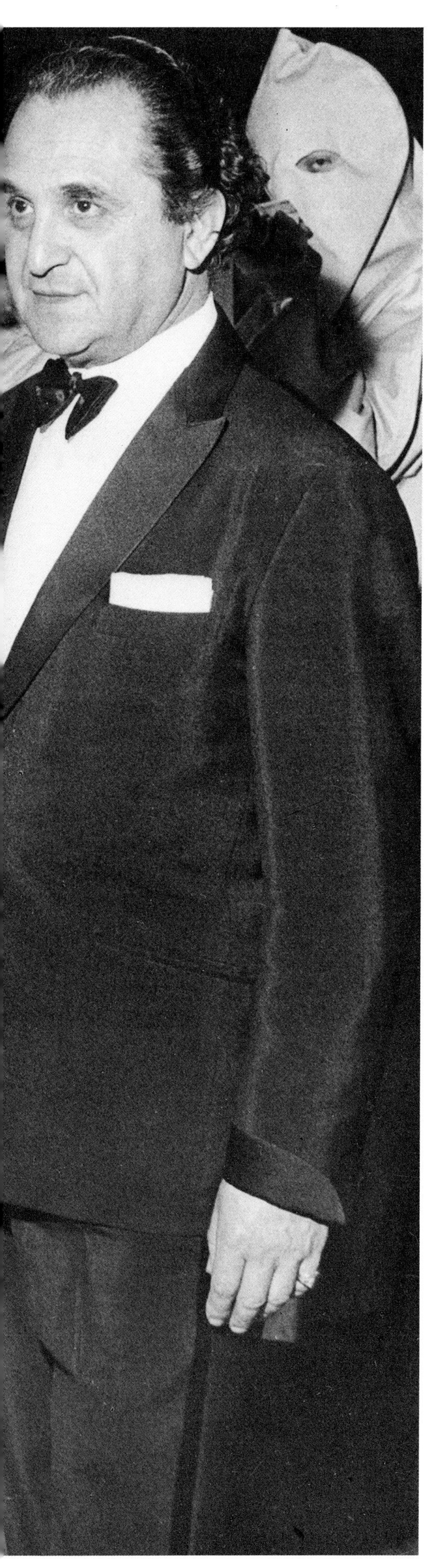

The Piddington broadcasts became the number one talking point throughout the country and the newspapers had a ball. They raised questions regarding the authenticity of the broadcast demonstrations and set telepathy tests for their readers.

Some journalists, assisted by magicians seeking cheap publicity and basking in reflected glory, claimed that they knew the methods used by the Piddingtons. Despite the information given, the so-called exposures made little difference to the progress of the mindreaders, who filled the theaters wherever they appeared.

A thought-reader who appeared on the radio about the same time as the Piddingtons was an Englishman, Maurice (The Amazing) Fogel. Fogel is widely regarded as the greatest showman since Harry Houdini. For more than thirty years he captured newspaper headlines with way-out publicity stunts, ranging from a mindreading chicken to his disappearance from a space rocket, for which he issued invitations to Professor Sir Bernard Lovell, who was in charge of the giant radio telescope at Jodrell Bank, England, and the Russian Ambassador to Britain.

Fogel caused nationwide controversy when he broadcast on a BBC radio show called "Starlight Hour". In this act, he told members of the studio audience their names, addresses and occupations. Approaching one man, the mindreader told him the name of a dead person, about whom the man was thinking. A sealed envelope, which had been in the possession of the BBC for a fortnight, was opened, revealing a prediction of the newspaper headlines published on the day of the broadcast. The prediction read "Railway Disaster". Fogel had made an error in the date: five days previously a railway accident had been reported in the papers.

One of Fogel's most famous and dangerous feats was his version of Russian Roulette. He selected six marksmen from the audience and gave each of them a number from one to six. Drawing attention to a revolving stand on which six rifles were displayed, Fogel spun it. When it had stopped turning, he asked each man to choose a rifle. Five of the rifles were loaded and one was empty. Before the rifles were selected, the mindreader had made a note of the number of the man who would, in a few moments, aim his rifle at a human target. He was asked to aim between Fogel's eyes, while the other marksmen aimed at five dinner plates displayed on a shelf behind the mindreader. At the word of command the rifles were fired. The plates were smashed but Fogel remained unscathed. The gun selected by the marksman was empty, even though he had apparently had a free choice of gun.

Far left: Maurice Fogel (1911-81) at the 1970 first showing of his dramatic mental mystery, Russian Roulette. Fogel apparently "divined" which one of the six thoroughly mixed rifles had already been fired and ordered that particular marksman to aim at him while the others shot at plates, shattering them: Fogel survived!

Left: Al Koran (Edward C. Doe, 1914-1972) who specialized in mental and psychic mysteries. He was frequently seen on television in Britain, and in 1969 settled in the USA.

"BRAIN BUSTERS" AND THE SECRET SERVICE

The accolade for being the most successful mindreader on radio must be awarded to an American, Joseph Dunninger, who was a star attraction on the ABC radio network, broadcasting on 160 stations every week. He was described as "The man who does the impossible, the world's foremost mentalist". When he later appeared on television, his sponsors paid him $1,500 for each program and he was one of the highest-paid society entertainers in the United States, receiving several thousand dollars for an hour's after-dinner entertainment.

The highest-paid mindreader before Dunninger had been Alexander, billed as "The Man who Knows", also an American. When he played the Keith Circuit in the States he received $3,000 a week.

During his broadcasts, Dunninger "read" the minds of spectators in the studio audience, revealing serial numbers on banknotes, social security numbers and names and addresses of people about whom they were thinking. Included in each program there was a "brain-buster", which was usually the main feature of the broadcast. "Brain-busters" were apparently impossible tests set for Dunninger by a panel made up of spectators and a guest celebrity.

In one of the tests, a film actress and the audience panel were asked to go to a book-store and purchase a book of their own choice. The book, in its original wrapping, was placed in a safe which was locked. Later in the program, the panel was asked to concentrate on the title of the chosen book, which was successfully revealed by Dunninger.

The Chief of the United States Secret Service, U.E. Baugham, was invited to appear on the Dunninger radio show and the producer explained to him a challenge suggested by Dunninger. Baugham was to obtain a large number of envelopes and number them in sequence. He was requested to place a counterfeit banknote into all but one of the envelopes. In the remaining envelope, he was to put a genuine bill. Dunninger claimed that, despite all the precautions that would be taken, he would be able to discover the envelope containing the genuine money, the denomination and the serial number.

The secret service man made his preparations in secret and would not even tell his secretary what he was doing. He decided to use fifty envelopes and placed the genuine bill in number forty-four. He took all possible precautions, placing the envelopes in his briefcase and not, for one moment, allowing it to leave his possession.

During the broadcast, Dunninger correctly divined envelope number forty-four as containing the genuine note and, concentrating on the folded note within the envelope, stated that it was a fifty dollar bill and revealed the serial number. The secret service chief, who had dealt with many forms of deception during his long and distinguished career, was at a complete loss over this one!

It is usual to find this type of act being presented indoors but one man who specializes in open-air demonstrations is Jon Marshall, who is known on the British Gala Circuit as The Man with the X-Ray Eyes.

Audience volunteers assist in blindfolding him with thick pads of cotton, layers of adhesive tape and a hood, made of thick black material. He is led to a waiting car, supplied by a local dealer, and, having checked the various controls by touch, begins his sensational Blindfold Drive.

He picks up speed as he travels around the arena, avoiding cones which have been placed in position while he was being blindfolded. During his second circuit, local personalities are used as obstacles in the arena. The car hurtles by, missing them by inches.

In his cabaret act, Jon Marshall presents a thought-provoking demonstration of

Above: Jon Marshall, "The Man with the X-Ray Eyes", about to present his thrilling Blindfold Drive. Securely blindfolded and hooded, he drives with panache round a circuit littered with obstacles and local celebrities, missing them by inches to the great excitement of the large crowd.

Right: Kreskin (George Kresge Jr), an American mentalist whose apparent ability to read minds astonishes audiences. A feature of the show involves volunteers from the audience hiding his salary check in the theater while he is taken outside under guard. On his return, he asks one of the volunteers to concentrate on the hidden check and, as seen here, asks her not to speak but to take the end of his handkerchief. Unerringly, he proceeds to locate his missing fee.

Above: Frances Willard and her husband, Glenn Falkenstein, himself an accomplished magician and mentalist who features Blindfold Vision and other impressive feats on stage and television.

Left: Michel de la Vega's Sword Suspension. The girl is initially supported by three swords, beneath her neck, back and feet. Even when two are removed, she remains suspended from the single sword at her neck, while a hoop is passed over her.

pseudo-psychometry, in which he is assisted by several spectators. They are each handed a red cloth bag, into which they are asked to place a small article, preferably something that has been in their possession for some considerable time, and to close the bag by means of an attached drawstring.

One of the spectators collects the bags and is asked to mix them so that there is no possibility of anyone knowing which of the bags was given by a particular person. The bags are handed to Jon Marshall, one at a time. Removing each article, he is able to identify the owner. This procedure is continued until all of the items have been returned to the people who loaned them.

A completely different blindfold mental act is that of American Glenn Falkenstein. Members of the audience assist in blindfolding him, placing a half dollar over each eye and holding them in place with strips of adhesive tape. Padding covers the coins and is held by a securely-fastened steel mask.

Four spectators are asked to take part in an experiment. Each one is asked to think of a number between 100 and 1,000. While they are engaged in writing their chosen numbers on a blackboard, Falkenstein writes on another blackboard what he believes will be the total of the numbers. When the numbers are added, the total is exactly the same as the one predicted by the blindfolded mindreader.

For his next demonstration, a spectator assists by taking a tray and collecting from members of the audience various items such as a ring, a pocketbook or a cigarette lighter. Upon receiving the tray, Falkenstein takes each article and, after a few moments concentration, describes it in detail and takes it to the person to whom it belongs.

TV Telepathy

Television has brought many mindreading acts to the attention of its millions of viewers. One person who has fired the public's imagination with his truly extraordinary demonstrations is the great American performer Kreskin. His appearances at concert halls, at colleges or on the small screen always lead to lively discussions among those who have witnessed his astounding feats of mentalism.

During one of his demonstrations, he asked a young woman to stand and, concentrating for a moment, told her that she was thinking of her boyfriend. She was asked to think of his name. In seconds, Kreskin revealed the name John, which the young lady acknowledged as being correct. His address and telephone number followed. She was asked to think of other members of her family and, wherever possible, their dates of birth. This took much longer but eventually the correct information was provided by Kreskin.

One of his experiments that causes a lot of comment is the hiding of his paycheck. Kreskin states that he will find the place where it has been concealed. If he is unsuccessful, the evening's entertainment will be given free of charge. Unusual hiding places used so far include the barrel of a gun, the leather binding of a book, a lady's brassiere and an envelope securely attached to the underside of a board taken from the stage and replaced. Kreskin has found them all.

Guns and Dollars

John Calvert, the globe-trotting magician and movie actor, includes in his magical spectacular Magicarama a blindfold act, which both thrills and mystifies his audiences and requires great skill and accuracy.

Taking a rifle, he fires at a number of selected targets, including bursting a balloon held between the lips of a spectator.

For the second part of his act, members of the audience are invited to blindfold the magician, using two silver dollars which are placed over his eyes and held in position with strips of adhesive tape. More tape is applied, covering most of the upper half of his face.

On being handed the rifle, Calvert fires at a number of targets, hitting them with uncanny accuracy, and brings the act to a close by hitting a walnut, precariously balanced on the head of an assisting spectator.

A mystery described in his program as Halley's Comet involves levitating a large silver sphere, which slowly rises from a box held by an assistant to float mysteriously around the stage, even passing through a wooden hoop held by the magician. It finally returns to the box, bringing to a conclusion a delightful routine which, with the specially selected background music and John Calvert's showmanship, makes this item one of the highlights of the show.

Master Showpieces

Suspensions and levitations have been seen in the programs of most of the master magicians. John Nevil Maskelyne, Harry Kellar and Howard Thurston all included a version of The Floating Lady illusion, each with his own particular presentation.

Doug Henning made a great impression with his version of this illusion during a recent television show, when he suspended a young lady above the "dancing waters", a series of fountains illuminated by colored lights.

In the late 1840s, when many new discoveries were being made in science and medicine, the French magician Jean Eugène Robert-Houdin presented a suspension that was topical because it tied in with the use of ether as a general anesthetic. He called his mystery The Ethereal Suspension, a title soon to be copied by some of his competitors. It was described in his programs as "Suspension in equilibrium by atmospheric air, through the action of concentrated ether".

In his introduction, Robert-Houdin explained: "When this liquid is at its highest degree of concentration, if a living person breathes it, the body of the patient becomes, in a few seconds, as light as a balloon."

Three stools were placed side by side on a wooden plank that was supported by two small trestles. Robert-Houdin's six-year-old son, Eugène, stood on the center stool at his father's bidding. He rested his elbows on two canes, balanced on the two outside stools.

The magician removed the cork from a glass bottle, which he held under the boy's nose for a few seconds. Members of the audience became aware of ether fumes drifting across the auditorium. Eugène's eyes then closed and his father removed the center stool, leaving the boy precariously suspended on the canes. The cane and stool at his left were then taken away, so that all of the boy's weight rested on the remaining cane. Placing his hand under the boy's feet, the magician raised him into a horizontal position, where he remained.

Right: Kalanag, the German illusionist, making his wife levitate until she floats mysteriously high above his head.

Far right: Indian magician Gogia Pasha (1910-76) presenting the exciting Sword Suspension during a Magic Circle Christmas Show.

GOGIA PASHA

Finally, lifting the plank of wood slightly, Robert-Houdin eased away the trestle supporting the boy's weight. Not only was the boy balancing on one elbow in a horizontal position but also the plank remained in position although supported at only one end.

A fine presentation of this mystery was given before an audience of almost 1,000 magicians, who attended the Annual Convention of The International Brotherhood of Magicians (British Ring), held in Britain in September 1985. Jon Marshall included the illusion in a program dealing with the history of magic.

Many magicians presented suspensions of various types in their programs but it was John Nevil Maskelyne who originated the levitation of a lady. She was hypnotized and lowered into a stone sarcophagus from which, a few seconds later, she arose, stayed suspended in the air for a while, then gracefully returned to the sarcophagus and was brought out of her trance.

J.N. Maskelyne's son, Nevil, added an extra convincing touch to the illusion. He introduced a large steel hoop, which he passed over the lady as she remained suspended, "proving" that there were not any attachments.

The Maskelyne levitation was presented in the United States by Harry Kellar and later by his successor, Howard Thurston, who both used the same title for the illusion, The Levitation of Princess Karnac. It is believed that Kellar witnessed a presentation of the mystery during a visit to Maskelyne's Egyptian Hall and, recognizing its drawing power, decided that it should become a featured item in his own program. He offered large sums of money for the secret of the illusion but was refused.

Right: Readers of *Scientific American* in the 1890s were regaled with exposures of illusions, including "The Illusion of Trilby" as performed by Alexander Herrmann (1844-96), seen here in the role of Svengali. The board on which Trilby reclines is initially supported by two chair backs, which are then removed, leaving the board in mid-air. The board and Trilby float up and down at Svengali's command.

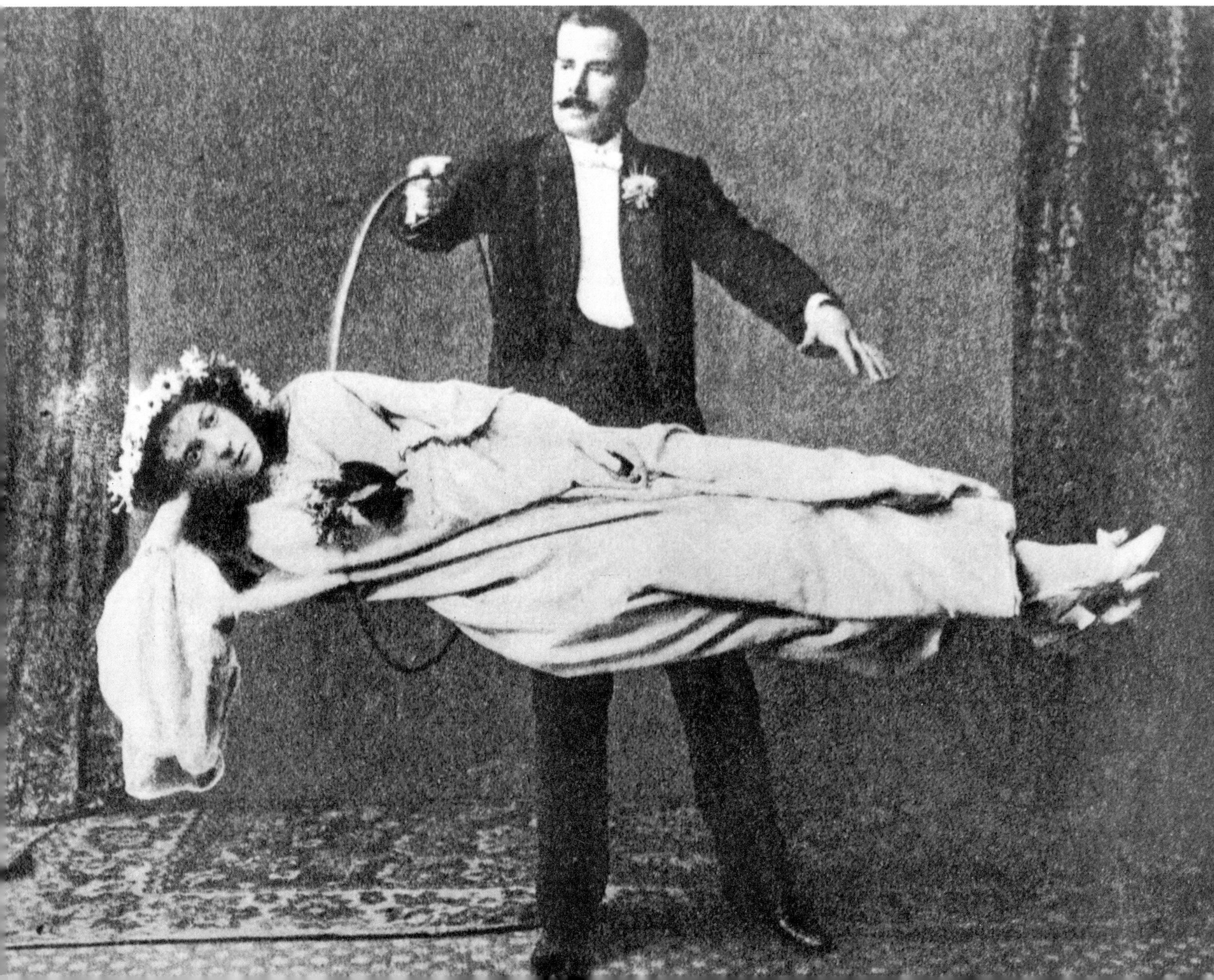

Below: David Devant passes a hoop over the floating girl to prove there are no supports holding her in the air. At the height of his career Devant was stricken by a progressive disease that eventually left him paralyzed.

Kellar nonetheless introduced the levitation into his show, helped, probably, by Paul Valadon. Valadon had worked for Maskelyne for the previous three years, before joining Harry Kellar's company. He hoped to become the successor to the great magician. Valadon was disappointed, however, as Kellar chose another successor. Howard Thurston purchased the Kellar show, including the Princess Karnac illusion.

One of the most mysterious and impressive presentations of The Floating Lady was that of the German magician, Kalanag. The title of his show, Sim Sala Bim, was "acquired" from Dante, the great Danish-American showman, who had presented his magical revue of that name in Berlin in 1939. Kalanag's chief assistant was Gloria de Vos, who has been described as "the most beautiful woman in magic".

The curtains opened for the levitation sequence, revealing an Indian backdrop dominated by a large, eight-armed idol. Kalanag positioned two wooden chairs in the center of the stage and placed a board across the chair backs. The lovely Gloria reclined on the board while Kalanag made a few mesmeric passes, apparently causing her to fall into a trance.

The illusionist carefully removed one of the chairs and then the other. Gloria remained lying on the board with no visible means of support. The board was then removed and she remained in mid-air. A large hoop was handed to Kalanag, who passed it over and around his assistant. She then slowly began to rise high in the air. After a few moments, she slowly descended and stood beside the magician, as they took their bows to tremendous applause. It was a wonderful piece of magical stagecraft.

6

CARD MYSTERIES

Left: A colorful stage setting for Le Grand David and his own Spectacular Magic Show at the Cabot Street Theatre, Beverly, Massachusetts.

Above: The American magician Carter the Great (Charles Joseph Carter, 1874-1936) toured the world with his big illusion show. He was generally successful, apart from the Temple of Mystery that he performed at the Chicago World's Fair in 1933, which proved a failure.

Some Victorian magicians added the prefix "Professor" to their names to lend an air of scientific authority. Professor Hoffmann, the author of what has become known as the magicians' "bible", *Modern Magic* published in 1876, and the American Professor John Wyman, a well-known entertainer of his day, both used the title. Whenever a modern magician talks about The Professor, however, there is only one man to whom he can be referring: David Frederick Wingfield Verner, known to his many admirers throughout the world of magic as Dai Vernon.

He was born in Canada in 1894 and at the age of ninety-one still retains his interest in magic. In his teens he was performing tricks for his fellow students at Ashbury College, Ottawa, and entertained dukes, lords and ladies at Government House there. In later years, he played theaters and night clubs to supplement the family income which came from his work as a silhouette artist.

In the late 1930s, he created a special "Harlequin" act for the prestigious Radio City Music Hall that was described as "an artistic triumph" but he preferred the intimacy of close-up magic, which he considered to be his real medium. Dai Vernon was able to take ordinary tricks and transform them into minor miracles, by simple sleight-of-hand.

A knowledgeable magician, who knew many of the "greats" personally, said that Dai Vernon was "the greatest man with a deck of cards in the world today".

"I Only Cheat a Little"

"Honest to goodness, Ladies and Gentlemen, I only cheat a little" was a favorite saying of Max Malini, who had a completely different personality to either Cardini or Dai Vernon. He has been described as "bold, brusque and offensive" but in spite of these criticisms he

CARDINI

A magician who took some of the items used in his act and made them part of his name was Welsh-born Richard Valentine Pitchford, who moved to America and became a world-famous manipulator, using the stage name Cardini.

Dressed in top hat and tails, wearing white gloves and sporting a monocle, he was the complete "man about town". Rather tipsily, he discovered fans of playing cards in his gloved hands. No matter how quickly he disposed of them, more appeared, followed by billiard balls and lighted cigarettes. He made his exit smoking a pipe, which suddenly appeared, and received thunderous applause, on occasion stopping the show.

Cardini's act was copied by hundreds of magicians but none of them achieved the greatness of the original. Sadly, Cardini never received the rewards he so richly deserved. He played many of the top hotels and theaters in Britain and the United States, including an appearance in a Royal Variety Show at the London Palladium in 1933, in the presence of King George V of Britain and Queen Mary.

His act was described by one reviewer as being as near perfect as humanly possible and the Society of American Magicians made a special award to him, naming him as "the greatest sleight-of-hand man of all times".

rubbed shoulders with royalty and commanded very high fees for his private performances.

He was born Max Breit, in the little town of Ostrow on the Polish-Austrian border. When he was a small child, his family emigrated to the United States and settled in New York. He was introduced to magic by a Professor Seidon but his real learning came from the hard school of experience. He busked in saloons for money, working in the most difficult conditions. He became an accomplished sleight-of-hand performer and a master of misdirection – that is, of distracting and confusing his audience to increase the impact of a trick. His hands were small and when he palmed poker-sized playing cards he was unable to conceal them completely but his skill was so great that he could perform this sleight without his audience seeing the cards.

He worked mainly in hotels and drew attention to himself by mixing in the bar with the guests and showing what appeared to be impromptu magic, using items that were to hand like glasses, corks, coasters or coins. The most talked-about of his impromptu mysteries was the production of a block of ice, or on some occasions a house brick, from under a borrowed hat.

When he had established himself, he approached guests and asked them to buy tickets for a program of magic that he was presenting in the hotel ballroom. They had been impressed by his impromptu mysteries, so they bought the tickets and Malini made a substantial profit from his two-hour performance.

His most remembered mystery is the Card Stab, a classic which Malini brought to perfection. A number of cards were selected by members of the audience and returned to the pack. A spectator assisted by borrowing a couple of handkerchiefs and blindfolding the magician, who then scattered the pack of cards on a small table. Using a borrowed penknife, he asked the name of the first card to be selected and, without hesitation, thrust the penknife among the apparently mixed cards. He impaled one, which he then showed to be the card named. This procedure continued with the remaining cards but when he came to the final selected card he stabbed right through the card and into the table, which he tipped, causing all the cards to slide to the floor, leaving only the stabbed card. Retrieving the knife from the table, he showed the card to be the one selected.

He was once admonished by a friend for damaging a valuable table belonging to his hostess, with the final stab. Malini remained imperturbable. "In years to come," he said, "she will be able to tell her friends that upon this table the great Malini performed one of his famous tricks".

Right: Cardini (Richard Valentine Pitchford, 1896-1973) pioneered the immaculate, manipulative style of magic act and was one of the most imitated conjurers of all time. Fans of cards, cigarettes and billiard balls materialized at his finger tips as he portrayed the slightly tipsy English gentleman in full evening dress. He was assisted by his wife Swan who dressed as a page boy.

Below: Max Malini (Max Breit, 1875-1942) is legendary for his skill and audacity. Principally he entertained royalty and the aristocracy in their own homes, rarely appearing in theaters. He was born in Poland and emigrated to the U.S.A. at an early age.

TH' FANS GO FOR THOSE CARD-(INI) TRICKS
IN A GREAT BIG WAY ~ AN' THIS CLEVER
AN' SOPHISTICATED MAN O' MAGIC HAS
WHAT IT TAKES TO AMUSE-THRILL-
AN' MYSTIFY TH' AUDIENCE!
BELIEVE IT
OR KNOT!
OUT O' TH' AIR
FOR TH'
LADY FAIR!
MONARCH OF
ALL HE SURVEYS ~
IN MAGIC!
D. E.

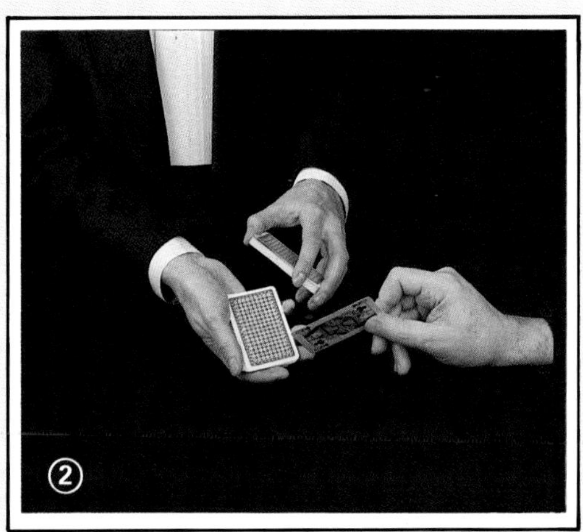

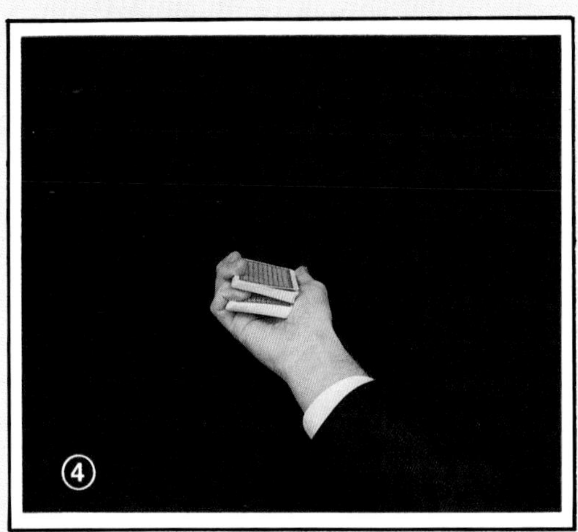

The Card Stab I

1 A pack of cards, shuffled by a member of the audience, is returned to the performer, who asks another spectator to select a card.
2 The performer cuts the pack and offers the lower half for the card to be replaced.
3 The upper half of the pack is placed on the spectator's card and, from the audience's point of view, everything seems fair. The card has been buried somewhere in the pack.
4 What actually happens is that, as the upper half of the pack is placed on the selected card, the performer inserts his little finger between the two halves, making a "break".
5 The performer shuffles the pack by taking the stock of cards above the finger break and depositing them underneath the lower cards. This is simply a cut, which brings the selected card to the top of the pack.
6 Without hesitating, the overhand shuffle is continued, but throughout the spectator's card is retained in its position, at the top of the pack. The simplest way to retain the top card while performing the overhand shuffle involves shuffling the cards with their faces, i.e. the bottom of the pack, towards the audience, and the top card nearest the palm. A block of cards is taken from the rear, i.e. the top of the pack and packets of cards are dropped alternately in front and behind those in the left hand, but the final packet is dropped behind the other cards, which leaves the top card in position. This procedure can be repeated.
7 The cards are haphazardly spread on the table, face down, but the performer keeps track of the selected card. The right forefinger shows the position of this card.
8 Making a circular movement around the cards using either a knife, ball point pen or pencil, the performer stabs the chosen card.
9 Finally, the performer reveals the card to the spectator.

The Card Stab I

Max Malini, in his version of the Card Stab, used sleight-of-hand to bring about the desired result. The version about to be described is simpler, with a minimum of sleights, yet quite effective.

From a shuffled pack, a spectator selects a card and writes his signature on the face. The card is returned, the pack shuffled, and the cards spread haphazardly on a wooden tray. The peformer is blindfolded with one or more handkerchiefs and, taking a dagger or ball-point pen, he thrusts it downwards among the cards. Raising the dagger and removing the blindfold, he shows the signed card, impaled upon the blade, or pinned beneath the pen.

There are a number of basic magical principles used in this mystery, which can be applied to other tricks, but they should be carefully studied and rehearsed before presenting the effect to an audience.

An ordinary pack of cards is used and may be shuffled by a member of the audience. When the pack is returned, the magician fans the cards and asks for a card to be selected and the person's name to be written on the face. In receiving back the card, the performer cuts the pack somewhere near the center and offers the lower half for the chosen card to be placed on the top. The two halves of the pack are brought together, but not before the left-hand little fingertip is inserted above the selected card and a "break" is held. From the audience's point of view, the cut has been completed and the card lost somewhere in the center of the pack.

The pack is given an overhand shuffle (see page 113), which is begun by lifting the stock of cards above the little finger and depositing them behind the lower cards. This cut is simply a way of bringing the selected card to the top, where it is kept as, without hesitation, the overhand shuffle is continued.

The cards are scattered on the tray but in the mixing the performer keeps his finger on the selected card and notes its final position. He is blindfolded by a spectator but can in fact still see down the sides of his nose. As he takes the dagger, he already knows the position of the chosen card. Thrusting the dagger among the cards, he impales the signed card and shows it to the spectator, who acknowledges that it is his selected card.

Card Stab II

This version of the Card Stab relies on another principle widely used in card magic.

The performer shuffles a pack of cards and asks a spectator to cut the cards and place his cards on the table. The performer completes the cut but places the cards across the lower cards. He explains to the audience that the cards have been shuffled and cut by a spectator and it is impossible to tell at what card the cut has been made.

He removes the upper cards, asks the spectator to look at the top card of the lower heap, remember it, and push it into the heap of cards on the table. The performer then hands him the rest of the cards, with a request to shuffle the cards and then to spread them face-down on the table.

A sheet of newspaper is spread over the cards and, taking a dagger, the magician stabs through the newspaper and the scattered cards. The newspaper is torn away, revealing a card impaled on the dagger blade, which proves to be the one chosen by the spectator.

The mystery is dependent on the "conjurer's choice". The card is apparently freely selected by the spectator but he has in fact been forced to take the card that the magician wanted him to have. There are many ways of "forcing" cards but the simplest is the best.

Deciding which card is to be used in the Card Stab, the magician prepares for the trick by placing that card on the top of the pack. To present the mystery, he shuffles the cards, keeping the "force" card at the top. The pack is placed on the table and a spectator is asked to cut the cards. The magician takes the remaining cards and lays them crosswise on the spectator's cards. The "force" card is on the top of the lower heap.

The audience is reminded that the cards have been shuffled and cut by a spectator. This is merely misdirection, in which the audience's attention is turned away from the cards. In fact, of course, it is the performer himself who has shuffled the pack. Removing the upper half of the pack, the magician asks the spectator to take the top card to which he has cut, remember it, and replace it somewhere in that pile. He is given the rest of the cards and asked to mix them thoroughly, then to spread them on the table.

The magician then takes a sheet of newspaper and spreads it over the cards. The newspaper has a pocket that contains a duplicate of the "force" card (or the duplicate may simply be attached to the back of the newspaper with a dab of wax). Knowing the position of this card, the magician stabs through it and, tearing away the newspaper, reveals the chosen card impaled on the dagger.

The Overhand Shuffle *(right)*
1 A block of cards is taken from the rear of the pack.
2 The cards are dropped alternately in front and behind those held in the left hand.
3 More cards are taken, and the procedure is repeated.

A Forcing Pack

It was mentioned in Card Stab II that there are many ways of forcing cards. Special packs are available from magic dealers for this purpose. The simplest is the "all alike" pack, which contains fifty-two identical cards; for instance, the queen of hearts. The cards may be cut and shuffled and a card selected from anywhere in the pack, and naturally the card chosen will always be the queen of hearts.

It is a good idea to place an indifferent card on the face of the pack, so that if a spectator catches a glimpse of the bottom card he will not become suspicious. An ordinary pack with the same back design should be at hand, so that it can be switched for the "all alike" pack, if necessary, to allay suspicion.

Below: This is an "all alike" forcing pack, in which all the cards are the same, with the exception of the face card.

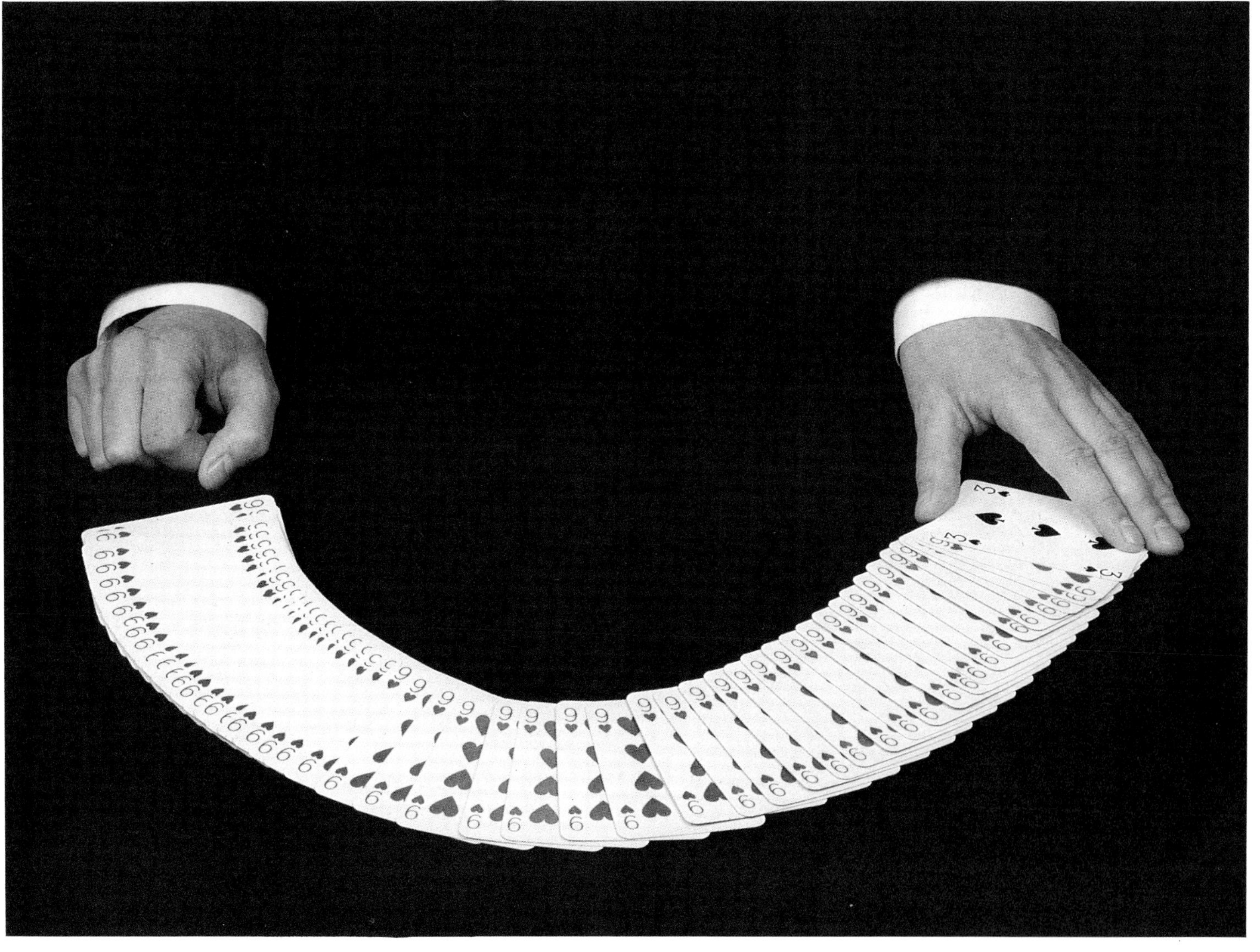

A Prearranged Pack

Some great mysteries can be presented using a pack of cards set in a prearranged order. To make it convincing, however, it is necessary to appear to mix the cards beforehand. One of the oldest, and most often used, prearrangements is known as the "Eight–King–Three" system.

When it is written down, the system seems to require a gigantic feat of memory but it is easily remembered by a couplet.

Eight kings threatened to save
Nine fair ladies for one sick knave

The couplet includes all the cards from Ace to King.

8 K 3 10 2 7
9 5 Q 4 A 6 J

The order of the suits is clubs, hearts, spades, diamonds; this can be memorized by the word CHaSeD. The pack is arranged by starting at the beginning of each sequence – eight of clubs – and running through, repeating the sequence as necessary.

To make everything clear, the table set out below shows the position of every card in the pack, starting from the top left. The first card should be the eight of clubs then the king of hearts, the three of spades and so on.

8C	8H	8S	8D
KH	KS	KD	KC
3S	3D	3C	3H
10D	10C	10H	10S
2C	2H	2S	2D
7H	7S	7D	7C
9S	9D	9C	9H
5D	5C	5H	5S
QC	QH	QS	QD
4H	4S	4D	4C
AS	AD	AC	AH
6D	6C	6H	6S
JC	JH	JS	JD

No matter how many times the cards are given a single cut, the pack remains in the same sequence.

To give the appearance of mixing the cards, a number of single cuts may be used but a better way is to take the pack in the left hand, push off a few cards with the left thumb and take them in the right hand. Push a few cards from the bottom of the pack onto the cards in the right hand. Push off more cards with the left thumb and place them below the cards in the right hand. Carry out this procedure until all the cards are in the right hand. With practice, this can be done swiftly so that it appears to the spectators that the cards have been thoroughly mixed.

Here are some tricks using the prearranged pack:

Card Revelation

The cards are mixed and fanned before a spectator, who is asked to take a card. The performer turns his back while the person looks at it, and eventually the performer reveals the name of the chosen card.

The cards are fanned while the spectator selects a card. Immediately, the performer takes all the cards above the one being selected and puts them underneath the rest of the pack. He turns his back, ostensibly so that he will not catch a glimpse of the spectator's card, but really to take a quick look at the bottom card of the pack. Knowing the sequence, he mentally moves one ahead in the number and in the suit. If, for instance, the bottom card is the seven of clubs, he knows that the next number in the sequence is a nine (8 – K – 3 – 10 – 2 – 7 – 9) and the following suit is hearts (CHased). By the same method, if the bottom card had been the ace of diamonds, he would have known that the chosen card was the six of clubs.

Once learned, the system can be used in many different ways, but it is not enough to say, "And your card is the seven of spades". The performer should appear to be searching for inspiration and reveal the name of the card a little at a time. For example:

> "Sir, your card is, I believe, a red card, it's a heart, no – wait a moment, it's a diamond. It's a red, it's a diamond. I don't think it's a picture card, no, it's a smaller card. Yes, I would say that your card is a red card, a diamond, it's the four of diamonds."

①

A Plural Revelation

Still using the prearranged pack, here is another mystery which, to an audience, seems impossible.

The pack of cards is mixed and a spectator asked to cut the cards. He is then told to take approximately ten cards from the top of the pack, mix them and distribute them to the people around him, keeping one for himself.

When this has been done, the magician concentrates for a moment, then reveals one by one the cards held by the spectators. As each card is called, the person holding it is asked to hold it up so that everyone can see that the revelations are correct.

③

A spectator takes about ten cards from the pack and the performer, in returning the remainder of the pack to the table, looks at the bottom card. Because of the sequence, he then knows the name of the top card. The spectator is asked to count his cards, mix them and distribute them to members of the audience. The shuffling of the cards does not mean a thing so far as the working of the trick is concerned but it implants in the minds of the spectators the idea that a shuffled pack was used throughout the demonstration. The magician, remembering the system, discloses the identities of the cards by mentally counting through the sequence until he arrives at the number specified by the spectator.

⑤

The Short Card

This is a device that is easily made and has many uses in card magic. A card is trimmed at one end and the corners rounded like those of the other cards. A joker may be preferred to avoid damaging other cards. The difference between the short card and the others is so slight that it will not be noticed.

When the card is mixed in the pack, it can be located by riffling one end of the cards. To riffle a pack of cards, the pack is held firmly in the left hand, face downwards, with the fingers underneath and the thumb on the top. The right fingers raise the end of the pack nearest the audience and, by releasing the pressure, the cards are allowed to spring back into position. When the riffling stops momentarily, the magician knows that he has arrived at the short card. Another name for this card is the "locator" card.

To force a card, for instance the five of spades, the card is put on top of the short card and both are placed together in the pack. The magician tells a spectator that he is going to riffle through the pack and asks the man to shout "Stop" whenever he wishes.

If the magician is stopped before he arrives at the short card, he allows the cards to run until the short card is reached. It is done so quickly that it is hardly noticed. Without hesitation, the magician asks that the face card of the cards he is holding be remembered. It is, of course, the force card.

The spectator may not call "Stop" until after the short card has been passed. The

⑦

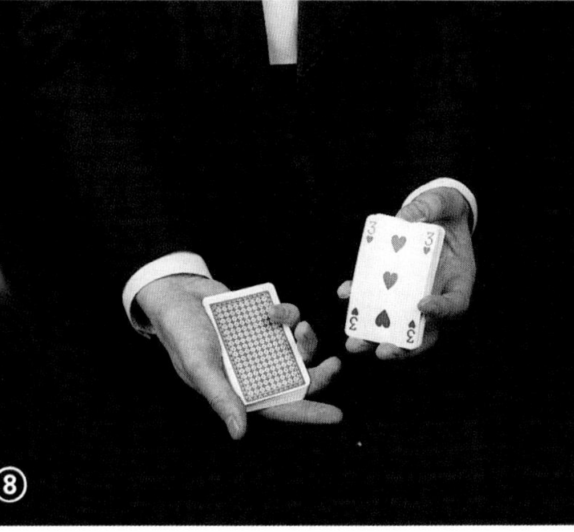

magician allows the rest of the cards to riffle through, asking the spectator to be quicker in calling. The pack is riffled once more and stops at the short card.

Just a Thought

Another "thought-reading" mystery in which the short card is employed has a simple plot.

A spectator takes from a shuffled pack any card, which he replaces in the center of the pack. He is asked to concentrate on first the color, then the suit and finally the number on the card. The identity of the card is gradually revealed by the performer and confirmed by the spectator as being his "thought-of" card.

A pack of cards is shuffled and cut, bringing the short card to the top. The cards are fanned to allow a spectator to choose a card. The pack is closed and an undercut made. To undercut the cards, the pack is held between the left thumb and fingers, face-down. It does not rest on the palm of the hand. The right thumb and fingers draw away the lower half of the pack and the cards in the left hand, with the short card on top, rest on the left palm. These cards are offered to the spectator so that his card may be placed on the top, and the cut is completed.

"Somewhere in the pack," says the performer, "is the card about which the gentleman is thinking". While he is speaking, the performer casually riffles through the pack, noting the spectator's card and eventually revealing its identity.

It may be preferable simply to cut the pack at the short card, which will bring the chosen card to the bottom. While he is speaking, the performer catches a glimpse of the card.

One final point. It is more impressive to ask the spectator to concentrate on the card "of which he is *thinking*," rather than for him "to remember the card he selected". This form of words means that members of the audience who talk about this mystery later will remember how the performer revealed a card that was simply "thought-of" rather than one in which a card was physically chosen.

The Short Card *(left)*
1 This card is made by trimming a thin piece from one end only and rounding the corners (it may be preferable to use a joker). The difference between the short card and the rest is so slight, it is not noticeable.
2 The short card is placed on the top of the pack. You can see it in the photograph immediately beneath the performer's left thumb.
3 A card is chosen by a spectator; while he is looking at it, the pack is closed.
4 The performer undercuts the pack. In other words, he draws away the lower half. The short card is on the top of the cards held in the right hand.
5 These are now held forward for the return of the spectator's card, which is placed on the top, and the cards in the left hand are dropped onto the selected card.
6 The performer riffles the cards, which automatically stop at the short card.
7 The card above the short card is the one chosen by the spectator.
8 The top portion of the pack is removed, showing that the face card is the chosen one.

Extraordinary Aces

One of the great classics of card magic is the Four Ace Trick, which has been demonstrated by magicians for several centuries. Through the years, there have been many variations in presentation and many methods of working but the basic plot remains the same.

The four aces are removed from the pack and laid face-down on the table. Three regular cards are placed on each of the aces and one heap chosen by a spectator. This heap is laid aside.

Taking the other heaps, one at a time, the performer deals the cards face-up on the table, revealing that the three aces have disappeared. When the spectator's heap is dealt, it is seen to contain the four aces.

Sleight-of-hand is used in many versions of this trick, but in this one the use of a short card helps to simplify matters. To prepare for the mystery, the short card is placed on the top of the pack and covered with three low-numbered cards.

To perform, the four aces are removed from the pack and handed to a spectator, who is asked to make sure that they are regular cards. The spectator affirms that they are and returns them to the magician, who lays them on the top of the pack and informs the spectator that they may seem ordinary but actually they are not. They are in fact extraordinary aces.

The four aces are apparently taken from the top of the pack but actually all the cards above the short card are lifted and held at a downward angle, so that the audience will not become suspicious that there are more than four cards in the performer's hand. Taking the first three aces, one at a time, the performer shows them and replaces them underneath the heap in his hand. The fourth ace is shown and replaced on the top. The cards are then dropped on top of the pack.

From the top, the cards now read: ace, three other cards and three aces. The performer lays the first four cards in a row, face-down on the table, claiming that they are the four aces. Starting with the first ace, three cards are dealt onto each of the four cards. All the aces will now be in the first heap, while the other three heaps contain other cards. The heaps are mixed, by exchanging the first heap for the third and the second for the fourth.

The aces are now in heap number three. The spectators are asked for a number between one and four. Usually someone calls "Three" and that heap is laid aside and is

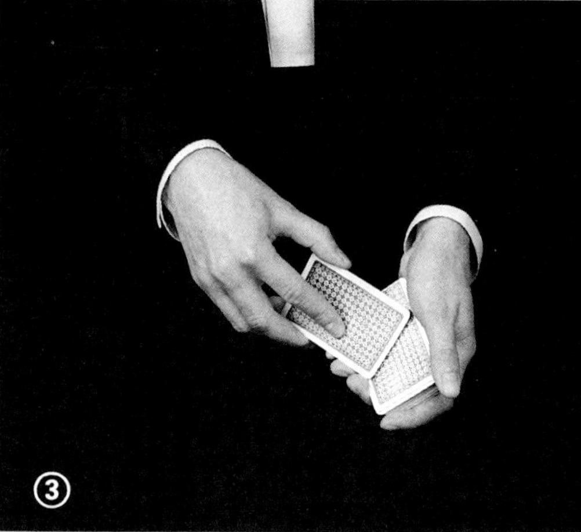

Extraordinary Aces *(right)*
Preparation The short card is placed on top of the pack, and three more cards are placed on the short card. The aces are scattered throughout the pack.
1 The four aces are removed from the pack and shown, face up, on the table.
2 The aces are collected and placed face down on the pack.
3 Asking the spectators if they can remember the order of the suits, the performer takes the aces from the top of the pack and shows them, one by one. In fact, he takes not only the four aces, but also the three other cards above the short one. These are held at a downwards angle so that the spectators are unable to see that he has taken more than four cards.
4 The top card is turned, shown and replaced beneath the rest. The second and third are shown and replaced underneath the other cards. The fourth ace is shown, but it is replaced *on top* of the cards.
5 Do *not* reveal the seven cards as shown here. This photograph has been taken to show the order of the cards. Reading from the bottom there are three aces, followed by three ordinary cards, and the last (top) card which is an ace.
6 These cards are dropped onto the rest of the pack. The top four cards, believed by the audience to be aces, are placed separately, face down, on the table. Three cards are placed on each of the four cards. Unknown to the audience, the first heap contains the aces. Apparently mixing the heaps of cards, the performer exchanges the first heap for the third, and the second for the fourth. The aces are now in third place.
7 A spectator is asked for a number *between* one and four. If he says "Three", count from the left. If he says "Two", count from the right. The chosen heap is put to one side.
8 The remaining three heaps are shown, one by one, revealing that the ace in each heap has disappeared.
9 When the heap selected by the spectator is shown, it is seen to consist of the four aces.

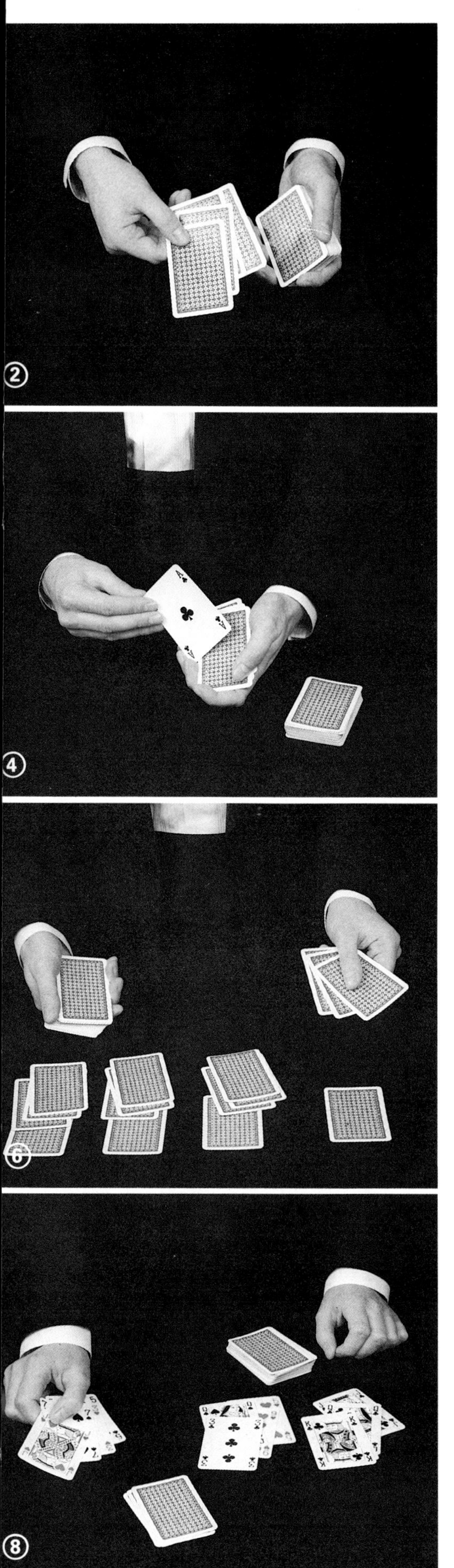

later shown to contain the aces. If "Two" is called, the heaps are counted from the opposite end of the line, with the same result. If "One" or "Four" is called, the performer emphasizes that he asked for a number between one and four.

Another way to force a heap is to ask the spectator to put his hands on two of the heaps. If the ace heap is one of them, he is asked to raise one hand. If the aces are left under his hand, he is asked to place the other hand on top, to prevent any trickery, and the other heap is removed. If the ace heap is the one from which his hand is lifted, the performer asks him if that is his final choice, the spectator agrees and the performer says that he will use that heap. The cards are taken from under the spectator's hand and discarded with the other two.

If, however, the spectator does not put his hands on the aces heap in the first place, the performer says, "You have left me with two heaps, please select one". If the aces heap is indicated, all well and good. If not, he says "So, you have left me with one heap". The performer manipulates the heaps so that the one chosen is that which contains the aces.

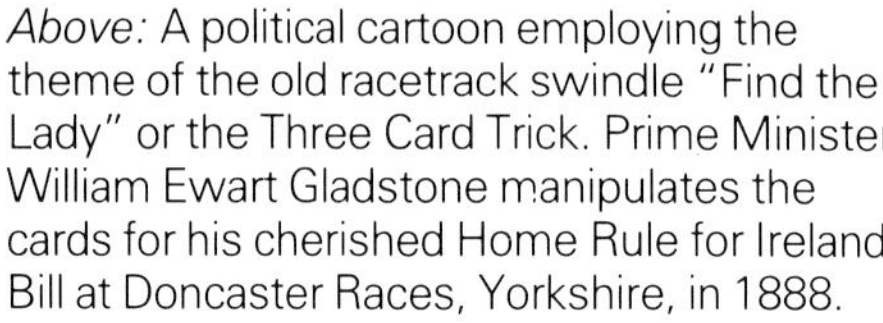

Above: A political cartoon employing the theme of the old racetrack swindle "Find the Lady" or the Three Card Trick. Prime Minister William Ewart Gladstone manipulates the cards for his cherished Home Rule for Ireland Bill at Doncaster Races, Yorkshire, in 1888.

Find the Lady

The Three Card Trick, or Find the Lady, is an age-old swindle that is still being demonstrated today, by street and race-course tricksters. No matter how often members of the public are warned not to take part in these "games", they foolishly believe that they can beat the man running the game.

Three cards are shown, the center one being the queen. They are thrown face-down on an improvised "table" and the victim is invited to bet money on the card he thinks is the "Lady". Although it seems obvious that the queen is in the center, the performer rearranges the cards by a sleight-of-hand. When the central card is revealed, it is one of the other two cards and the Lady is on one side.

This trick relies on sleight-of-hand. The cards are held between the thumb and second finger and thrown onto the table with a smooth action. The performer must be adept at releasing the bottom card while appearing to release the top one. This leaves the spectator confident that he has followed the Lady with his eye when in fact he has been misled. A great deal of practice is needed in learning how to "throw" the cards but once the operator has mastered it, the spectator will always be the loser.

Find the Lady *(right)*

1 To prepare for this mystery, the queen of diamonds is placed on top of the pack, and the short card is placed on the queen.
2 Presentation. The top two cards are turned as one, showing the queen, and replaced on top of the pack.
3 The top card (short), believed by the audience to be the queen, is inserted somewhere near the center of the pack.
4 Riffling the cards, the performer shows that the top card is the queen.
5 The pack is cut at the short card, to receive the queen.
6 The queen is placed on the short card.
7 The remainder of the cards are dropped onto the queen, completing the cut.
8 The performer claims that, by cutting the cards once, he can make the queen re-appear on top of the pack. He cuts at the short card, placing the upper half of the pack underneath the rest. The top card is turned, but it is not the queen.
9 Undeterred, the performer says that he will "control" the queen, moving her to the bottom of the pack. Riffling the cards, he pauses.
10 Slowly turning the pack he shows that the bottom card is the queen of diamonds.

2

3

4

5

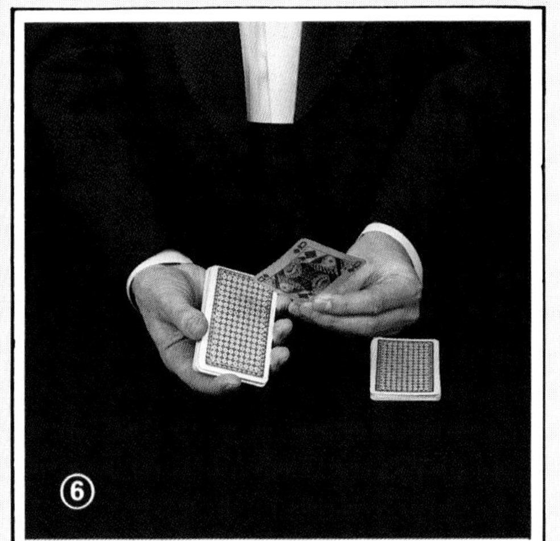
6

8

9

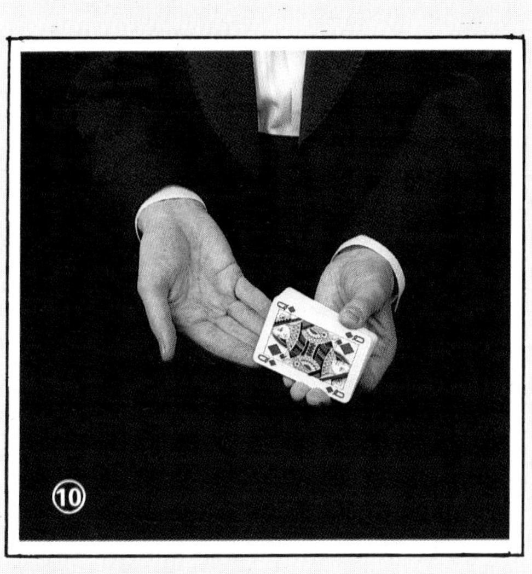
10

While the version just discussed is practised only by swindlers, similar principles can create excellent card tricks that do not involve stealing from the audience! Interest can be created by talking about the street-corner swindlers, while demonstrating how it is possible to make the Lady vanish and appear in different parts of the pack.

The Lady (queen of hearts) is laid face-up on the top of the pack. It is then placed face-down in the center of the pack. Immediately turning over the top card, the performer reveals the queen of hearts. It is placed once more in the center and the magician says that he will find the Lady by cutting the cards once. He cuts the pack and, turning over the card, discovers that it is not the queen. It appears that he has failed but he says that he will "control" the queen so that she will travel to the bottom of the pack. He taps the cards and, turning them over, shows that the bottom card is indeed the queen of hearts. He then leaves the cards on the table, so that the onlookers can check to see if more than one queen of hearts was used in the demonstration.

To prepare for the trick, the queen of hearts is placed next to the top card in the pack and the short card is near the center. In presenting the mystery, the top two cards are turned as one and laid face-up on the top of the face-down pack. The right thumb and fingers retain their hold on the card(s) which are then turned face-down on the pack again. Only the top card is removed and pushed into the center. The new top card is now tapped and, when turned, is shown to be the queen.

The pack is cut at the short card and the queen laid on top of it. The rest of the cards are placed on top. The onlookers are informed that the magician will, with one cut of the cards, reveal the queen of hearts. The pack is cut at the short card and the upper cards placed under the rest.

The magician appears to have failed when he turns the top (short) card and it is not the queen but redeems himself when he "controls" the queen to the bottom of the pack.

Dual Discovery

In this card mystery, everything seems to be under the control of two volunteer assistants but despite this restriction the performer is able to work his magic.

Two volunteers are each handed half of the pack to shuffle. They each select a card, memorize it, and place it face-down among the cards held by the other person. Again, the cards are thoroughly shuffled. The magician invites the volunteers to try and find the other person's chosen card and, when they are unable to do so, he takes one card from

The Riffle Shuffle *(below)*
1 The pack is divided into two halves, which are held with the thumbs at one end, and the fingers at the other. The bent forefingers apply pressure, causing the cards to bend.
2 The thumbs release the cards which fall onto the table.
3 As the cards fall alternately from each packet, they interweave.
4 At the conclusion of the shuffle, the cards are picked up, still interwoven.
5 The outer ends are held in place, at the base of the fingers of each hand. The hands are brought together forcing the cards into an arc. The thumbs, at the top of the arc, prevent the cards from springing apart.
6 The hands release pressure, and the cards fall into place on the fingers.

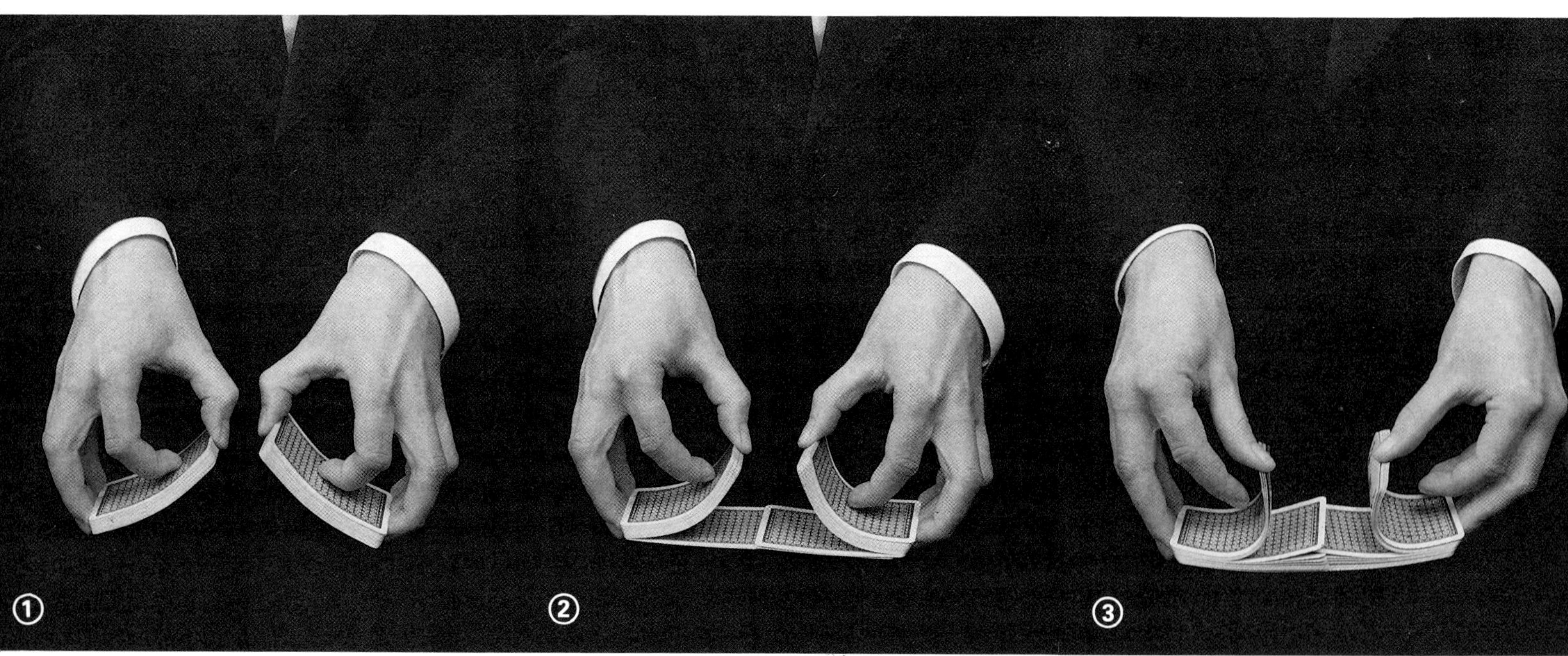

each person and lays them face-down on the table. The volunteers are asked to name their cards and, turning over the two cards, the magician shows that they are the ones named.

The pack of cards is prearranged by putting all the odd-numbered red cards and even-numbered black cards in one half, and all the even-numbered red cards and odd-numbered black cards in the other. Picture cards count: jack = 11, queen = 12, king = 13. This arrangement will not be noticed by the volunteer assistants, as there are cards of all suits, high and low, in each half. The shuffling convinces the onlookers that it is impossible for the magician to discover the two cards but does not affect the original division of the pack. When the volunteers have exchanged their chosen cards, the magician can easily identify the "stranger" cards.

Class Distinction

The magician claims that through constantly handling playing cards, he is able to distinguish between court cards and spot cards by touch. As most people can tell the difference only when looking at the faces of the cards, his claim meets with derision.

A spectator shuffles a pack of cards and counts twelve out on the table, face-down. Without turning them over, the magician takes the cards, one at a time, between his thumb and second finger, apparently weighing them. He drops the cards into two heaps. When the heaps are turned over, the spot cards are in one heap and the court cards in the other.

Members of the public who have witnessed a demonstration of card magic sometimes dismiss the performer's ability by saying that he was using marked cards. "Readers", as they are called in the magical profession, are in fact rarely used, as so many good tricks can be performed without them.

In this mystery, however, marked cards are used. Nonetheless, at the conclusion of a demonstration, anyone who is suspicious may closely examine the designs on the backs of the cards, without anything being discovered. Only the twelve court cards are marked, not on their backs, but on their edges.

The court cards are taken and squared so that all the edges are even, and a line is drawn with a pencil across the edges of the cards, near the right top corner. The cards are turned and a line is drawn across the diagonally opposite corner. When the cards are separated, only a dot appears on the edge of each card, which is rarely noticed by a spectator but is easily recognized by the magician who knows its location.

Class Distinction *(below)*
The picture cards are marked along the edge so that when they are distributed through the pack they can easily be distinguished by a dot.

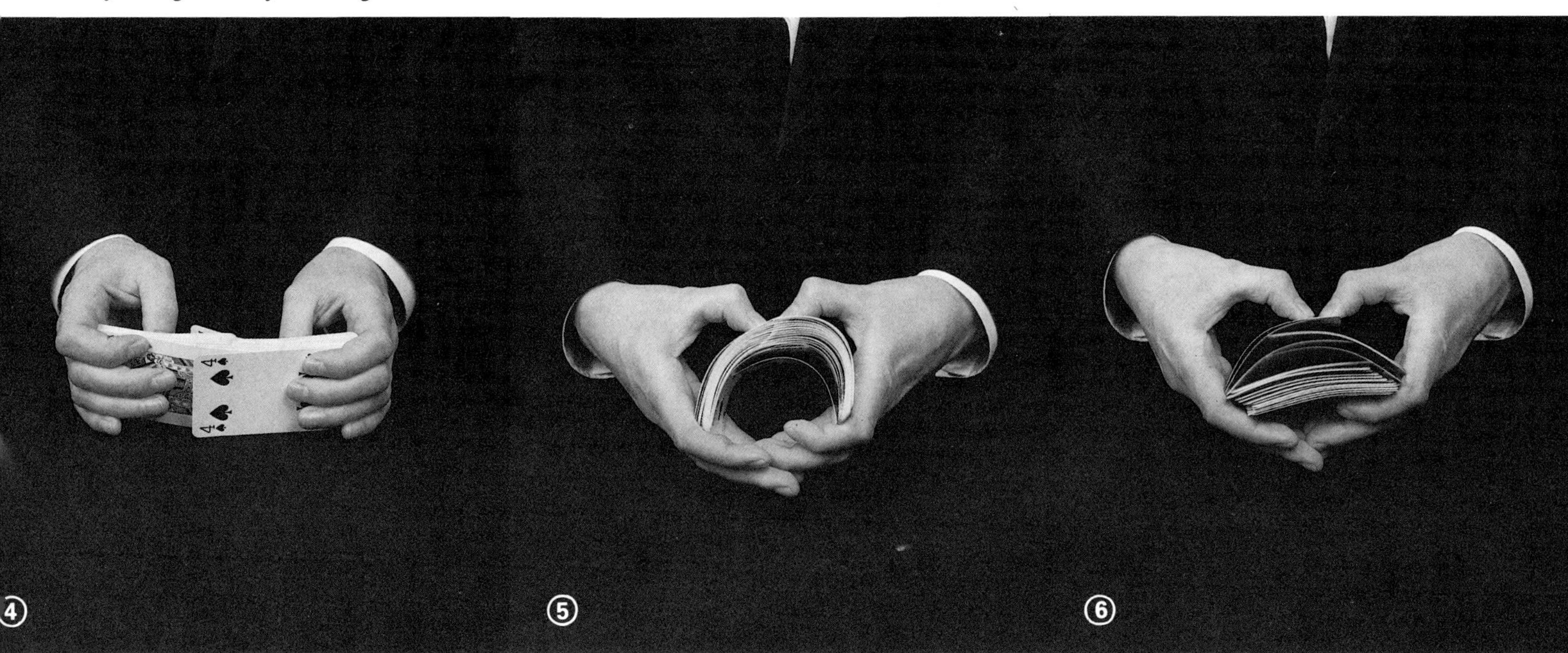

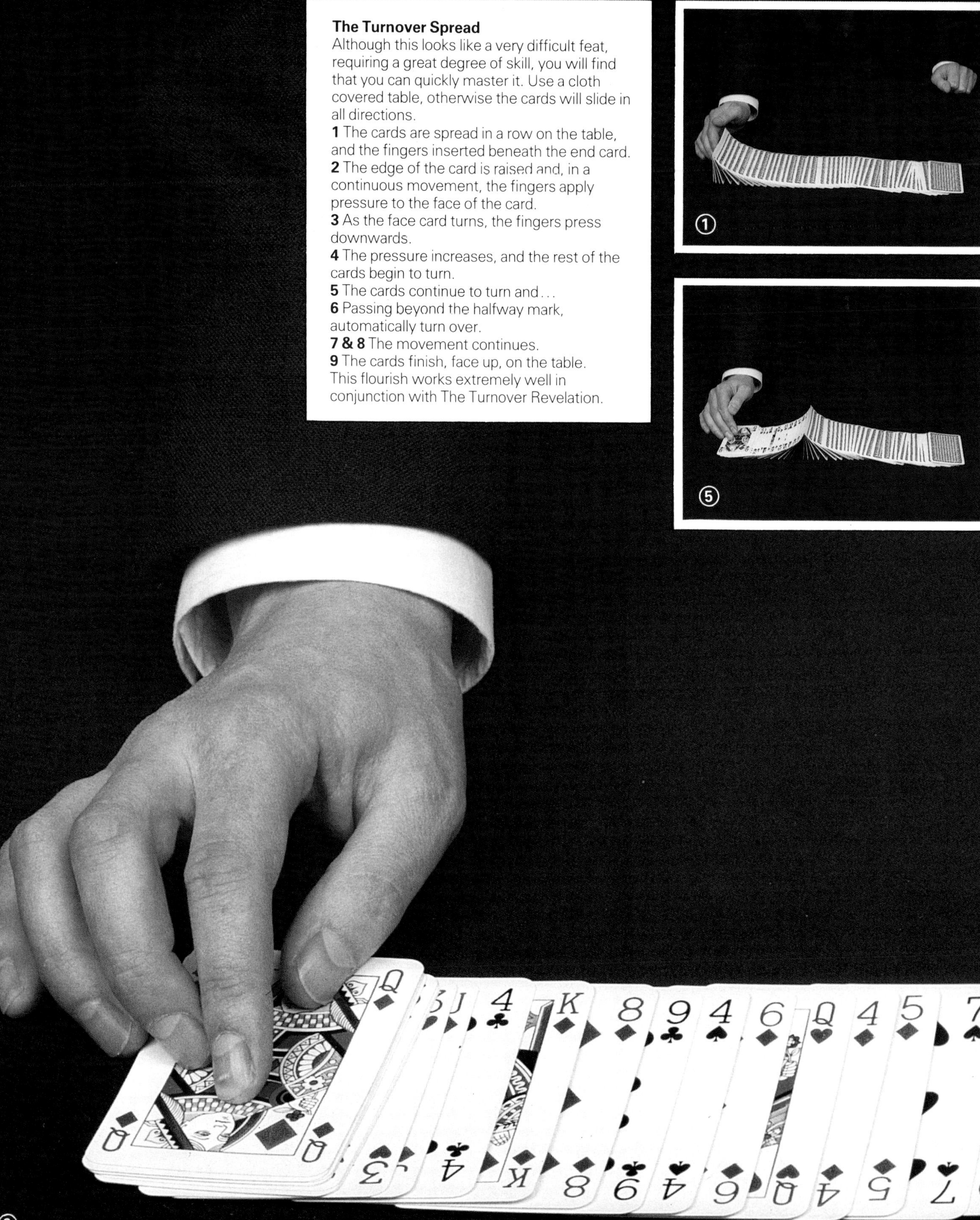

The Turnover Spread

Although this looks like a very difficult feat, requiring a great degree of skill, you will find that you can quickly master it. Use a cloth covered table, otherwise the cards will slide in all directions.

1 The cards are spread in a row on the table, and the fingers inserted beneath the end card.
2 The edge of the card is raised and, in a continuous movement, the fingers apply pressure to the face of the card.
3 As the face card turns, the fingers press downwards.
4 The pressure increases, and the rest of the cards begin to turn.
5 The cards continue to turn and . . .
6 Passing beyond the halfway mark, automatically turn over.
7 & 8 The movement continues.
9 The cards finish, face up, on the table.

This flourish works extremely well in conjunction with The Turnover Revelation.

①

⑤

⑨

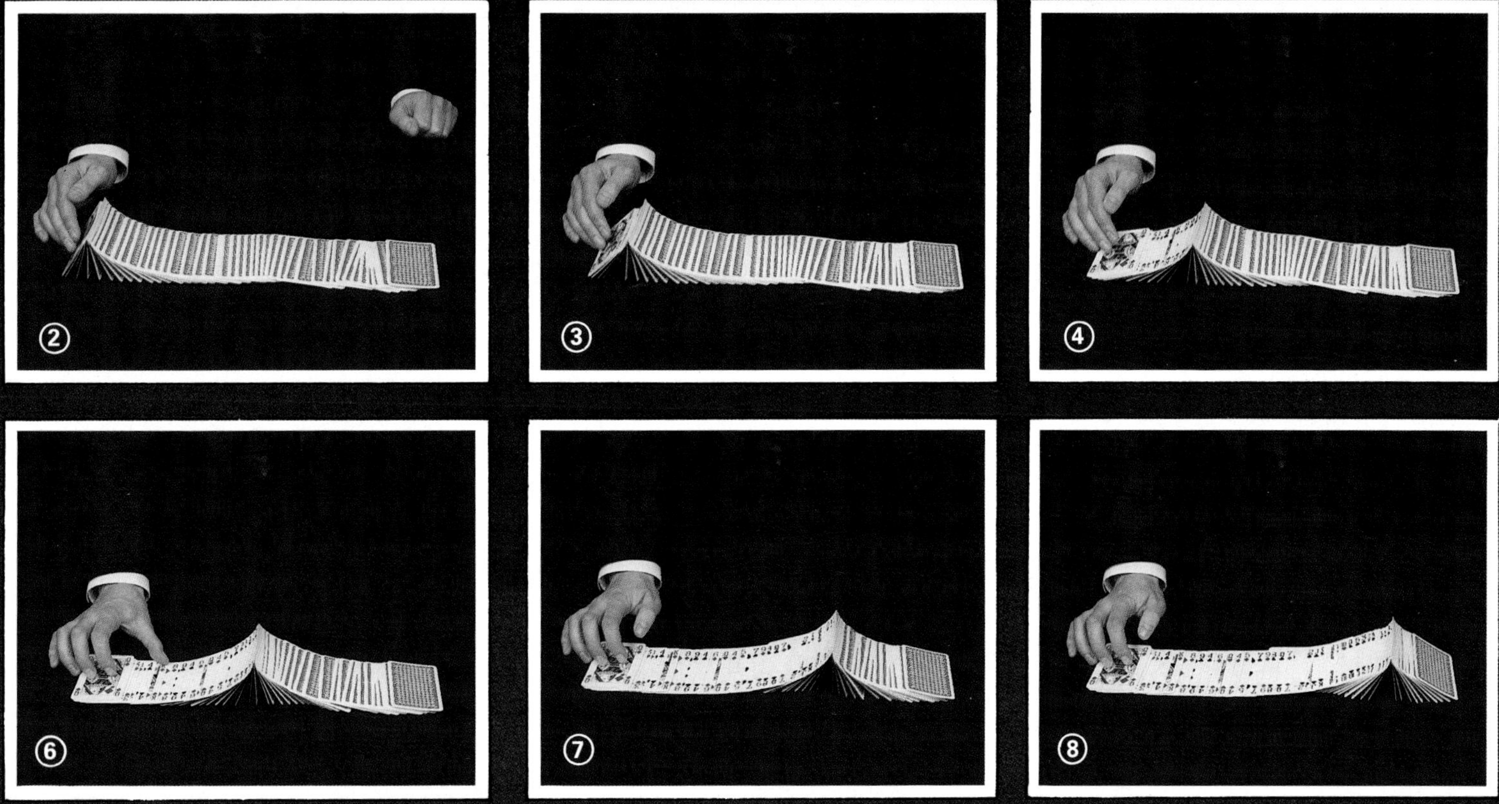

Left: World-famous Geoffrey Buckingham "springing the cards" – seemingly easy but in fact quite tricky. Buckingham won the Grand Prix in Paris in 1951 for his superb sleight-of-hand act. In January 1986, aged 83, he received a standing ovation at a Magic Congress in Germany for a lecture on his methods followed by a performance of his act.

The One-handed Pass *(below)*
This sleight is attributed to Charlier, a mysterious French magician who, in Victorian times, was an acknowledged expert with playing cards. The pass was originally used to bring a chosen card from the center of the pack to the top but, nowadays, is usually regarded as a flourish.
1 The pack of cards is held flat on the fingers. The thumb reaches across to open the pack.
2 The stock of cards, held by the thumb, is raised until it is vertical. The lower half of the pack is held at the first joints of the fingers, and the bent forefinger pushes it upwards.
3 The thumb releases the cards and is withdrawn, so allowing the remainder of the cards to fall into position.
4 The pack of cards is then squared up.

The Turnover Revelation

From a pack of cards, shuffled by a spectator, a card is chosen by another member of the audience, looked at, and returned to the pack. Placing the cards behind his back, the performer says that he will discover the spectator's card.

Removing a card, he brings it into view. It is not the chosen card. Replacing the card, he tries once more, again without success. Bringing the cards to the front, he says that he will now make the card reveal itself. Spreading the cards in a row on the table he shows that all of the cards are face-up, with the exception of one. The spectator is asked to name his card. When the face-down card is turned over, it is seen to be the one named by the spectator.

A spectator is asked to shuffle the cards, which gives him a chance to see that an ordinary pack is being used. A second spectator is asked to take a card, and the performer turns away while the spectator looks at his chosen card. As he turns away, the performer turns over the face-down pack, removes the top card and turns it over. To the spectators, the pack now appears to be face-down, but in fact it is only the top card which is face-down. The closed pack is offered for the chosen card to be inserted. The card is inserted face-down. There are now two face-down cards, the chosen card and the top card.

The performer says that he will produce the chosen card. Placing the cards behind his back, he removes one card — it is the top (reversed) card — and shows it to the spectator. It is not his card. Turning the pack over (still behind his back), he replaces the card so that it faces the same way as the rest of the pack. Taking another, he shows it, with the same result. Bringing the cards to the front, the performer spreads them in a row on the table. All the cards are face-up, with the exception of one. When it is turned over, it proves to be the chosen card.

The Q Mystery *(left)*
The actual size of this shape has no bearing on the successful performance of the trick; the key element is the number of cards used to form the tail.

The Q Mystery

A spectator is asked to shuffle a pack of cards, cut it in half and hand one half to the performer. The cards are laid face-up on the table in the form of a capital letter Q. The performer writes something on a piece of paper, which he folds and places in the center of the Q.

The volunteer is asked to count the cards forming the Q, starting from the tip of the tail and proceeding clockwise up the left-hand side of the circle, touching each card in turn as he counts and stopping whenever he wishes. He is then asked to start with that particular card and count back again to the same number, but this time avoiding the tail and continuing up the right-hand side of the circle, touching each card as before.

All the cards are removed, with the exception of the one on which the count finished. Unfolding the piece of paper, the spectator reads the message, written before he started to count. The paper contains the name of the card remaining on the table.

The secret lies in the number of cards in the tail. The counting process will finish as far up the right-hand side of the circle as there are cards in the tail. If, for instance, there are five cards in the tail, the counting will finish five cards to the right of the tail. The card at this position is noted and the name written on a piece of paper which, when read, brings the mystery to a successful conclusion. It makes no difference to the success of this trick if the Q is large or small, nor does it matter how many cards are used for the tail.

Right: The popular Norm Neilsen plucks cards out of thin air during his act, which also features such unusual novelties as a floating violin (see page 171) and bow, and a coin "ladder" that plays a tune like a dulcimer when coins cascade down it.

Preceding pages: David Berglas with Omar Sharif in the 1986 TV series *The Mind of David Berglas*. From the bowl containing twenty-four new packs of cards Sharif has taken a pack for himself and handed another to Berglas. The seals are broken and they each shuffle their respective cards, place them face down and simultaneously cut the packs – incredibly, they both cut to the same card, the eight of hearts! The procedure was repeated three times, always successfully.

7

MAGIC FOR THE JUNIOR MAGICIAN

The tricks described in this chapter are for the junior magician and use items that are easy to obtain or simple to make. They should not be passed over as being *too* simple, as some of them have been included in the programs of famous magicians.

Ring-a-ding

A ring is threaded on a piece of string, each end of which is held by a spectator. A handkerchief is draped over the center of the string and the magician, under cover of the handkerchief, releases the ring from the string.

Two identical rings, a piece of string and a pocket handkerchief are required. The pocket handkerchief and one of the rings are in the performer's right-hand pocket.

To present this mystery, the string and one ring are passed around for examination and the ring threaded on the string. Two spectators each hold one end of the string. The performer takes out the handkerchief and drapes it over the ring on the string. He takes out the duplicate ring along with the handkerchief and keeps it hidden in the right hand.

Under the handkerchief, the magician pushes part of the string through the duplicate ring and, taking the loop, passes it over the ring, which temporarily secures the ring to the string.

The performer takes hold of the original ring and covers it with his left hand. He asks the spectator at his left to feel the (duplicate) ring through the handkerchief. When the spectator confirms that the ring is still there, the magician asks him to tap the ring with his finger and to hold his other hand underneath to catch it. As the spectator releases his end of the string in order to do this, the magician slides his left hand, with the ring concealed, to that end. When the spectator fails to remove the ring, the magician offers to show how it can be released.

The spectator is asked to take hold of his end of the string again and, as he does so, the magician removes his left hand with the concealed original ring, which he disposes of at an appropriate moment. Removing the handkerchief, he takes the tiny loop and, enlarging it, passes it over the ring. He hands the ring to one of the spectators for examination.

Left: The highly inventive Ali Bongo (William Oliver Wallace) presenting his internationally famous comedy act, "The Shriek of Araby". Bongo is a magical author and an "ideas man" who has spent much of his time as an adviser for TV magic shows but who has also had his own children's TV show.

The Mysterious Indian Vase

A brass vase and a piece of rope are passed around for examination. Taking the vase, the performer lowers one end of the rope into it. The vase is turned upside-down but the rope remains in position. The magician holds the end of the rope and stands the vase on his other hand. Still holding the rope, he carefully moves his other hand away and the vase remains suspended on the rope. The items used may, again, be examined by the audience.

A brass vase, or an opaque bottle, with a narrow neck is required. Some shampoos are sold in long-necked containers, which are ideal for this trick. Also required is a small rubber ball, or a rounded piece of cork, which will loosely roll into the neck of the vase, but should not be too small.

To perform, the rope and vase are given out for examination. The performer has the rubber ball concealed in his right hand. When the vase is returned to him, he takes it by the neck, allowing the ball to roll into the vase. He passes the vase into the left hand, as he takes the rope from the spectator. Holding the vase, he inserts one end of the rope (**1**) and turns the vase over, which causes the rubber ball to fall into the neck. A tightening of the rope causes the ball to jam and the rope is held in place (**2**). When the vase is placed on the hand and the rope held taut, the hand holding the vase can be taken away and the vase remains attached to the rope. The vase can be swung gently to and fro (**3**). If it is then placed back on the hand with a slight jolt, the ball will be dislodged and fall to the bottom of the vase. The rope is then handed around for examination. In the act of passing the vase out for

Woolly Wizardry *(right)*
1 The coin is placed in the center of a square of paper and the bottom edge is folded up to about ¾ inch from the top.
2 The ends of the paper are folded inwards, *away* from the performer.
3 The top is now folded over.
4 Unknown to the audience, there is an opening at the top of the packet down which the coin slides into the performer's hand.
5 The coin is slipped down the slide, which protrudes through the far side of the paper bag.

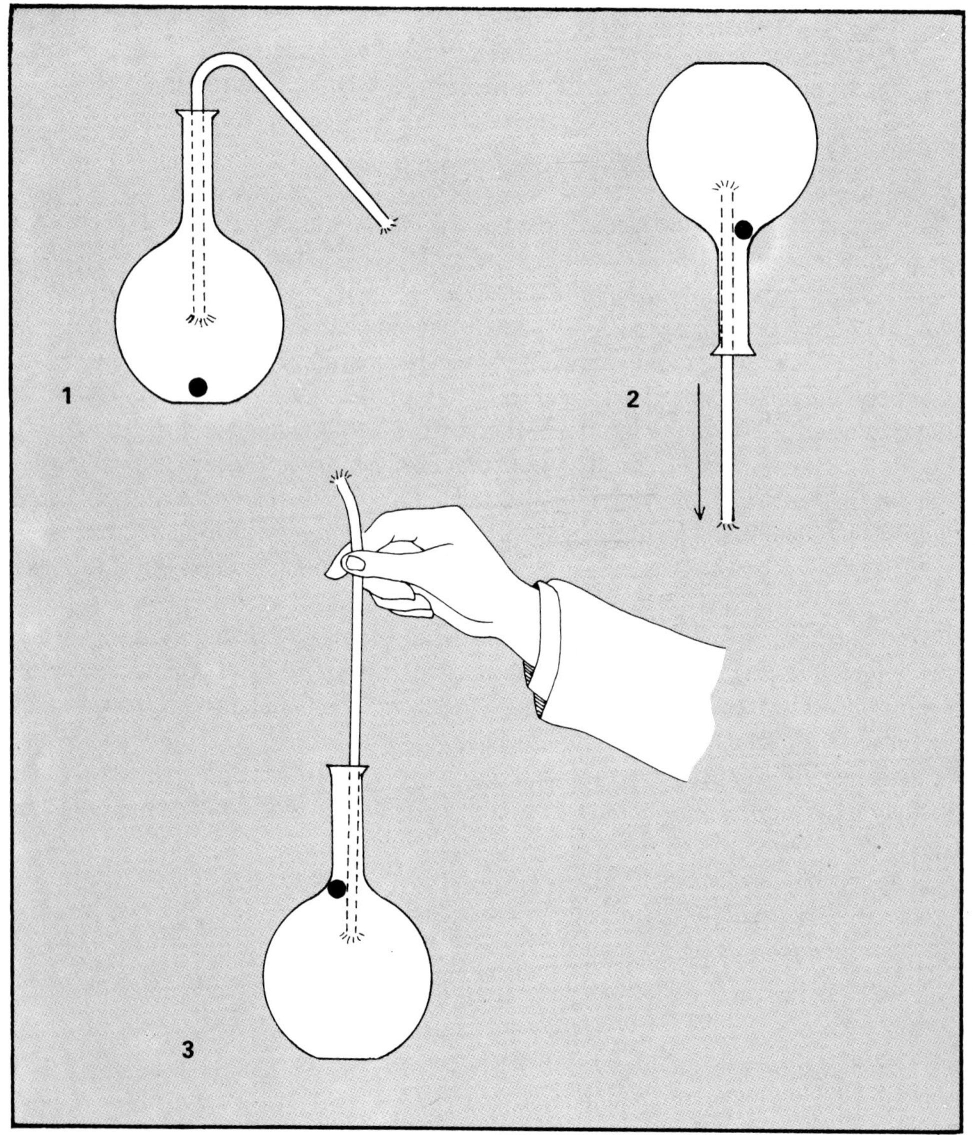

The Mysterious Indian Vase *(left)*
1 The rope is inserted into the vase which contains a rubber ball.
2 When the vase is turned over the ball jams between the rope and neck.
3 The vase, turned back to its original position, can now be gently swung to and fro.

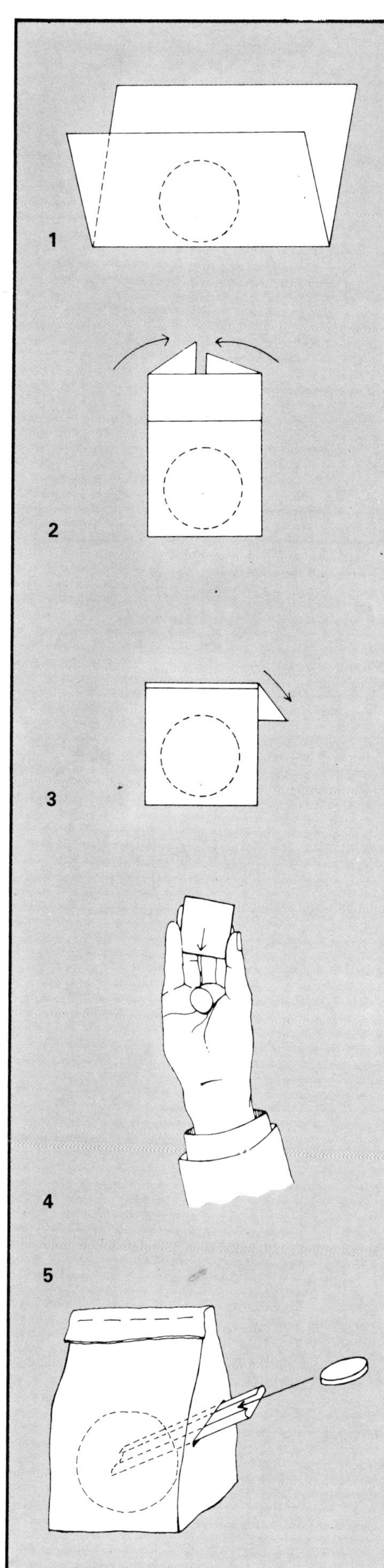

inspection, the magician inverts it, holding it by the neck. This allows the ball to roll out into his hand. Practice will show how easily the rope can be trapped and the ball dislodged at the conclusion of the mystery.

Woolly Wizardry

The performer borrows a coin from a member of the audience, who has noted its date. It is wrapped in a small square of paper and held in a spring clip, which is placed on a wire hook. A paper bag, stapled across the top, is placed some distance away and, taking the packet from the clip, the magician declares that he will cause the coin to travel from the packet into the paper bag.

He tears the packet into pieces. The coin has gone. Showing his hands to be empty, he tears open the paper bag and reveals a ball of wool, which he drops into a glass jar. Taking one end of the wool, he unwinds the ball. As he nears the center, a clinking sound is heard and a coin falls to the bottom of the glass. A spectator is requested to remove the coin, which is restored to its owner, who checks the date and acknowledges that it does in fact belong to him.

The requirements are: a ball of wool, a metal or cardboard slide, a square of paper, a wire hook, a paper bag, a spring clip, a glass jar and a borrowed coin. To prepare for the mystery, the square of paper is folded and opened out, which makes it easier to fold during the actual performance. The bottom edge is folded upward to about 3/4 inch from the top (**1**). The right side of the paper is folded *away* from the performer, taking about a third of the width of the paper, and the left side is folded in the same manner (**2**). The top of the paper is also folded over, toward the audience; just less than 3/4 inch is folded, leaving a slot at the top (**3**).

The slide, which is large enough to take the coin, is wrapped around with wool, allowing a portion of the slide to protrude. The wool is put in the paper bag and a slit made in the back of the bag, through which the slide is pushed. The top of the bag is stapled or tied. A piece of wire (coat hanger wire is ideal) is fixed into a wooden block and the top bent into the form of a hook.

To present the mystery, a spectator is asked to take a coin from his pocket and note the date on it. The magician places the coin in the center of the piece of paper, and folds it as above. The coin appears to be securely trapped. If the packet is turned upside-down, however, the coin will slide out into the performer's hand (**4**).

The packet is slipped into the spring clip and hung on the wire hook. The paper bag containing the wool is then placed some distance away and, in putting it exactly where he wants it, the performer inserts the coin into the slide (**5**). He then removes the slide from the ball of wool, and leaves it in the bag. This can be done quite quickly with practise.

The packet is removed from the clip and torn into pieces. The bag is torn open and the ball of wool revealed. The torn remnants of the bag are crushed and laid aside (the slide is recovered later). The performer drops the ball of wool into the jar and, taking one loose end, unwinds it until the coin drops out. A spectator is asked to remove the coin, which is checked by its owner. The mystery is thus brought to a satisfactory conclusion.

Magical Magnetism *(illustration overleaf)*

The performer takes his magic wand and strokes it lengthwise, as though to create a mystic force. He stands with his left side to the audience, grasping the wand in his left hand. With his right hand, he holds the left wrist and slowly opens the fingers holding the wand, which remains attached to the palm of the left hand. The fingers are closed and the right hand removes the magic wand. (Other articles such as a walking stick, a knitting needle or a large spoon may be used in place of the wand.)

The secret lies in the position of the right hand. The thumb and second, third, fourth and little fingers encircle the wrist but the forefinger presses the wand against the left palm, which is turned away from the audience (**1**). The audience, looking at the back of the left hand, sees the wand apparently suspended across it (**2**).

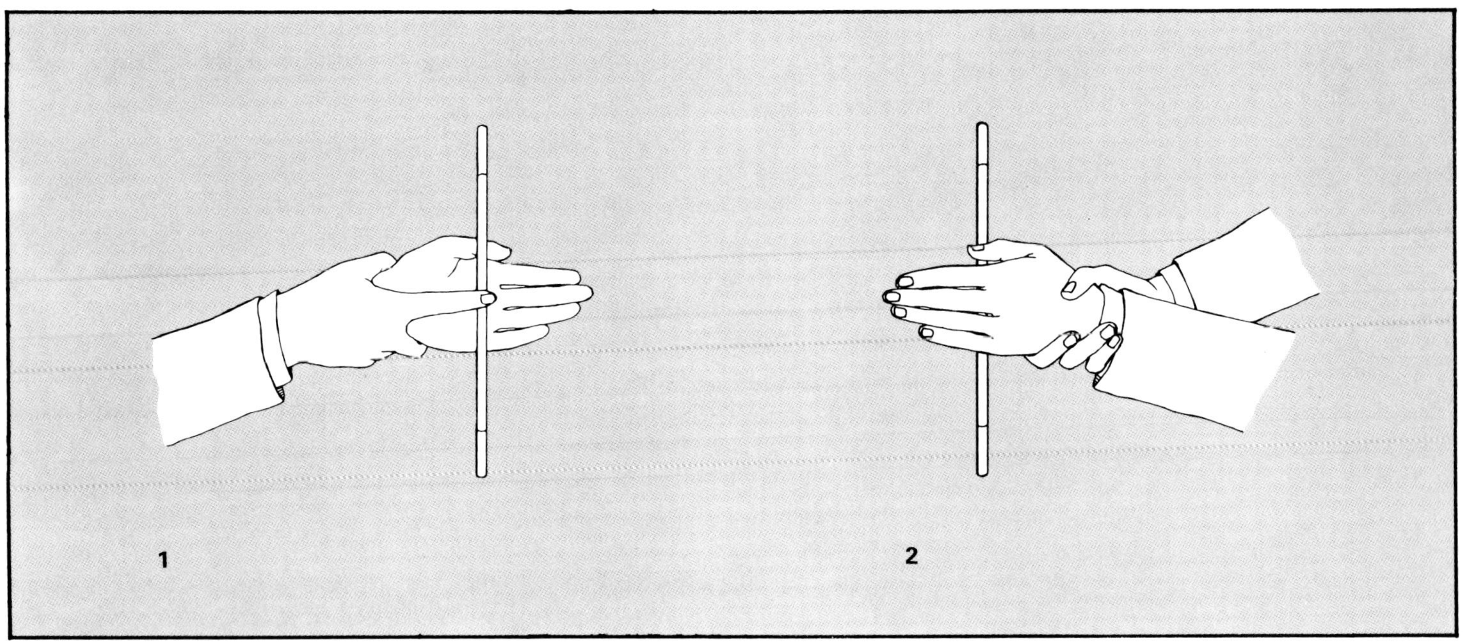

A Surprise Release

The performer's wrists are tied together with a handkerchief. A long piece of cord is passed through the space between the tied hands and behind the handkerchief (**1**). A spectator holds the two ends of the cord and another helper is asked to cover the performer's wrists with a cloth. The spectator holding the cord is asked to give a sharp pull and, to his surprise, the cord passes through the handkerchief, which is still fastened around the performer's wrists.

When his wrists have been covered with the cloth, the performer stands directly in front of the spectator holding the cord. If the cord is being held taut, he moves forward slightly to obtain some slack. He bends the fingers of one hand inward between the wrists, and picks up the loop of rope. He slides the loop of rope over the back of one hand (**2**). When the spectator pulls the cord, it then comes away quite easily.

Magical Magnetism *(above)*
1 The forefinger of the right hand holds the wand in position.
2 The magic wand appears to be attached to the hand.

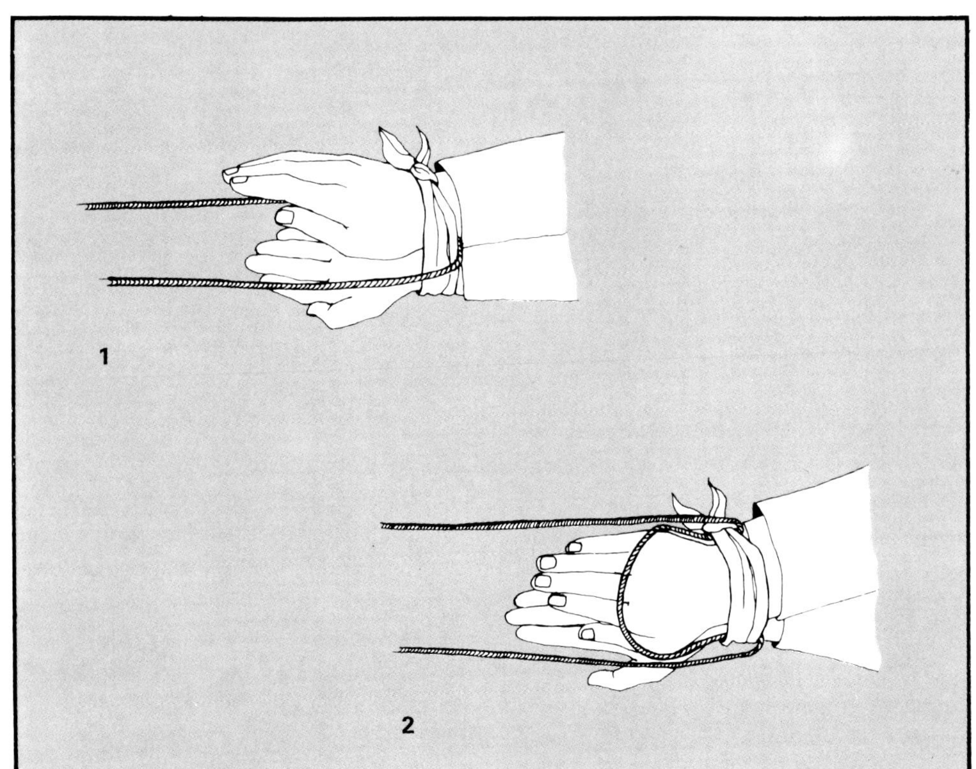

A Surprise Release *(left)*
1 The cord is threaded between the performer's wrists, behind the handkerchief, and the ends held by a spectator.
2 The fingers of one hand bend inward and pull the loop of cord up between the palms and over the back of one hand. When pulled, the cord appears to penetrate the handkerchief.

The Slip-Away Knot

Two silk handkerchiefs are held, one in each hand. Bringing them together, the performer pushes them completely into a decorative tube. Holding the tube to his lips, he blows and the handkerchiefs emerge, tied together. They are replaced in the tube and, when removed, are seen to have separated once again.

A nicely decorated cardboard tube is needed and two brightly colored handkerchiefs, preferably silk, as linen ones are more difficult to blow out of the tube. A small elastic band, slipped over the thumb and forefinger, is the only preparation required.

The two handkerchiefs are held, one in each hand, just below one corner. As they are brought together, a small movement of the forefinger and thumb holding them allows the elastic band to snap onto the handkerchiefs (**1**). Where the band grips the material, it gives the appearance of a knot (**2**) but this is not revealed at this time. The handkerchiefs are pushed into the tube and then blown out, apparently tied together.

As they are put in the tube a second time, the elastic band is removed. When the handkerchiefs are blown through the tube again, they have become separated.

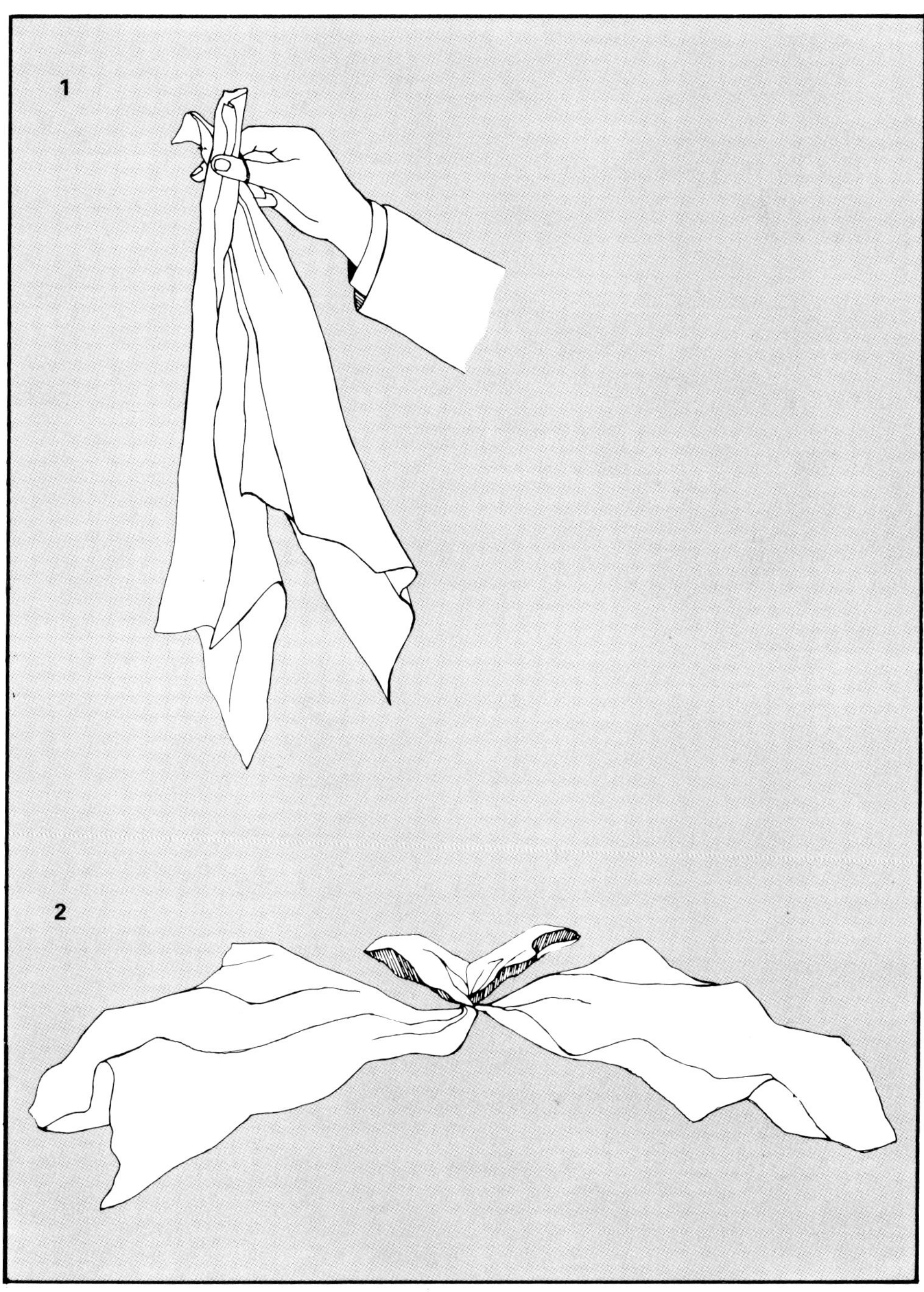

The Slip-Away Knot *(right)*
1 The small rubber band encircles forefinger and thumb. When the handkerchiefs are picked up, the band snaps around them.
2 The handkerchiefs now seem to be tied together.

Ribbon Restoration

A piece of ribbon is threaded lengthwise through an envelope. The performer takes a pair of scissors and cuts through both the ribbon and the envelope. The envelope is, naturally, in two parts but the ribbon remains in one piece.

The envelope is prepared by cutting two slots, one at each end, and a square hole in the back (**1**). A length of ribbon is threaded through the envelope (**2**). Just before cutting, the performer hooks a loop of ribbon out of the cut-out square with his thumb. When the envelope is cut, the scissor blade goes under the loop of ribbon (**3**). The two parts of the envelope are held together while the ribbon is slowly pulled through, completely undamaged.

The French Drop *(right)*
This sleight is used to make a small object – such as a coin or a die – vanish. In the following sequence a key is used.
1 The key is held between the thumb and middle finger of the right hand.
(continued overleaf)

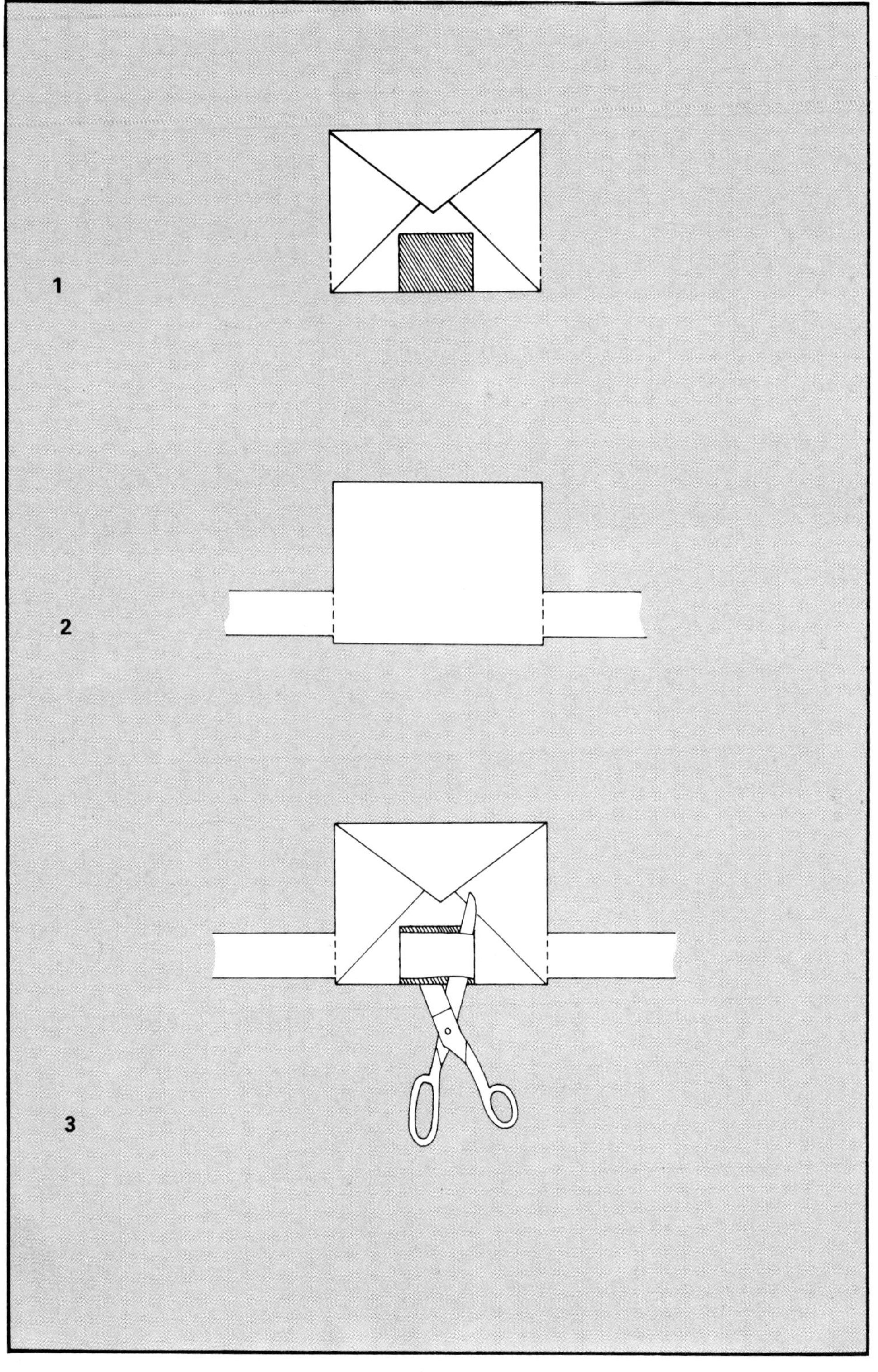

Ribbon Restoration *(left)*
1 The rear view of the prepared envelope, showing the cut-out and the slots at each end.
2 A piece of ribbon is threaded through the slots; from the front, the envelope appears intact.
3 The scissors cuts through the envelope but the blade passes under the ribbon.

①

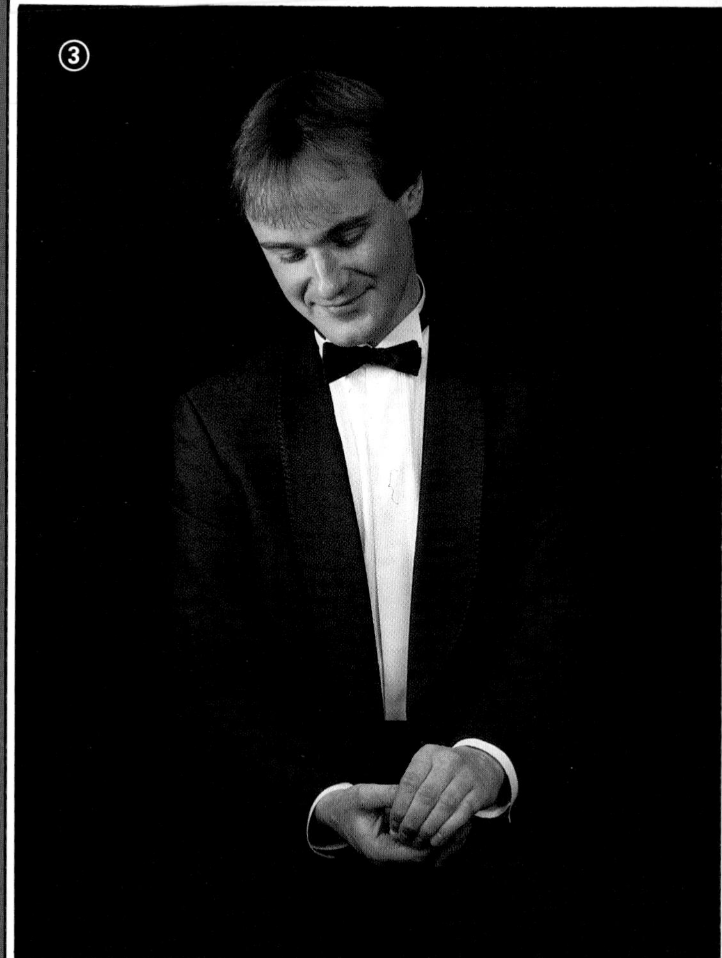

The French Drop *(continued)*
2 The left hand moves closer to take the key.
3 The left hand apparently takes the key but, while hidden by the half closed fingers, it has dropped into the right palm.
4 The left hand moves away, apparently holding the key. By looking at it, the performer directs the audience's attention to this hand. The right hand must not be moved at this stage.
5 Slowly opening his hand, the performer reveals that the key has disappeared.
(continued overleaf)

④

⑤

The French Drop *(continued)*
6 Holding the key, concealed in his right hand, he rubs his left elbow.
7 He produces the key, apparently from his elbow.
Practise is required to make the movements seem natural.

Deceptive Dice *(below)*
The dice are mixed and stacked up. The performer, knowing that the top and bottom of each die total seven, only needs to see the face of the top die and subtract that number from 21, to be able to provide the total of the numbers on the hidden faces.

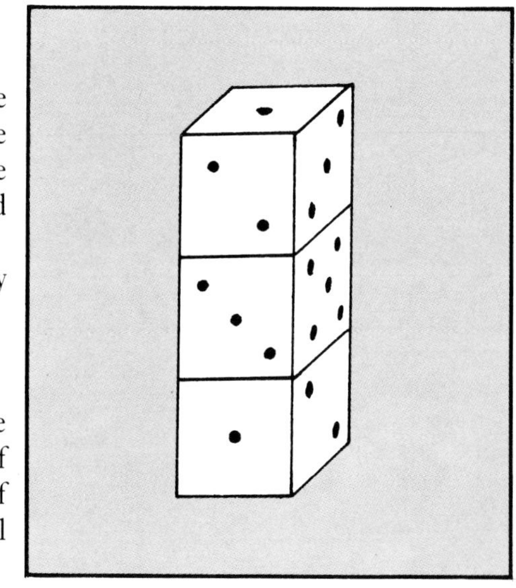

Deceptive Dice

The performer turns his back while a spectator takes three dice, rolls them on the table and stacks them one on top of another (see diagram). The spectator is asked to add the numbers on the five hidden faces of the dice. As he then concentrates on the total, the performer reveals the number. This is a nice presentation, as no questions are asked and it seems impossible for the performer to know the thought-of total.

It is not generally known that the numbers on the opposite faces of correctly manufactured dice add up to seven:

6 and 1   5 and 2   4 and 3

The total for three dice, therefore, is twenty-one.

When the performer asks the spectator to count the numbers on the hidden faces, he turns to ask if he has finished adding the total. It is at this moment that he catches sight of the number on the top die. He subtracts this number from twenty-one to find the total of the numbers on the hidden faces. For example, if the top number is three, the answer will be eighteen.

The Growing Wand

The magician says that, to perform good magic, a magic wand is needed but his wand is far too small. He asks his audience to help him by saying, "Grow, grow, grow". Holding the wand between his hands, he begins to pull and, slowly but surely, the wand begins to grow until it becomes twice its original length. When handed out for examination, it is found to be perfectly solid.

The wand measures approximately 14 inches and has a loose white collar, identical to one of the wand tips (**1**). The collar is made by rolling a strip of white, glossy paper into a tube and sticking it securely. It is a good idea to present this as an opening trick because the collar is held halfway down the wand and the rest of the wand is concealed in the sleeve.

The performer pulls on the wand and it appears to grow as the hidden part is brought into view (**2**). When the concealed end of the wand emerges from the sleeve, the white collar is slipped off and remains concealed in the hand. It may be disposed of at an appropriate moment.

The Growing Wand
1 The wand has a glossy paper collar, which is identical to the white tip.
2 Part of the wand is hidden up the performer's sleeve. The performer holds the collar. With his other hand, he slowly pulls the wand through the collar, creating the illusion of growth, until the whole wand is in view.

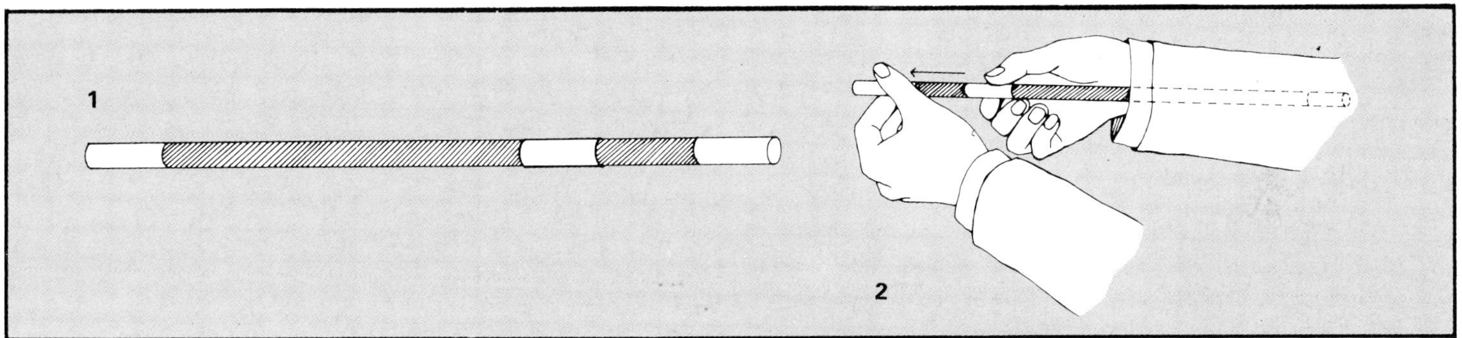

PAGED THOUGHTS

This is a mystery which, if presented well, will really make the audience believe that the performer has mystical powers.

Taking a book from his table and a playing card from a pack, the performer announces that he is going to attempt an experiment in thought reading. He hands the card to a spectator, inviting him to push the card somewhere in the book, leaving part of the card protruding. The book is then given to another member of the audience, who is asked to open it at the place where the card has been inserted.

While the person is opening the book, the performer reminds the audience of what has taken place. A card has been thrust into the book between pages of the spectator's own choice. The book has been opened at these pages, which no-one could possibly have identified in advance.

The person holding the book is asked which of the two pages he or she would prefer to be used in the experiment. Whichever page is selected, the performer closes his eyes, concentrates and slowly proceeds to describe the contents of that page.

The secret lies in the fact that two duplicate playing cards are used, one of which has been placed between two pages briefly memorized by the performer. The book is offered to a spectator, who partially inserts his card into the pages. While this is being done, the performer covers his own card with the hand holding the book. While he is looking for someone to read the pages, he pushes the spectator's card into the book, turning the book and bringing his own card into view. He hands the book to a member of the audience, who decides which of the two marked pages is to be used in the demonstration. The performer gradually reveals the information to be found on that page, from memory.

Banana Split

A playing card is chosen by a spectator and a banana is held by the performer. The spectator is asked how many spots there are on his card. His reply is "Three". When he has made mysterious passes over the banana, the performer removes the peel, showing that the banana has been cut into three pieces.

The card is forced (a suitable method will be found in Chapter Six). The banana is prepared by threading a length of sewing thread through a needle, which is pushed under the skin of the fruit. The needle is directed under the peel, not through the fruit (**1**). When the needle emerges, it is reintroduced into the same hole and pushed a little further around the circumference, making sure that the thread is not pulled through. This procedure is continued until the needle returns to the hole from where it began. If the two ends of thread are then pulled, the thread will cut through the fruit without damaging the skin (**2**). One more cut is made in the same way. This "sewing" must be done with care, to avoid damaging the peel and to give a clean cut. When the banana is peeled, the fruit will be seen to have been cut into three pieces (**3**).

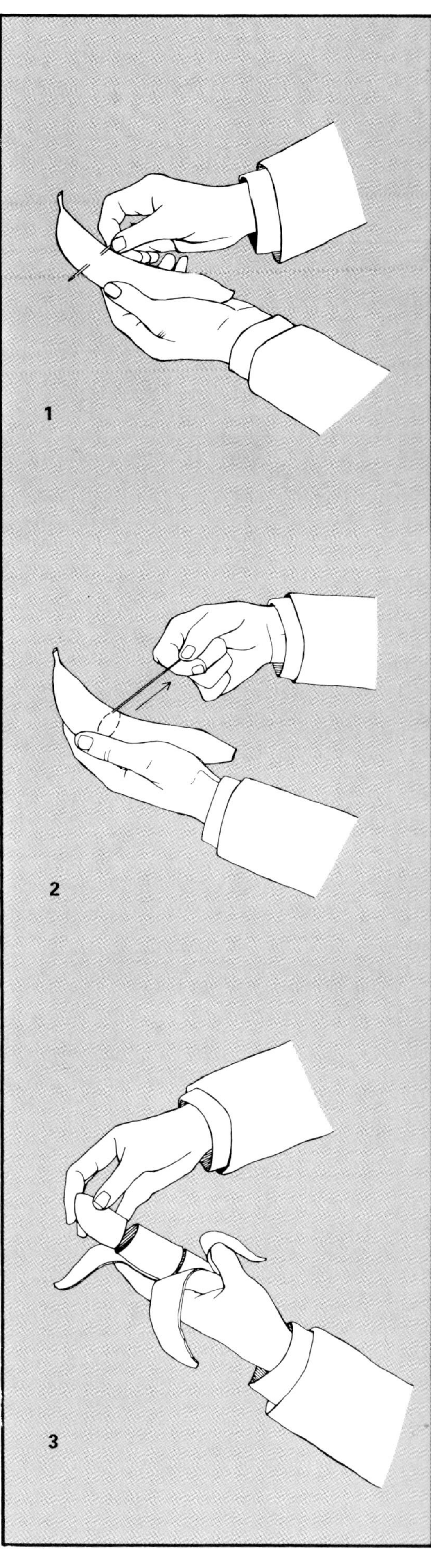

Domino Magic

The performer writes a prediction, which he seals in an envelope and hands to a spectator. A box containing dominoes is tipped on the table and the performer asks the volunteer to lay out the dominoes as he would when playing a game. When all the dominoes have been used, the spectator notes the numbers at each end of the line.

The envelope is opened and the spectator removes the sheet of paper, on which is written "My prediction is that the numbers at each end of the row of dominoes will be six and two". The numbers at the extreme ends of the row are indeed six and two, as predicted.

The only preparation required is to remove one domino from the set. Any domino may be used (in this case the "six–two"), with the exception of doubles. In every instance, the end numbers will correspond with the domino removed. Care must be taken not to allow the spectators to see that one domino is missing, when tipping them out of the box.

Magic in Rhyme

Two little dicky birds,
Sitting on a wall,
One named Peter,
One named Paul,
Fly away Peter,
Fly away Paul,
Come back Peter,
Come back Paul.

This old nursery rhyme is used to illustrate a little mystery which young children find quite amusing.

Two moistened pieces of paper are stuck on the nails of the index fingers. Both of the hands are closed into fists with only the two fingers showing. The tips of these two fingers are placed on the edge of a table.

The first two lines are recited with the fingers resting on the table. When reciting the next two lines, at the word "Peter" one finger is lifted then, on "Paul" the other, indicating that the two pieces of paper represent the birds. The fingertips are returned to the table after each of them is named.

Continuing the rhyme, "Fly away Peter", the right arm is raised and the fingertip replaced on the table but the paper has gone. On "Fly away Paul", the same action is repeated with the left hand and that paper has also disappeared. On "Come back Peter"

Banana Split *(left)*
1 A sewing needle, threaded with a length of cotton, is pushed just under the skin of the banana. When it emerges, the performer pulls on the cotton, and re-inserts the needle into the same hole from where it was withdrawn. Continue in this way around the circumference of the banana until the needle finally appears through the hole into which it was first inserted.
2 The performer pulls on the two ends of the cotton, forcing it to cut through the fruit without damaging the skin. The process is repeated at another position on the banana.
3 When the banana is peeled by a spectator, the fruit is found to have been cut into three pieces.

and "Come back Paul" the action of raising each arm is repeated but, when the finger returns to the table, the paper has "come back".

The secret of this trick is simply an exchange of fingers. The arm is raised and, when returned to its former position, the tip of the *second* finger rests on the table and the index finger is bent inwards so that it cannot be seen. The part of the finger showing should be from the first joint only. The rest of the hand must be kept out of sight, below the level of the table. The trick should be well practised, so that the exchange of fingers can be done quite quickly.

The Bewildering Boomerangs

Two boomerangs, one red, one yellow, are shown together. The red one appears to be shorter than the yellow. The red one is taken and "stretched". When it is compared with the yellow, it is now the larger of the two. Finally, the boomerangs are reversed and both are seen to be exactly the same size.

The boomerangs are made of cardboard, plastic or wood, and their size is dependent on where the mystery is being shown. An optical illusion is used in this trick – the boomerangs are, in fact, identical in size. If the boomerangs are shown together with ends A and C lined up with each other, the lower boomerang seems to be longer than the other (**1**). If the upper one is apparently stretched and placed below the other, it will now appear to be the longer. If the boomerangs are turned so that ends A and D, and B and C, are touching, they appear to be the same size (**2**).

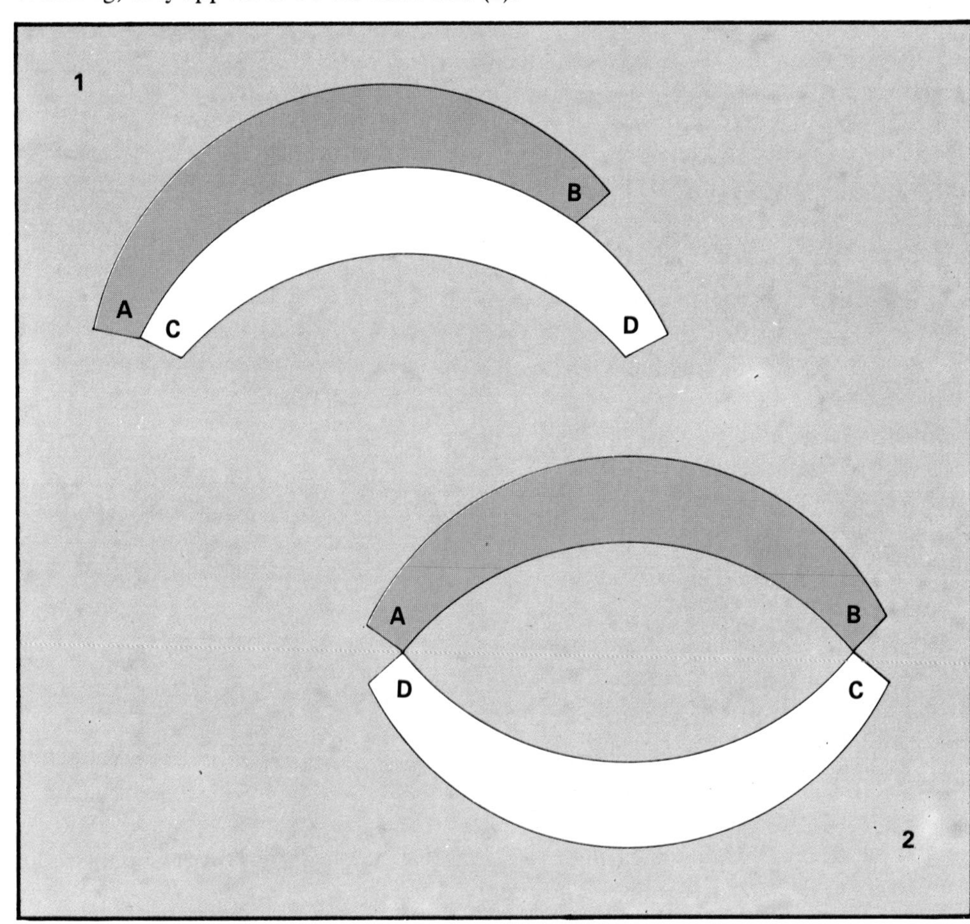

The Bewildering Boomerangs *(right)*
1 When the boomerangs are placed together, the lower one appears to be the longer. If the upper boomerang is placed below the other, it appears to have stretched.
2 If the boomerangs are placed point to point, they are found to be of the same size.

Aerial Addition *(illustration overleaf)*

A number of silver coins are counted into the hands of a volunteer assistant, who is asked to cup his hands around them, so that they cannot be tampered with in any way. The performer apparently produces three coins from the air which, he says, will pass invisibly into the cupped hands of the assistant. When the coins are counted, three more coins have been added to the original number.

Twelve coins and a magazine are required. Before starting the demonstration, three coins are concealed under the cover of the magazine. They should be near one end, so that during the counting a tell-tale clink will not create suspicion.

At the commencement of the demonstration, a spectator is asked to assist and is handed the coins to count onto the magazine (**1**). He is requested to count them aloud so that the audience can be sure how many coins are being used. The performer excuses the use of the magazine "tray", by saying that its use will ensure that at no time during the demonstration can he touch the coins.

When they have been counted, the coins are poured from the magazine into the assistant's cupped hands (**2**), the three hidden coins automatically being added to the nine. He is asked to close his hands to make sure that nothing can get in or out.

The performer reaches in the air, pretends to grab an invisible coin and makes a throwing motion in the direction of the assistant's hands. This action is repeated twice more, and the assistant is asked if he felt the extra coins join the others. When asked the number of coins with which he started, he says, "Nine". When the coins are counted again, he discovers that he now has twelve.

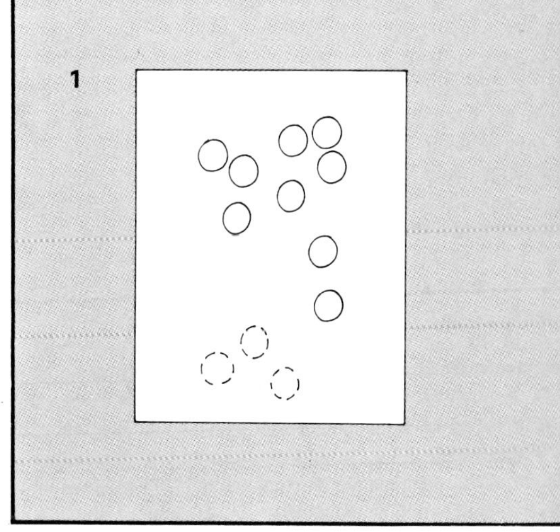

Aerial Addition *(above)*
1 Nine silver coins are counted on to a magazine, which acts as a tray. Three other coins have previously been concealed within its pages.
2 When the coins are poured from the top of the magazine, the concealed coins are automatically added.

Star Prediction

The performer asks members of the audience to call out the names of famous television or sporting personalities. The performer writes the names on separate slips of paper, which are folded, dropped into a glass bowl and well mixed.

Taking a different-colored piece of paper, the performer writes a name and places the paper in a drinking glass. A spectator is asked to select one of the slips and read aloud the chosen name. Another spectator removes the colored sheet of paper and reads the identical name.

About ten slips of paper are required, also a glass bowl, a larger sheet of different-colored paper and a drinking glass. To present the mystery, the performer writes the first name called on one of the slips, folds it and drops it into the bowl. When a second name is called, the performer takes another slip but writes, not the name that is called, but the first name again.

As each name is called, the original name is written and dropped among the other slips in the bowl. The performer must ensure that the slips are folded up so that the deceit cannot be detected. There are now ten slips with identical names. The name that has been written on the slips is also written on the larger sheet of colored paper, which is placed in the glass. The slips in the bowl are well mixed, one chosen and the prediction checked. The unused slips should not be left lying around after the show; they should be disposed of as soon as possible.

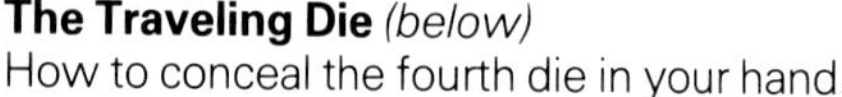

The Traveling Die *(below)*
How to conceal the fourth die in your hand.

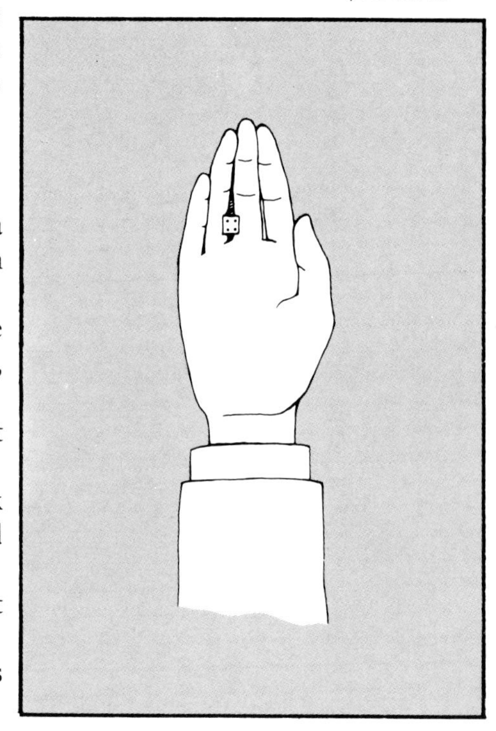

The Traveling Die

The performer takes three dice from the table, placing them in his left hand, one at a time. He removes one of the dice and places it in his trouser pocket. When the dice from the left hand are rolled on to the table, the third die is seen to have returned.

The three dice are once again taken from the table and placed in the left hand, and one removed. He places it in his trouser pocket, yet when the dice are rolled on to the table, once again the die has returned.

Use a fourth die, concealing it at the base of the second and third fingers of the right hand. Your fingers need be only slightly bent to hold the die in position (see picture).

Pick up the first die from the table and place it into the slightly cupped left hand. Pick up the second die and place it too in the left hand, simultaneously dropping the concealed die there as well. Finally, pick up the third die and put it into the hand.

Remove one of the dice and appear to put it in your trouser pocket, but actually retain it in the hand, replacing it in position at the base of the fingers, ready to repeat the trick.

The three dice are rolled from the left hand and you are ready to repeat the trick, as often as you wish.

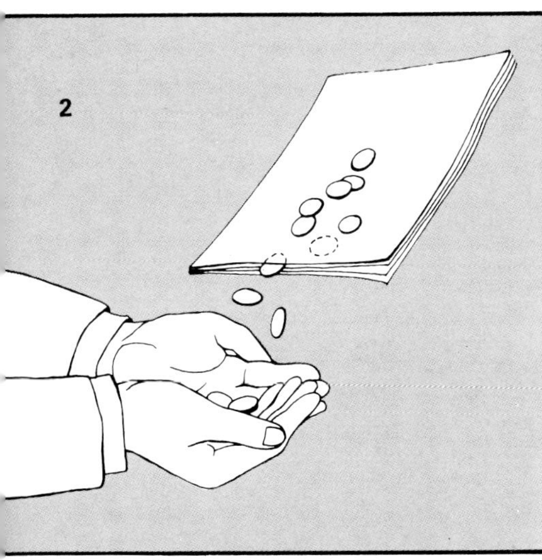

Rope and Ring

The performer shows a large metal ring, which he passes out for examination. A spectator ties the performer's wrists together with a piece of rope. When the ring is returned, the performer turns his back for a moment. When he faces his audience again, the ring is on the rope. The rope has to be untied before the ring can be removed.

A length of rope about 3 feet in length and two identical rings or bracelets, large enough to slip over the hand, are needed. In preparation for this mystery, one of the rings is slipped over the left wrist and pushed up the arm, where it remains hidden in the sleeve.

The other ring is given out for inspection to prove that it is a regular ring. A spectator ties the performer's left wrist, followed by the right, leaving about 10 inches of rope between the wrists. When the ring is returned (**1**), the performer turns his back and slips the ring into an inside pocket of his coat (**2**). He then allows the hidden ring to slide down his arm, over his hand and onto the rope.

He turns to the audience, revealing that the ring is threaded on the rope (**3**). He may allow the knots to be examined and the ring to be inspected.

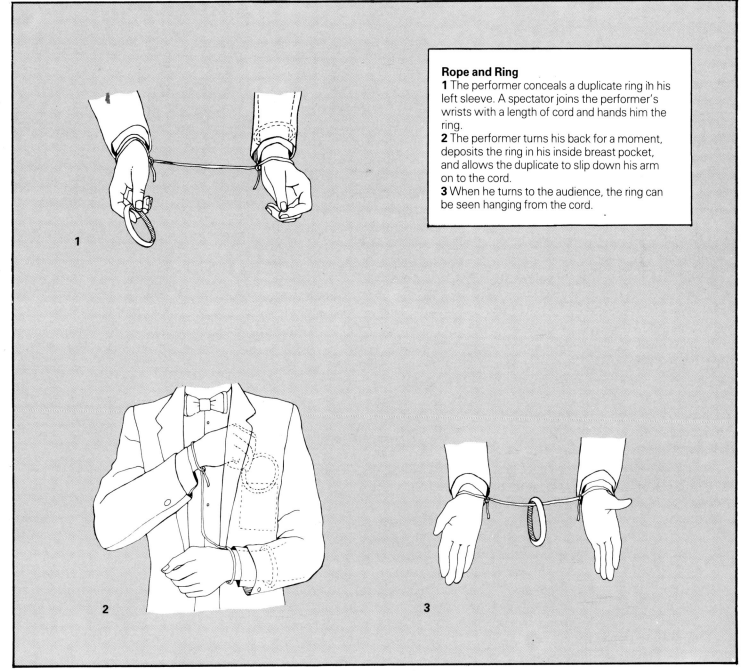

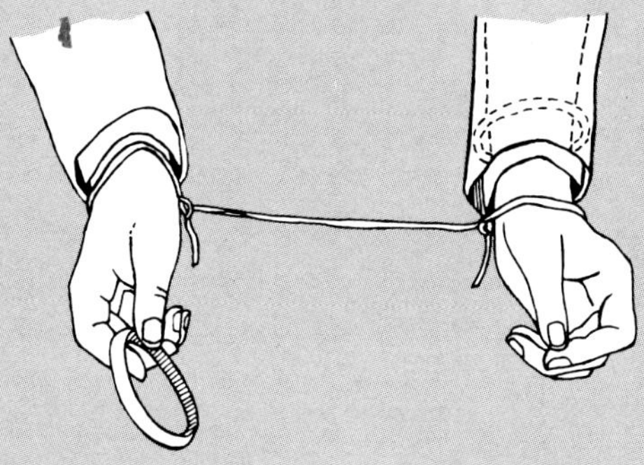

Rope and Ring
1 The performer conceals a duplicate ring in his left sleeve. A spectator joins the performer's wrists with a length of cord and hands him the ring.
2 The performer turns his back for a moment, deposits the ring in his inside breast pocket, and allows the duplicate to slip down his arm on to the cord.
3 When he turns to the audience, the ring can be seen hanging from the cord.

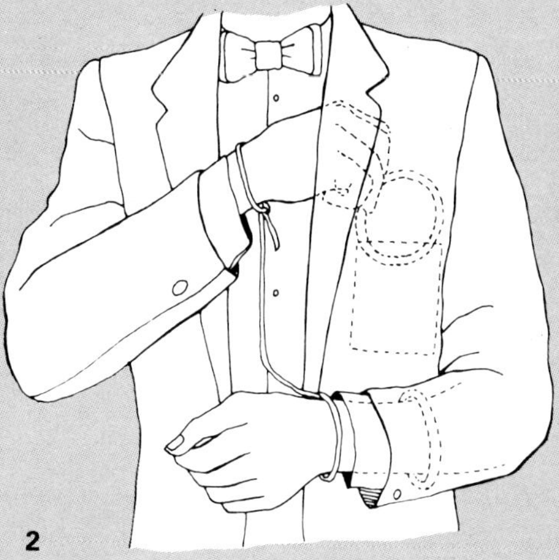

1

2

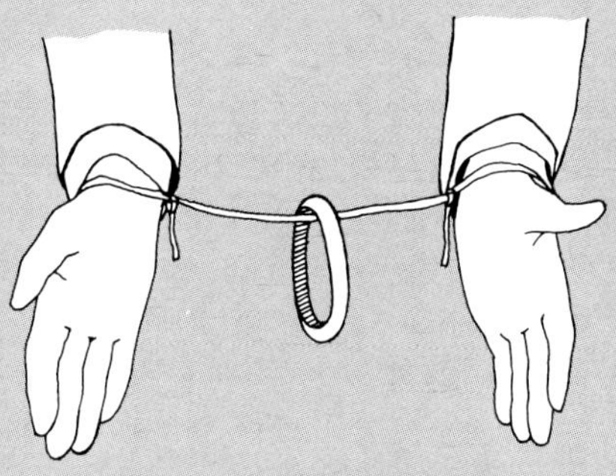

3

Fantastic Figures

A spectator is asked to think of a number between one and ten. When he has decided on a number, he is asked to double it and add four. He is then told to divide his total by two and subtract the number he first thought of. The performer informs him that his answer is two.

The nice thing about this mystery using figures is that the performer does not have to make any mental calculations.

Here is an example:

The number thought of is	5
When doubled it becomes	10
Four is added	14
Divided by two	7
Subtract the first-thought-of figure (five)	
The answer	2

The answer will always be one half of the number added. In the above example, four was added, so the answer will be two. If the mystery is repeated, the number added should be changed so that the answer will be different.

It's Matchic

This trick will delight young children.

Seven matches are required. To begin the presentation, the performer places seven matches on the table, alternately head at the top, head at the bottom, head at the top, etc.

The performer tells the story of Daniel, a not-very-bright boy who volunteered to go to market and collect some pigs for his master. "He put them in the farm cart and, to make counting easier, he arranged them head, tail, head, tail and so on. (*The seven matches are laid on the table as described.*) He went to one side of the cart and counted 'One-two-three heads'. Then he went around the other side and counted, 'One-two-three tails'. (*Point to the matches while counting.*) He climbed onto the cart and began his homeward journey.

Unknown to him, one of the pigs jumped out of the cart. (*Remove one match.*) A quarter of an hour later, he decided to check the number of pigs. There were one-two-three heads on this side, and one-two-three tails on this side. Satisfied, he continued his journey. He was almost asleep when the cart hit a large stone, abruptly awaking Daniel and jolting one of the pigs off the back of the cart. (*One match is removed.*) Five minutes later, Daniel thought that he ought to check the pigs and, counting the heads, one-two-three, on this side and the one-two-three tails on that side, he was happy. (*Recount as before.*)

He was not far from home when Roger the Dodger, a local thief, waited in a hedge at the side of the road and, as the cart passed, stole two of the pigs and made himself scarce. (*Remove two matches.*)

Arriving at the farm, Daniel counted the pigs for the last time, one-two-three heads, and one-two-three tails. Happy at the thought that he had completed the journey with the same number of pigs with which he began, he reported to the farmer that his mission had been successfully accomplished. However, you and I know differently."

During the telling of the story, the performer is careful not to touch the matches in positions two-four-six. These three matches are laid with their heads at the bottom.

When the performer counts the matches, he counts the heads of these three matches as "One-two-three heads", and the other ends of the same matches as "One-two-three tails". During the recounting of the narrative, any of the matches may be removed, with the exception of the three with heads at the bottom, and the performer will still be able to count three heads at the bottom, and three tails at the top. Actually, the same three matches are counted each time, but this goes unnoticed by the spectators.

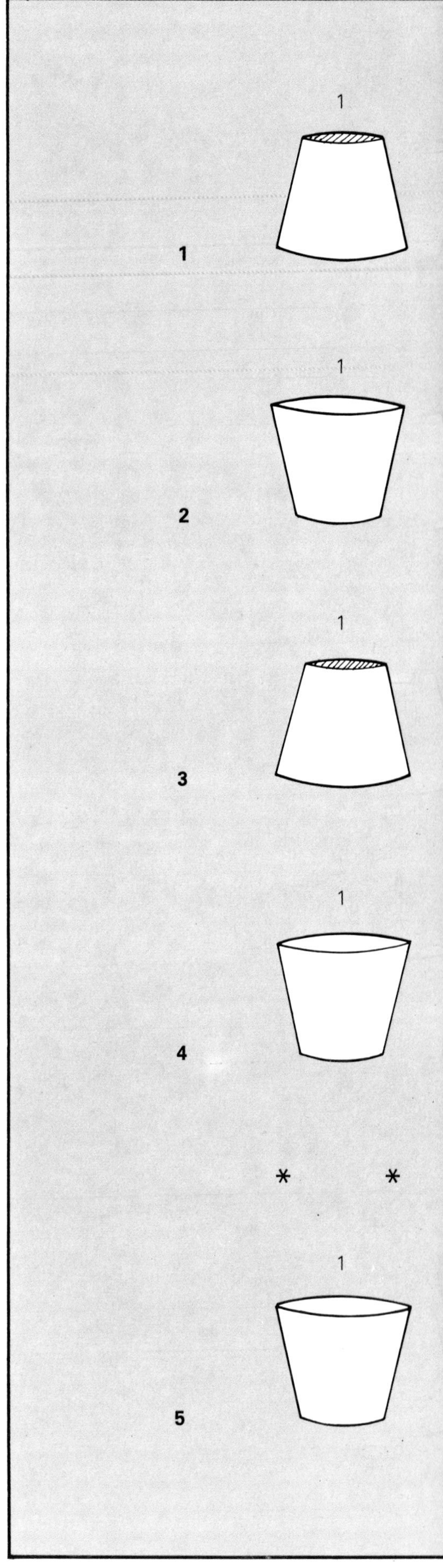

A Tumbler Teaser *(left)*
1 The glasses are placed with the center one the right way up and the other two upside down.
2 The performer turns over glasses 1 and 2.
3 Then he turns over glasses 1 and 3.
4 Finally, he turns over glasses 1 and 2. The glasses are now all upright.
5 In arranging the glasses for a spectator to attempt the feat, the performer places the center glass upside-down and the other two right way up.

A Tumbler Teaser

This demonstration looks very simple when shown by the performer but, when attempted by a spectator it is discovered to be impossible.

The performer stands three drinking glasses in a row on the table. The center glass is the right way up and the end glasses are upside-down. He says that with the aid of the glasses he has set a problem, which he will ask various spectators to try to solve.

He explains the problem, which is to turn the glasses over, two at a time, one in each hand, and to finish with all the glasses standing the right way up in just three moves. The performer demonstrates that it can be done but when the spectators try to duplicate the feat, they are unsuccessful. Usually, they finish with the three glasses upside-down.

In showing that it can be done, the performer may turn over No 1 and No 2, then No 1 and No 3, and finally No 1 and No 2. When he has demonstrated that it can be done, he arranges the glasses for the spectator to try. He alters the arrangement, however. The glasses are set up so that the center one is upside-down and the two others are the right way up. Very few people notice the difference in the arrangement but it makes success impossible.

Balancing a Coin

A silver coin is used in this trick, and may be borrowed from a member of the audience. It is carefully balanced on its edge on the tips of the left fingers. The hand is kept moving as though keeping the coin upright. It is finally thrown upward, caught with the right hand and returned to the lender.

The secret of the balance lies in a straight pin, which is hidden between the first and second fingers of the left hand, with the head nearest to the fingertips. Taking the borrowed coin, the performer balances it on the tips of the first and second fingers. The thumb of the right hand raises the point of the pin to an upright position against the coin. This action will not be seen as it is hidden by the coin.

The coin appears to be balancing on its edge and a natural hand movement, as though keeping it upright, helps to create the illusion. The coin is finally allowed to fall backwards and is then tossed into the air, to be caught in the right hand. This move is merely misdirection. While the audience is following the flight of the coin, the left hand drops to the side and releases the pin, allowing it to fall to the floor.

A Production Finale

Many magicians finish their acts with a colorful production, using boxes or tubes from which to produce the various items. Others, however, prefer the "ordinariness" of a gentleman's hat, either a derby or a top hat. It is not always easy to obtain these types of hat; you could use a plastic hat from a novelty store instead. It is necessary for the hat to remain rigid during the "handling" of this production.

A hat is passed out for examination and, taking it back, the performer places it on his table. Waving his magic wand over the hat, he produces from it a variety of items, such as ribbons, silk handkerchiefs, Japanese lanterns and colored boxes which, when displayed, make a colorful finale.

THE CHANGING BOX

A versatile piece of magical equipment, which is easy to make, is the Changing Box. Using this apparatus it is possible to place separate silk handkerchiefs into the box and remove them, seconds later, tied together. Or put some white handkerchiefs into the box and bring them out dyed in various colors. The box may be filled with cotton, which is transformed into rice, or sawdust that is changed to candy. The box has many uses and may be used on its own or in conjunction with another trick.

It measures approximately 6 inches by 2 inches by 2 inches and has a lid at each end. Inside the box, there is a diagonal partition which separates the box into two compartments (see diagram). If the cotton and rice transformation is to be performed, the rice is poured into one compartment and the lid placed on the box, which is turned so that the empty compartment is uppermost. In presenting the mystery, the cotton is put into the box and the lid put on. At the appropriate moment, the box is turned so that the rice is ready to pour from the box. It is a good idea to tease out the cotton so that it appears that far more is being used than is actually the case.

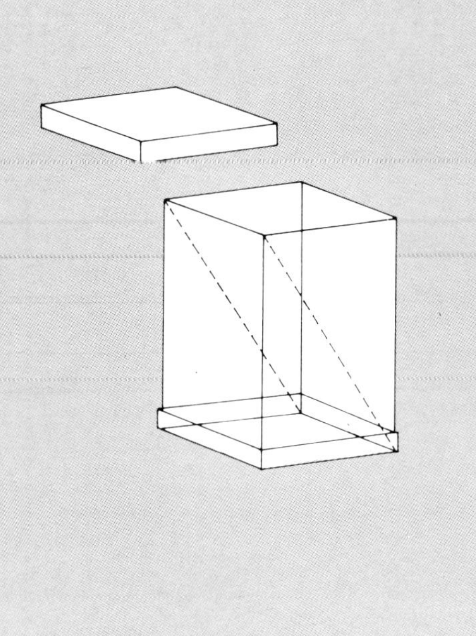

The Changing Box *(right)*
The box is divided diagonally, making two compartments. Lids are fitted to the top and bottom of the box. An article is placed in the upper compartment but when the box is put on the table, unknown to the audience, it is turned over. This move enables the performer to extract a different item from the box.

Hat productions were popular in the nineteenth century and the items produced were many and varied. Joseph Hartz produced a skull which rose out of his top hat and Jean Eugène Robert-Houdin, a cannon ball. Some magicians produced bundles of firewood and others baby dolls. Some were more traditional and, after producing other items, concluded by producing a rabbit.

The items to be produced are resting on a shelf at the back of the performer's table, hidden from view by the tablecloth (**1**). Magicians refer to the shelf as a *servante*. Some are made by pinning the bottom edge of the tablecloth near to the top of the table, making a deep pocket, from which items can be produced or vanished.

A large, colored silk handkerchief or cloth is wrapped around the items to be produced, the four corners brought together and an elastic band slipped over them. The goods remain intact and are easily released for production.

When the hat is returned to the performer after examination, he places it brim downward toward the back of the table. Standing to the (performer's) right of the table, he picks up his magic wand with his right hand and with his left raises the hat by the rear brim. As he does so, he grips the cloth-covered articles on the *servante* between his thumb and the brim (**2**), turns the hat, which causes the bundle to swing inside and, releasing the cloth, allows it to fall into the hat.

This movement should be practised until it can be smoothly presented. The performer walks forward and, waving his wand over the hat, makes the production, using the cloth as one of the production items (**3**).

A Production Finale *(right)*
1 The hat is shown empty and is placed on the table. The "load" is hidden behind the table, ready to be inserted into the hat.
2 The performer takes the hat by its brim and, as it is raised, swings the "load" into the hat as it is turned over.
3 Removing the rubber band, the performer produces the items, including the silk square which held the "load".

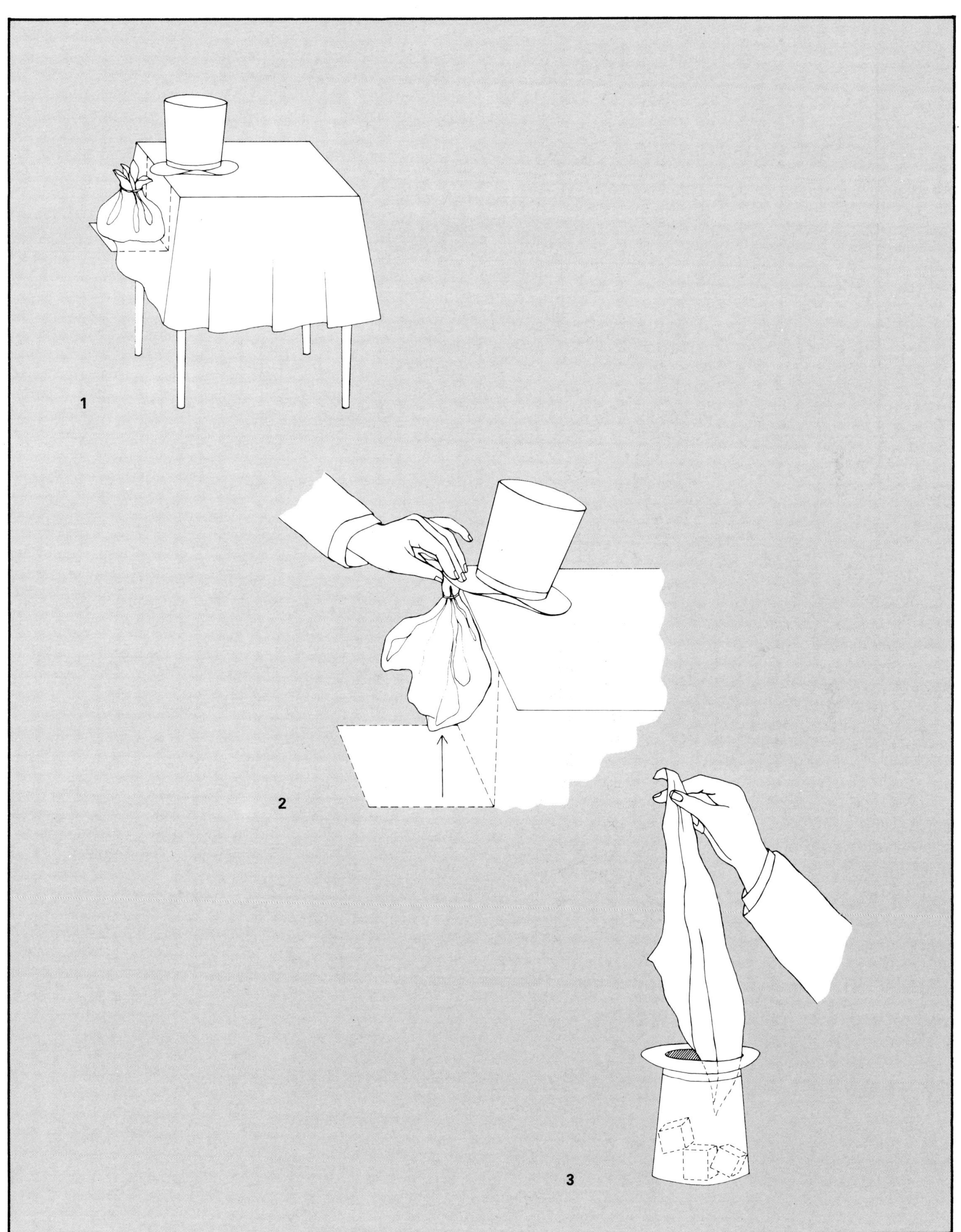
1
2
3

8

MASTER MAGICIAN

While reading this book you will have learned something of the master magicians and the mysteries that made them famous. Some people are envious of the stars of magic who appear on television, or on the stage, forgetting about the years of hard work, practise and perseverance that are required to make the grade. Everyone has to start somewhere and many of the lessons regarding showbusiness and entertaining the public can be learned only in the hard school of experience.

Beginners Please

There are basic rules to be observed if you wish to become a successful magical entertainer, whether on television or the stage or simply entertaining friends in your home. It is very important to like what you are doing. If you enjoy entertaining, this is transmitted to the audience. They will relax and enjoy your magic. You may not achieve great fame as a magician but you can still find pleasure in presenting magic in your neighborhood. The great British author, Charles Dickens, did not achieve fame as a magician but that did not prevent him from enjoying amazing his guests at social gatherings, and his children at their birthday and Christmas parties.

If you want to make a beginning in magic, read through the explanations of tricks given here and discover the ones that appeal to you most. Read the description of the trick carefully, then read it again with the required articles in your hands.

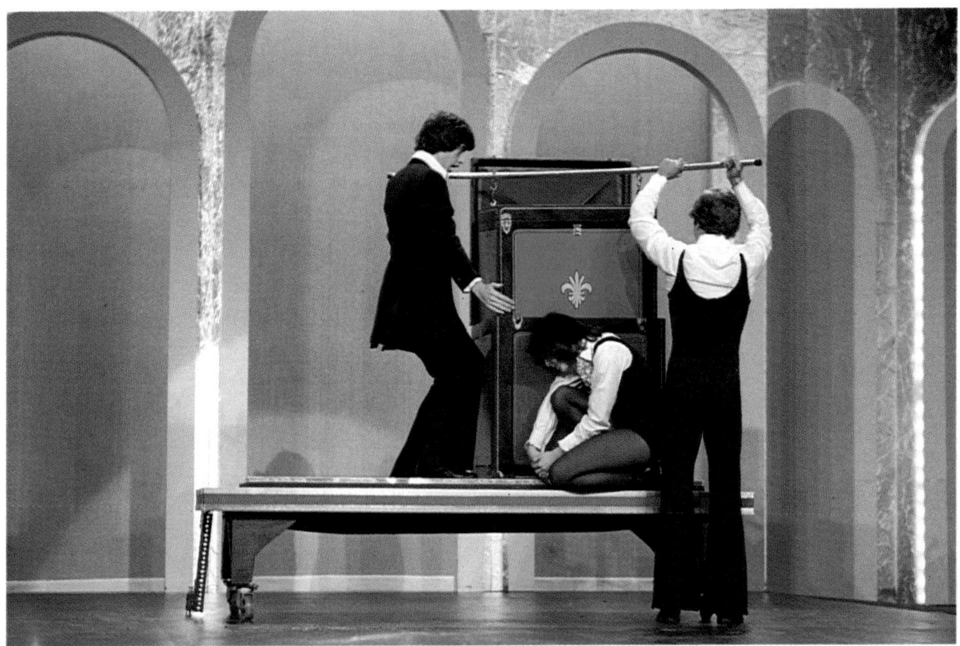

Above: David Copperfield presents Backstage with a Magician, a concept devised by Dante, in which the audience is led to believe that they are being shown how an illusion is worked, only to be surprised by an entirely unexpected denouement.

The blue box is taken out of the red box while the female assistant hides behind it. After the blue box has been shown to be empty she crawls in while the red box is now shown empty. The blue box, with the assistant inside, is then lowered back into the red box and the complacently relaxed audience waits for her to reappear. Instead, a guest celebrity steps from the nested boxes – the assistant has completely vanished.

Left: Marco the Magi with his Broomstick Suspension using a colorful set at the Cabot Street Theatre, Beverly.

The Dutch magician Tel Smit astounding his audience by producing flames at his finger tips.

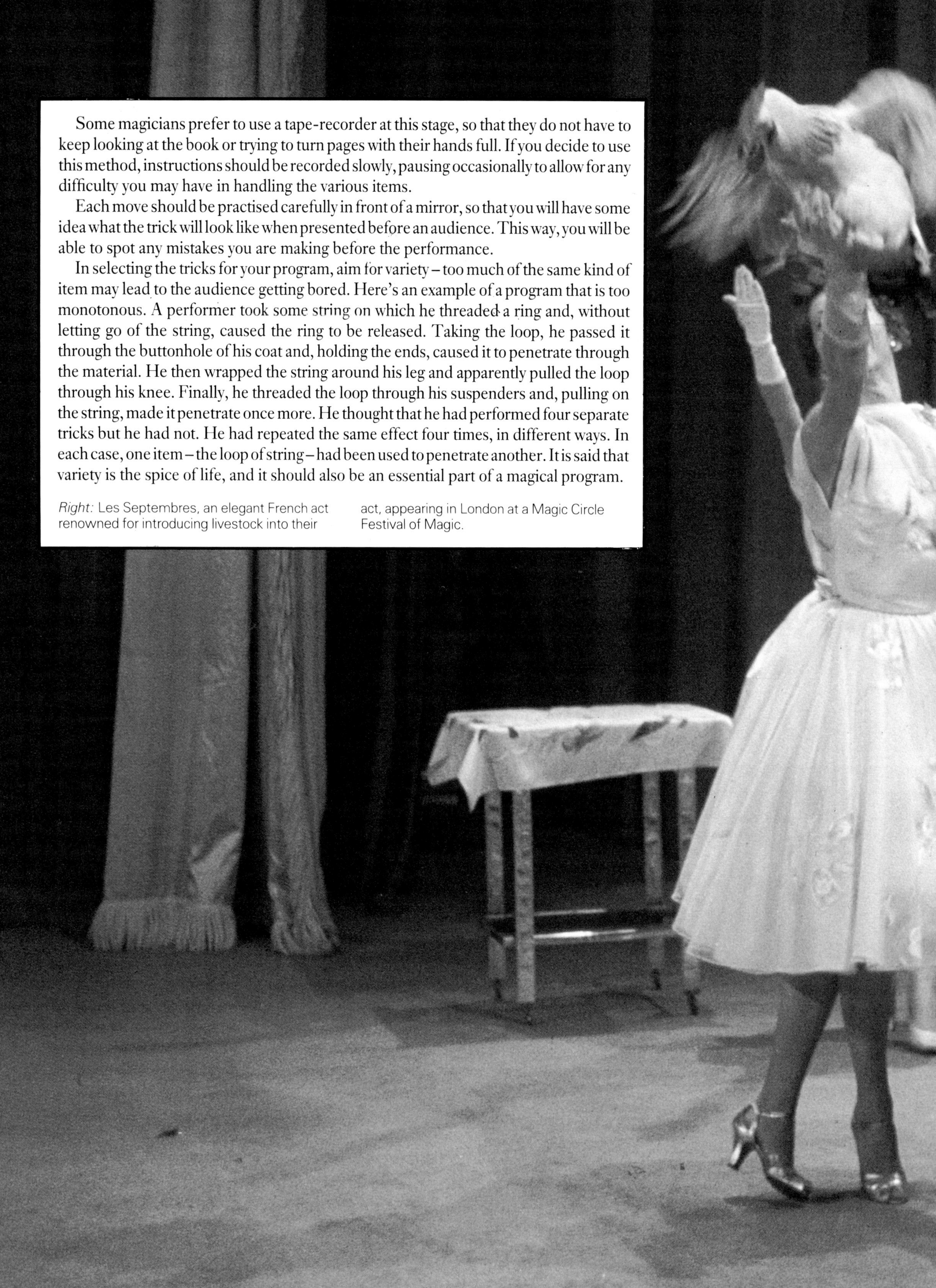

Some magicians prefer to use a tape-recorder at this stage, so that they do not have to keep looking at the book or trying to turn pages with their hands full. If you decide to use this method, instructions should be recorded slowly, pausing occasionally to allow for any difficulty you may have in handling the various items.

Each move should be practised carefully in front of a mirror, so that you will have some idea what the trick will look like when presented before an audience. This way, you will be able to spot any mistakes you are making before the performance.

In selecting the tricks for your program, aim for variety – too much of the same kind of item may lead to the audience getting bored. Here's an example of a program that is too monotonous. A performer took some string on which he threaded a ring and, without letting go of the string, caused the ring to be released. Taking the loop, he passed it through the buttonhole of his coat and, holding the ends, caused it to penetrate through the material. He then wrapped the string around his leg and apparently pulled the loop through his knee. Finally, he threaded the loop through his suspenders and, pulling on the string, made it penetrate once more. He thought that he had performed four separate tricks but he had not. He had repeated the same effect four times, in different ways. In each case, one item – the loop of string – had been used to penetrate another. It is said that variety is the spice of life, and it should also be an essential part of a magical program.

Right: Les Septembres, an elegant French act renowned for introducing livestock into their act, appearing in London at a Magic Circle Festival of Magic.

Left: Lance Burton, the suave and skilled young American who has been appearing in Las Vegas for several years. His superb manipulations won him the Grand Prix in 1982 at the triennial Congress in Lausanne, Switzerland.

A textbook on magic contains the following verse:

"The rules of a sleight-of-hand artist
Are three, and all others are vain,
The first and the second are, practise,
And the third one is practise again."

These rules apply not only to sleight-of-hand but to all types of magic, from close-up pocket tricks to stage illusions. If you carry out the necessary practise, the nerves that are usually felt by most beginners when presenting their first show will not be so bad because you will have confidence. Also, you will not need to wonder which trick comes next, or what is the best time to get rid of a concealed coin, or where did you put that piece of cord for the bracelet trick? If everything is studied, carefully thought out and practised beforehand, none of these problems need arise.

Patter

This is a term used by magicians and other entertainers to describe the words spoken during a show. Patter is very important. It creates interest, is often used for misdirection and provides humor. There are some non-patter acts, usually Oriental or manipulative, but it is not easy to present magic silently, particularly for beginners.

Patter should be interesting but not far-fetched, unless it is presented in a tongue-in-cheek manner. To listen to a nine-year-old boy, who is performing magic in a serious manner, saying "This is a mystery taught to me by a very wise man in India" sounds absurd – particularly if the spectators know that he has not been further than the next county!

Let us take an example of two magicians performing the same mystery, noticing particularly their patter. Their different approaches affect the impact that they will have on an audience.

The First Magician – The Great Alpha

"Ladies and gentlemen, I would like to show you a trick with an ordinary red handkerchief, which I place in this empty glass and cover with this ordinary cardboard tube. Now, ladies and gentlemen, I am going to make the red handkerchief disappear. I pick up my magic wand, and wave it over the tube. I take away the tube and the glass is empty and, ladies and gentlemen, I produce the handkerchief from my coat collar.

The Second Magician – The Great Beta

"Good evening, everyone. Here is a little mystery using a red handkerchief." (*He takes a red handkerchief from his breast pocket and, showing a drinking glass to be empty, places the handkerchief into the glass but makes no comment.*) "A mysterious tube." (*He smiles as he says this, shows the tube and places it over the glass.*) "And, of course, the magic wand." (*He waves the wand over the tube, which he removes, showing that the handkerchief has vanished.*) "I know that there's a solution to this mystery – somewhere!" (*He fumbles at the back of his collar.*) "Ah, here it is." (*He produces the handkerchief, which he displays.*) "That – is magic!"

Perhaps you have noticed the difference in the two sets of patter. Alpha's was full of "I place . . . I cover . . . I pick up . . . I produce". He was describing actions which the members of the audience can clearly see for themselves.

A famous magical writer once said "You never hear an acrobat say 'Look, I am standing on my head'. He gives the audience credit for having the intelligence to realize what he is doing. Why do magicians have to be different?"

Alpha describes the red handkerchief as being "ordinary". He does not normally describe handkerchiefs in this way, so why do it during a conjuring performance? If he thinks that he can prove its innocence, he is going about it the wrong way. He is more likely to arouse suspicion in the minds of the audience. If an item is innocent, why stress the point? If it is not, why tell unnecessary lies?

The Great Alpha uses the phrase "ladies and gentlemen" three times, when once would have been sufficient. He also speaks of an "empty" glass. Because of its transparency, the audience can see into the glass without the performer emphasizing the point. Another of his faults was to tell the audience what he was going to do, before he actually carried out the action. This not only eliminates any element of surprise but also limits the performer's options if anything should go wrong.

A performer took a cigarette and pushed it into his closed fist. When he opened his hand, the cigarette had changed into an egg, which he broke into a glass to show it to be the genuine article. He received great applause for this mystery. What the audience did not realize was that the trick had gone wrong. The magician had intended to change the cigarette into a silk handkerchief!

As he was introducing the mystery, he realized that the silk handkerchief was missing and, as he had an egg concealed ready for another trick, he palmed it and used it for the cigarette transformation. The audience thought that it was marvellous because the magician had not committed himself and told them to expect something different.

The Great Beta may not be everyone's ideal but he did manage to eliminate the repeated use of "I" and let the audience see for themselves what he was doing. The addition of a touch of humor would have helped his presentation.

When preparing your patter, do not imitate the styles of other people. Act naturally, be yourself. Some young people try to imitate Carl Ballantine, for example. Because of his slightly aggressive approach, when they copy him their patter seems false and they appear to be cheeky and sometimes downright offensive.

Patter helps an audience to know when to applaud or signals when the performer is finishing his act. Performers do not always make it clear that a trick is finished and spectators are confused as to whether they should applaud or not. There is nothing more embarrassing than a performer having to say "Thank you very much, ladies and gentlemen," almost begging for applause.

Right: Carl Ballantine, the American comedy magician whose act revolves around deliberately brash, unsuccessful attempts to perform a variety of tricks using ropes, newspaper and cards.

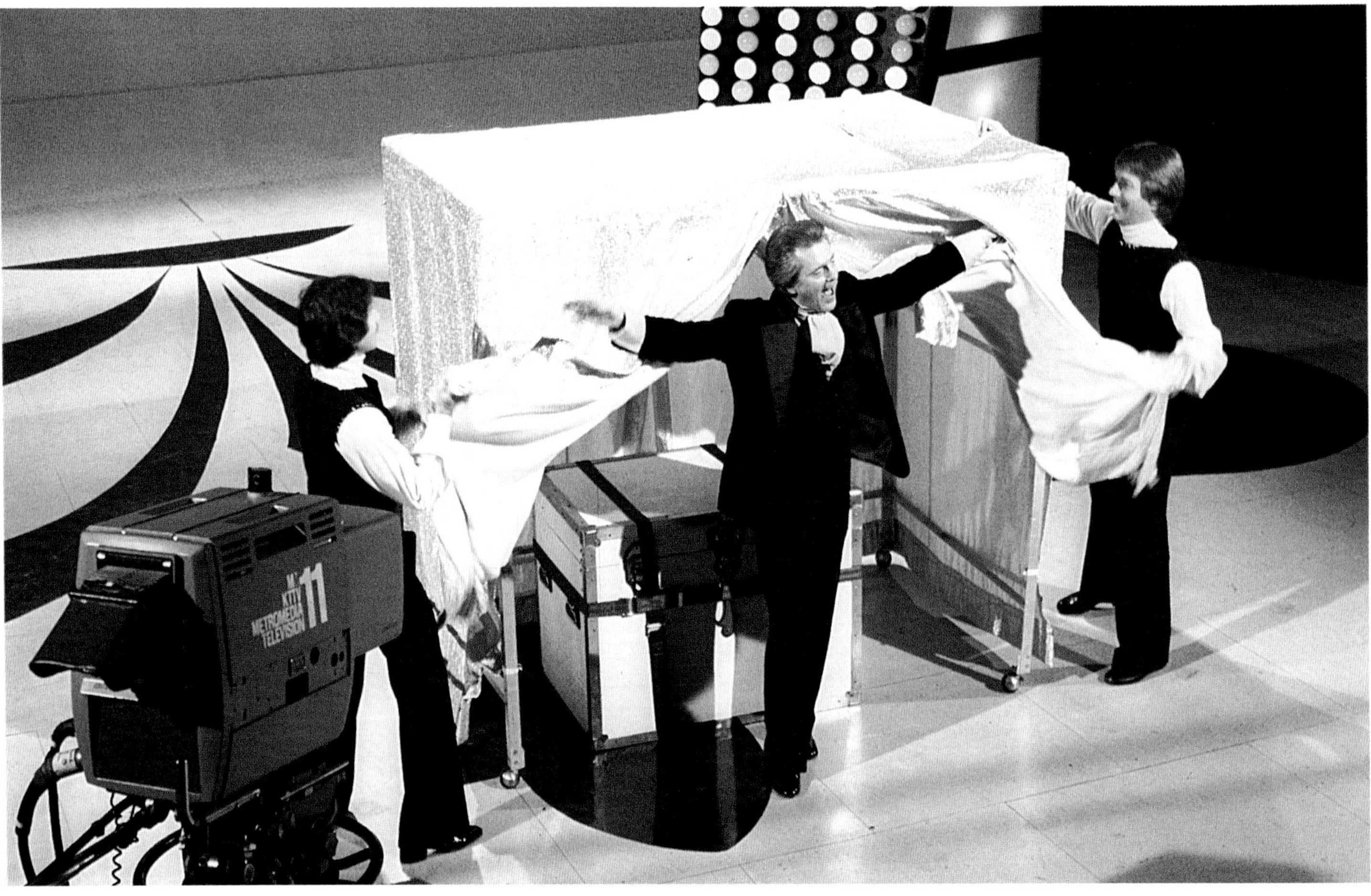

Below: Mark Wilson with the Substitution Trunk illusion during a Home Box-Office cable television special show.

BALLANTINE
THIS WORLD'S
GREATEST
MAGICIAN

One clue to help them realize that you are finishing your act is to begin your final trick with the words "And now for my final mystery", or "In conclusion, let me show you" or, if you prefer the comedy approach, "Now for the trick you've all been waiting for – my last".

Patter should be rehearsed along with the trick. There is little point in rehearsing the trick really well and trying to think of some suitable patter on the way to the show. There is nothing worse than a performer interspersing his patter with "er", "ah" or "um" because he does not know what to say next.

When speaking, make sure that you can be heard. This is a common fault, not only with magicians but with many speakers who have to address an audience. A great deal of time may have been spent in preparing what they have to say and it is wasted because they cannot be heard beyond the front row. So, speak up. Do not rush your patter and speak correctly. A good act can be killed through the use of slovenly speech.

Handling of Apparatus

The handling of items used in the act is also important. Learn, for instance, how to shuffle a pack of cards neatly. One magician took the shuffling and handling of cards very seriously and, because of the smoothness of his card work, he was given the credit for being a marvelous sleight-of-hand performer, whereas the tricks he presented relied mainly on a prearranged pack (see Chapter Six) or on an almost automatic result. With his showmanship, he fooled the spectators before he even started to show them his magic.

Faults in the handling of props are very common. For example, a card has vanished and, when it is produced, the magician says "And this was your chosen card". He shows the card for an instant and replaces it in the pack. It is done so quickly that some spectators are unable to see the card.

It is much better to hold up the card with its back to the audience and say, "A few moments ago, sir, you selected a card from a shuffled pack, returned it and shuffled the pack once more. For the first time, will you please tell me the name of your chosen card? The five of hearts? Thank you, sir. I also have removed a card from the pack and that card is (*pause*) the five of hearts". The card is turned in the fingers to face the audience and held. This not only gives the members of the audience time to see the card but is also a cue for applause.

Another tip with regard to handling concerns the picking up of a drinking glass. It should be picked up with the hand behind it. So often a performer picks up a glass with his hand grasped around the front, hiding whatever it contains from the audience's view.

Articles used in your act should always look clean. Silk handkerchiefs should be washed and ironed. Grubby packs of cards may be used in practise sessions but certainly not in your public performances. The same applies to your dress and appearance. Your hands are the focus of attention for a great deal of the time, so make sure they are clean and the fingernails neatly trimmed.

An important point to remember is to polish your shoes. Occasionally a magician appears on a platform or a stage and the audience can see the whole of the performer, instead of just his head and shoulders, so from head to toe he should look presentable.

Right: The magicienne Valeria (later known as Cleopatra) was the widow of the Greek performer Kasfikis. She is seen here with the assistants from her all-female illusion show.

Above and right: Doug Henning performs the Indian Sands Trick. Three differently colored sands are poured into a tank of water and thoroughly stirred. Having shown his hand empty, Doug plunges it into the cloudy water and then withdraws it, clenched. He now has his hand above one of the plates and squeezes his fist until pure dry sand of one single color pours forth. The feat is then repeated with the other two colors.

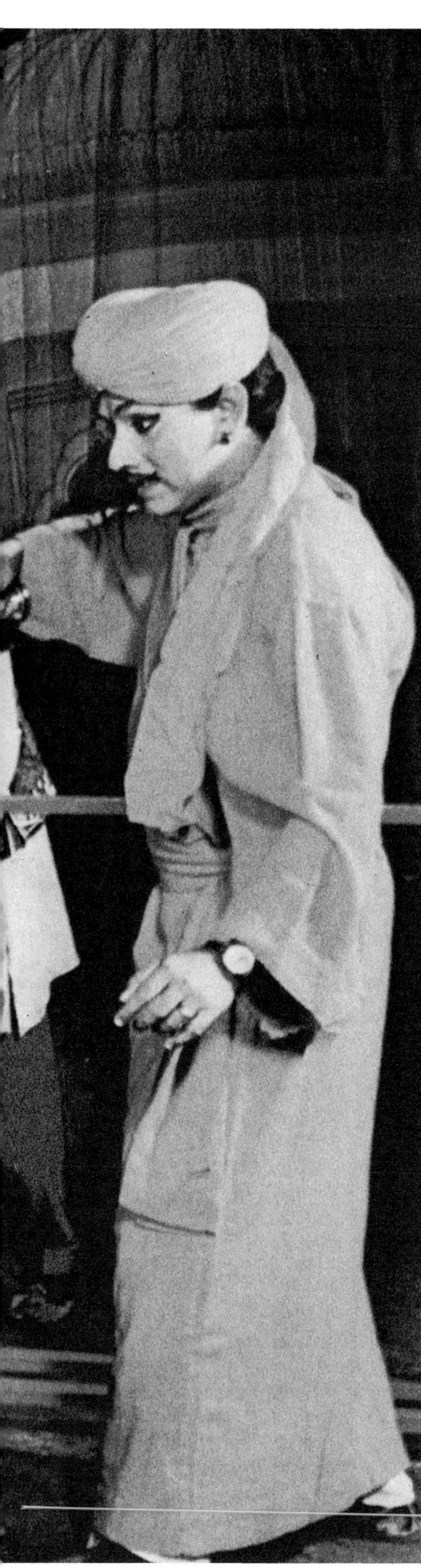

Left: Sorcar Junior, the Indian magician, following in his famous father's footsteps, is seen here performing the Temple of Benares illusion.

Building A Show

To put a magical program together requires certain guidelines. It has been suggested that so long as the opening and closing items are good, the rest of the program will take care of itself. There is a certain amount of truth in this statement but it should not be taken too literally. There is a lot of work to be done on the middle part of the program as well as the opening and closing items.

Your opening trick should be one that creates interest because if you fail to catch the attention of your audience at the beginning of your show, you will find it much harder to hold their interest in the rest of the program. So, a long-winded card trick is not a good choice with which to begin your magical extravaganza.

Let us look at some opening tricks that have been used by professional magicians.

- The magician wraps his cane in a sheet of newspaper, which he immediately unrolls, showing that the cane has disappeared.
- A cane held by the magician is suddenly transformed into two large, silk scarves.
- The magician shows a large cloth, back and front, and from beneath it produces a large bowl of water.
- A Japanese parasol is transformed into the magician's table.
- The magician removes his white gloves and throws them into the air, where they change to a bouquet of flowers.
- A number of silk handkerchiefs, shown separately, join up to become a large vari-colored square.

These half-dozen examples could be described as "quick tricks". They are eye-catching and create interest straight away.

Your closing mystery should be one that will bring applause. It is your final item and your last chance to make a good impression on your audience. Let us turn again to the professional magicians and see how they finish their acts.

- The magician shows three pieces of tissue paper, red, white and blue, which he changes into a large flag.
- A hat box is shown empty, from which the performer produces three baskets of flowers.
- From an empty cocktail shaker, various drinks are poured and passed around to members of the audience.
- A ball floats around the stage and finally comes to rest between the magician's hands. He pulls the ball apart and in each half there is an array of colored flowers.
- Showing a green bush, the performer takes a watering can and waters it. A visible growth of roses appears.
- The magician shows a large cloth, back and front. Then, holding the cloth by its center, he produces from the folds two large pocket watches, which he places on a display stand.

It is better to end on a production than a vanish because if an item disappears the audience is left wondering where it has gone and the applause suffers.

Some performers prefer to close their program with a contrasting item – for instance, a demonstration of thought-reading.

Do not close your show with volunteer assistants on stage with you. Thanking assistants and helping them off the stage is an anti-climax. This rule has been broken many times but, generally speaking, it is better to take your final bow alone.

Right: Richard Ross, the brilliant Dutch magician whom many regard as the natural successor to his fellow countryman, the late Fred Kaps, as the finest magician in the world. Working silently to music, he produces coins, uses four large rings in his routine for the Chinese Linking Rings and, as seen *far right*, produces a watch which multiplies to several, each dangling from its own chain.

Overleaf: A carnival atmosphere pervades the stage of the Cabot Street Theatre, Beverly, where Le Grand David (left) and Marco the Magi (center) are in action.

Once you have gained the attention of the audience with your opening mystery, it must be kept and your program should include plenty of variety. There should be variety in the properties used. The pace of the program should vary; for instance, a short item should be inserted betwen two longer routines. There should be a difference in the basic types of effects, too.

When a magician talks about basic types of effects, he is referring to the main headings used to describe certain categories of trick. Here are seven basic types:

1 Production, in which something appears or multiplies.
2 Disappearance, in which something vanishes from sight.
3 Transformation, in which something changes in color, size or shape.
4 Transposition, in which something moves from one place to another.
5 Penetration, in which one solid object passes through another.
6 Mentalism, which includes thought-reading and predictions.
7 Anti-scientific Laws. This category is specifically for those effects that include levitation or anti-gravity, invulnerability, unexpected "magnetic" attraction, etc.

There are more categories but they are, in the main, offshoots of the types listed above.

Your Program of Magic
Let us take some of the tricks described in this book and build them into a program.

The Growing Wand (Transformation) – page 141
The Changing Box (Transformation) – page 148
Aerial Addition (Transposition) – page 143
The Mysterious Indian Vase (Anti-scientific Laws) – page 132
Star Prediction (Mentalism) – page 144
A Production Finale (Production) page 147

You will see that there is plenty of variety in the properties used, and the basic effects are varied. Smaller items are interspersed with larger ones and there is variety in the presentation of each mystery.

The Growing Wand is a natural opening item in a program of magic, for a number of reasons. As part of the wand has to be hidden up your sleeve, it would be difficult to place the wand in position during the show. Also it is a reasonably quick trick and creates interest. Audiences expect to hear magic words and to see a magic wand, so why not use the wand in your opening mystery?

The second mystery is a little longer and adds color. Use the Changing Box to cause three long loops of colored ribbon to become linked together. Give the audience a chance to see the linked ribbons. If a thumb is inserted into the end links and the ribbons held at arm's length, this is a cue for applause.

Aerial Addition includes the participation of a member of the audience and a touch of humor is created with the production of the "invisible" coins.

The Indian Vase provides a different line in patter, with its eastern mysticism, and audience participation when it is passed around for examination.

Star Prediction introduces an experiment in thought. This routine, involving a number of spectators, is the longest item in the program but it should not be dragged out. Because the method is simple, greater attention can be given to the presentation. This type of mystery lends itself perfectly to showmanship.

Producing colorful items from a hat makes a fitting climax to the program. Silk scarves should be produced with a flourish. Do not load them folded in neat squares and spend time opening each one individually. It slows down the smooth flow of the production. They should be folded diagonally, in zig-zag fashion.

Do not forget to take your bow at the conclusion of your show.

Norm Neilsen with the *pièce de résistance* of his manipulative act, the Floating Violin. The bow is placed on the instrument, which then begins to float above and below the cloth in his hands, playing all the while.

There are times when friends, knowing of your particular interest, suggest that you demonstrate your skill as a magician. A close-up program with articles taken from your pockets, or borrowed, which can be presented with friends sitting around a table, could be made from the following tricks.

Ring-a-ding – page 131
Deceptive Dice – page 140
A card routine using the "Eight – King – Three" system – page 113
A Tumbler Teaser – page 147
It's Matchic – page 146

All of the items will fit in your pockets with the exception of the drinking glasses used in A Tumbler Teaser. If you are presenting the program in your own home, these should not be a problem. If you borrowed a set of dominoes, you could include Domino Magic, too (page 142).

When presenting your card routine, do not make it too long, otherwise people will become bored.

You should know the running order of your program and, when setting your table, begin with the items used in your last trick, then the next-to-last and so on, until you finish with the opening trick. The reason for this procedure is that sometimes the top of your table is not large enough to hold all your apparatus and you may want to stand something on a piece of tissue paper, a magazine or a book. It is most unprofessional to have to rummage among pieces of apparatus to find an item for your next trick.

Knowing the running order and practising your tricks in the same order is essential. It helps you to discover any snags and ways in which they may be eliminated.

A certain magician would have saved himself a great deal of embarrassment if he had taken this precaution. One of his mysteries concluded with the production of a quantity of confetti. His next trick was one in which a ball floated in the air. Throughout his performance, a black thread lay unnoticed across the stage for use in this mystery. When an off-stage assistant raised the thread, however, pieces of confetti were attached to it, exposing the method used to the audience.

Concluding Observations

Do not give away secrets. There is an old saying in magic that "when a secret is made known, it is a secret no longer". If someone enquires how a trick is done, do not tell him. You have had to put in a lot of practise, so why should he be told the secret?

If you see a magician on the stage, or on TV, and a friend who is with you asks how a certain trick was done, do not tell him. You may know, and it may give you a feeling of importance to divulge the secret of a brother magician, but your friend will not thank you. He will be thinking what an idiot he has been in allowing himself to be fooled by such a simple trick.

The best way of dealing with a person who wants to know how a trick was done, is to ask "Can you keep a secret?" Thinking he is going to learn something of the magic art, he will say "Yes". Your response is, "So can I".

Do not repeat a trick at the same performance. The only reason for a person asking to see a trick again is to try to learn how it is done. Do not give him the opportunity. The first showing of the trick created a surprise. He did not know what was going to happen. On the second showing, he already knows the end result and will be carefully watching for clues that will lead to solving the mystery.

There are occasions when someone will say, "I know how you do that trick". Do not argue with him because, feeling important, he will enjoy revealing your secret to all within earshot. The way to deal with this situation is, when he proclaims "I know how you do that", simply to say "So do I", or "Well, that makes two of us". This retort usually takes the wind out of his sails and brings chuckles from other members of the audience, which makes the knowledgeable person wish that he had kept quiet.

Left: Doug Henning with the Mismade Girl illusion. Having entered the cabinet, the assistant is apparently dissected into four segments which are separated and then "accidentally" reassembled in the incorrect order with hilarious results.

Above: Marvin Roy and his wife Carol have traveled the world presenting their clever magical routines, one featuring jewelry and the other electric light bulbs. In the former, fabulous jewels are produced throughout the performance.

Right: Marvin Roy at the climax of his Electric Act. Center stage is a huge 5000-watt lighthouse lamp on a skeleton stand. Marvin dons dark glasses before the theater is darkened, enabling him to concentrate on the lamp and make it glow dimly. Gradually the power increases and the lamp shines with incredible intensity, illuminating the entire theater.

THE MAGICIAN IS ALWAYS RIGHT

Tricks can go wrong and for a magician to apologize does not help his image as a master of mystery. It is at moments such as these that his knowledge of the subject and working experience can be particularly helpful. Earlier in this chapter, we described how a magician intended to change a cigarette into a silk handkerchief but instead transformed the cigarette into an egg. Because he had not told the audience what he was going to do, they were not aware that the trick had gone wrong.

A famous English music hall performer, Jack le Dair, introduced "The Vanishing Birdcage". It was a large cage, which he brought on stage at the commencement of his act. He told the audience of this famous mystery (see Chapter Three). He was just about to make the cage disappear when he said, "By the way, have you seen this?" and, putting the cage on a table, demonstrated another trick. He returned to the birdcage and was once more about to make it vanish, when he put it down and began another trick. The Vanishing Birdcage became a running gag throughout his act and finally, as he was about to make the disappearance, the bell of an alarm clock was heard and, with "Sorry, I haven't the time to do it", he made his exit to a big laugh.

This idea could be used if a trick goes wrong. Use it as a running gag, with the trick still unfinished at the end. It may be that, as you walk off-stage, the trick can be re-set, and when you return to take your final bow you will be able to perform it successfully. Do not, if it is at all possible, admit defeat.

A marvellous example of the elaborate kind of stage setting used by many magicians. Here the American Chung Ling Soo on the extreme right (with his wife on the far left) gets ready for his Chinese-based show (in about 1910).

Learning from Experience

If you hear entertainers talking about the famous old Chinese gentleman, you will know that the performer on stage is over-running his time. He is "On Too Long". This is a fault, particularly amongst amateurs, who once on stage seem reluctant to leave. To overstep the time you have been allotted, particularly if there are other performers on the program, is not the best way to win friends and influence people. You also run the risk of boring your audience.

A good way of learning the business, apart from reading books, is to watch entertainers – not only magicians but comedians, singers and specialty acts. Do not watch only *what* they are doing but also *how* it is being done. Notice their movements, their timing and their patter. Take note of their hand movements and how they pick up pieces of apparatus. See how applause is gained from the audience and notice the pace of the various items.

Watch the opening number and see how quickly they get into their act and hold the attention of the audience and watch out for the applause cues leading to the final item in their program.

Successful performers work hard to achieve their goal. They practise continually, search for humorous touches to include in their act, and in general try to present a polished performance. The one thing that makes an act better than average is the "selling" of the various items. In other words, it depends on showmanship.

Showmanship

The dictionary defines showmanship as "a flair for presenting something to the public effectively, especially by introducing theatrical techniques". People in showbusiness might agree with this definition, but would prefer to express it in their own way.

- "Showmanship is doing nothing, but doing it well."
- "Showmanship puts breath into clay and makes it a living thing."
- "Showmanship makes the ordinary – extraordinary."
- "It is the art that creates and sustains interest."

Shimada (Haruo Shimada), a stylish Japanese magician now living in the USA, is famed both for his superb sleight-of-hand and the marvelous costumes used in the Parasol Act and the Dragon Act. Here he is seen performing his Dove Act (*left*) which begins spectacularly with his cane bursting into flames (*below*).

YOUNG MAGICIANS

It is never too soon to start training as a magician. Fourteen-year-old Seth Bartlett, who stars as Seth the Sensational in Le Grand David show at the Cabot Street Theatre in Beverly, Massachusetts, started doing magic when he was four years old. That surely makes him the most experienced youngster in magic.

Teenager Johnny Hart built up an act, which he presented at The Magic Circle's Young Magician of the Year Competition in London. He was the first winner of this coveted title. Since then he has progressed and is now a busy professional magician appearing in London and Las Vegas. During the following years, other young amateurs have won this competition and some have later joined the ranks of the professionals, while others have made it a hobby.

The current Young Magician of the Year is an English teenager named Jeremy Dane, who, with a novel Japanese act which includes a great deal of humor and mystery, won over the judges and the audience with his act. There are opportunities for young magicians locally, nationally and internationally.

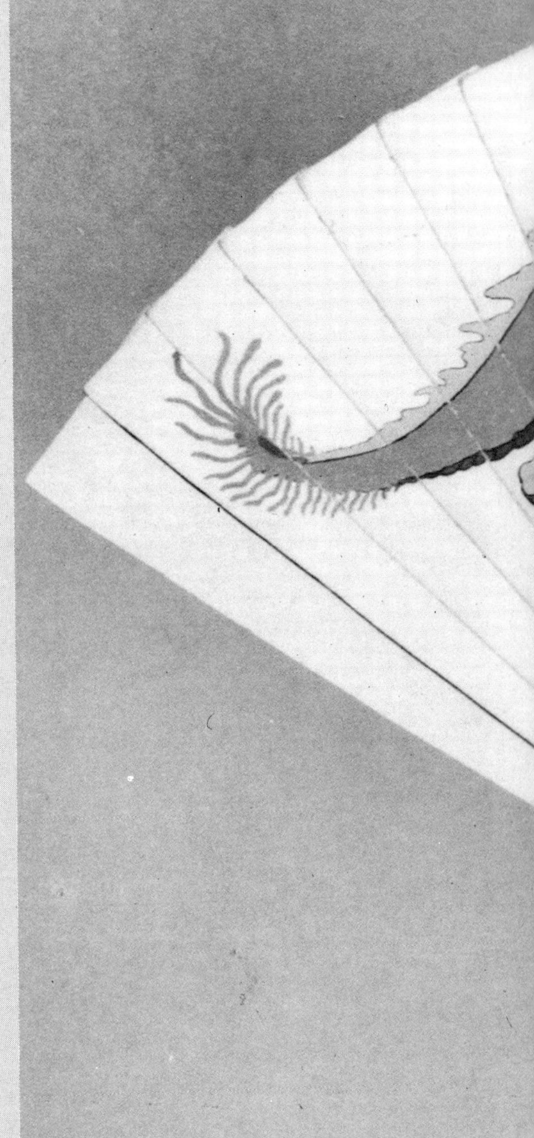

Above: Johnny Hart, international star of magic, produces parakeets at his finger tips. Johnny was the first to win the coveted Young Magician of the Year Award, instituted by The Magic Circle of London, and then embarked upon a highly successful professional career that has spanned the world. Though a skilled manipulator, he also features large and small scale illusions in his show.

Right: Jeremy Dane, winner of The Magic Circle Young Magician of the Year Award in 1985, with an unusual oriental act in which he entices his audience to sing with him to effect his magic.

Marco the Magi (*above*) and Le Grand David (*right*) showing the importance of showmanship. Marco is performing the Chinese Linking Rings which has astounded audiences since it was first introduced to Western audiences in the early nineteenth century. Le Grand David (David Bull) and Marco are performing the Substitution Trunk illusion in the course of a spectacular evening's entertainment at the Cabot Street Theatre, Beverly, Massachusetts.

Above: Dante's startling variation on an old theme using a pig instead of a rabbit.

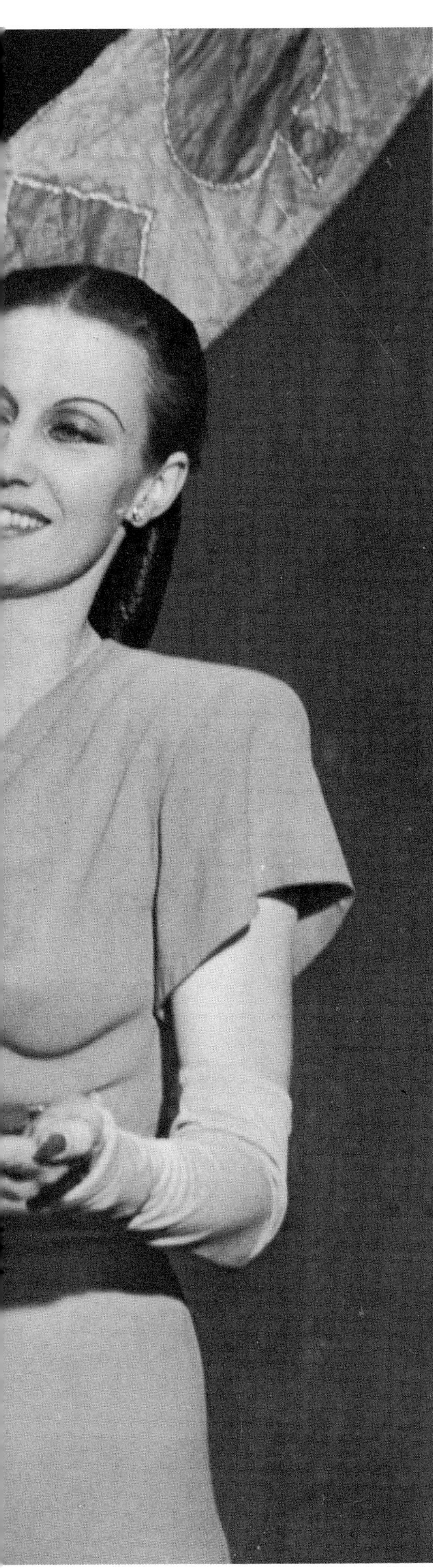

A magician is like the producer of a play, who uses the artifices of the theater to create an illusion. He can take a paint-daubed canvas, lighting, music, costumes and actors, and create a believable ballroom scene in a royal palace. The magician, through the use of his skills, can take his pieces of apparatus and create a miniature masterpiece.

Let us look at three examples of showmanship at its best.

1 – Dante

The great Danish-American magician Dante has already been mentioned as the ideal showman. He dressed well and was a commanding and dignified figure, with his white hair, clipped beard and mustache. He looked and played the part of a master magician, both on and off the stage.

During his last English tour, he played a London theater and stayed at one of the top hotels. One evening, the reception area was crowded with guests waiting for taxis. They suddenly became aware of a figure in evening dress, wearing a silk-lined cloak and top hat and carrying a silver-knobbed cane, descending the central staircase preceded by an Indian boy.

"Peter," commanded the magician, "call me a cab". The boy left the hotel and returned a few moments later. "Taxi, Mr Dante", he called. As they left the hotel, the guests looked in disbelief. Approaching the taxi, Dante said in a loud voice "Driver, take me to the finest theater in London, the Garrick, where the greatest show in the world, 'Sim Sala Bim', is being presented". The taxi drove away, leaving a crowd of people talking about Dante, the Magician. That is showmanship.

2 – Chung Ling Soo

The famous Chinese conjurer, Chung Ling Soo, who had one of the most colorful magic shows ever seen, occasionally held press conferences. To help him answer questions put to him by the newspapermen, he was assisted by an interpreter. Soo, whose real name was William Ellsworth Robinson, was an American, born in New York, and understood perfectly all the questions asked by the reporters. To add realism to the character he played, he used a translator. That, too, is showmanship.

3 – "The Lazy Magician"

The Cords of Phantasia or The Silks, Wand and Ropes is a trick that has been used by magicians for many years, particularly children's entertainers. Dante took this overworked mystery, lifted it out of the mediocre and made it one of the most talked-about items in his show. He called it "The Lazy Magician".

A chair stood in the center of the stage. Dante walked on, wearing his top hat at a rakish angle and carrying a silver-topped cane. He was smoking a cigar. Sitting on the chair, he crossed one leg over the other and waited while two girl assistants brought him two lengths of rope. Lazily, he held out his cane. The girls, finding the centers of the ropes, hung them over the cane. They tied a knot, securing the ropes to the cane, and held the ends of the ropes.

A third glamorous assistant brought on some colored silk squares, which she draped over the ropes, two on either side of the cane. Motioning to the girls to bring the ropes nearer to him, so that he would not have to leave his chair, Dante tied each silk square to the ropes, at the same time eyeing the glamorous assistant and occasionally blowing smoke into her face.

He slid the tied silk squares along the ropes to the center and, taking a rope end from each of the girls, he tied a knot around the bundle of silks and handed the ropes back to the girls. Removing his top hat, he held it beneath the bundle of silks, withdrew his cane and used it to tap the ropes. The silk squares, still tied, dropped into his hat, having penetrated the ropes.

The trick itself is not particularly out of the ordinary. It was Dante's presentation that made it a classic.

Within the pages of this book, you have read of the achievements of the famous magicians and you have been shown the basics of magic – the rest is up to you.

SUGGESTIONS FOR FURTHER READING

If this book has aroused your enthusiasm for magic and you would like to pursue the subject further, the following brief list of books should prove of interest.

History of Magic
Christopher, M. (1973) *The Illustrated History of Magic.* Crowell; Hale.
Dawes, E.A. (1979) *The Great Illusionists*. David & Charles; Chartwell.

Card Magic
Annemann, T. (1964) *Miracles of Card Magic.* Faber.
Gibson, W.B. (1969) *The Complete Illustrated Book of Card Magic.* Doubleday.
Hugard, J. (1961) *Encyclopaedia of Card Tricks*. Faber.
Hugard, J. and Braué, F. (1949) *The Royal Road to Card Magic.* Faber.

Impromptu and Close-up Magic
Gibson, W. (1980) *The Complete Illustrated Book of Close-Up Magic.* Hale.
Marshall, J. (1980) *How to Perform Instant Magic.* Bailey Bros & Swinfen; Quality Books.

Mental Magic
Kaye, M. (1975) *The Handbook of Mental Magic.* Stein & Day.

Magic for the Young Performer
Bongo, A. (1979) *Be a Magician*. Macdonald.
Daniels, P. (1980) *Paul Daniels' Magic Book*. Piccolo (Pan).
Eldin, P. (1985) *Pocket Book of Magic.* Kingfisher.
Wilson, M. (1975) *Mark Wilson Course in Magic.* Mark Wilson.

Left: Faust, in the Aladdin pantomime role of Abanazar the magician, performing his magic tricks in the Cave of the Magic Lamp.

General Index

Index of Magic Tricks and Techniques

PICTURE CREDITS

MARK WILSON Front cover, Contents page, 9 right, 70/71, 76/77, 82, 88/89, 158 THE EDWIN A. DAWES COLLECTION Endpapers, half-title, 6, 8/9, 10, 11, 12 right, 13, 14, 15, 16 left, 16/17 top, 18, 19, 20, 21, 22/23, 24/25, 26, 27, 28, 30, 31, 32, 33 left, 35, 36, 37, 40, 45, 49, 53, 54, 55, 56/57, 58, 49, 65, 66, 67, 68/69, 71 right, 72, 73, 75, 81, 83, 84, 91 right, 92, 93, 94 bottom, 96, 97, 99 top, 100, 104, 107 right, 108, 109, 118 left, 150, 160/161, 164/165, 176/177, 180, 181, 182 left, 186/187 REBUS INC. Title page, 42, 52 bottom, 90, 99, 129, 151 right, 159, 162/163, 166, 167, 171, 172, 174/175, 178, 179 ALDUS ARCHIVE 12 left, 34 MAC WILSON/THE MAGIC CIRCLE 16 bottom right, 33 right, 38, 43, 64, 78, 79, 95, 102, 103, 130, 154/155 THE MARY EVANS PICTURE LIBRARY 29, 41, 44, 62, 105 THE KOBAL COLLECTION 46/47 THE PHOTO SOURCE 48, 124, 152/153, 184 PAUL DANIELS 50/51 ALISTAIR MORRISON 52 top SIEGFRIED AND ROY/FRONTIER HOTEL 84/85 PHOTOREPORTERS/ALAN S. ADLER 86/87 GLENN FALKENSTEIN 94 top & middle, 101 LE GRAND DAVID/JOHN LAPURTA 106/107, 168/169, 182/183 MULTIMEDIA PUBLICATIONS/PHASE ONE PHOTOGRAPHY 110, 112, 113, 114, 115, 116, 117, 118 right, 119, 120, 121, 122, 123, 125, 128, 137, 138/139, 140 DAVID BERGLAS/TYNE TEES TELEVISION 126/127 LANCE BURTON/LAVALLO, RUFFALO & FARGNOLI 156

Endpapers: Le Grand David and his Own Spectacular Magic Company have been appearing at the Cabot Street Theatre in Beverly, Massachusetts since 1977. Lavishly produced, with beautiful costumes, unusual apparatus and a cast of over sixty, this remarkable show is the creation of Cesareo Pelaez, seen here in his role as Marco the Magi.

Page 1: This striking poster for The Great Carmo (Harry Cameron, 1881-1944) effectively combines a Pepper's Ghost effect with a devil's shadow.

Page 2: The popular American magician Doug Henning performs the Indian Sands Trick. See pages 162-163 for a full explanation.